English Grammar Today

Workbook

**Ronald Carter, Michael McCarthy,
Geraldine Mark and Anne O'Keeffe**

26/9/11

CAMBRIDGE
UNIVERSITY PRESS

CAMBRIDGE UNIVERSITY PRESS
Cambridge, New York, Melbourne, Madrid, Cape Town,
Singapore, São Paulo, Delhi, Tokyo, Mexico City

Cambridge University Press
The Edinburgh Building, Cambridge CB2 8RU, UK

www.cambridge.org
Information on this title: www.cambridge.org/9780521731768

First published 2011

Printed in the United Kingdom at the University Press, Cambridge

A catalogue record for this publication is available from the British Library

ISBN 978-0-521-73176-8 English Grammar Today Workbook
ISBN 978-0-521-73175-1 English Grammar Today Paperback with CD-ROM
ISBN 978-0-521-14987-7 English Grammar Today Paperback with CD-ROM and
Workbook

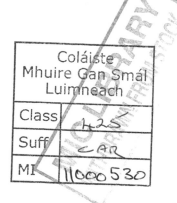

Contents

Contents

Contents

Introduction

The *English Grammar Today Workbook* is an up-to-date exercise and practice guide to the grammar of modern English.

This workbook is useful for all users of English but in particular for learners of English at an intermediate to upper-intermediate level (CEF B1–B2). It practises key areas of grammar and targets typical learner errors through real examples, texts and a wide range of exercises.

The book is organised in an A–Z format to make it easy to use. For example, if you want to practise the use of determiners in English, you can look up *Determiners* under D. The book includes key features of grammar such as *adjective, adverb, conditionals, conjunction, future, noun, ellipsis, modality, verbs* as well as individual words and pairs of words which are commonly confused such as *do* and *make* or *as* and *like*. There are also units on spelling, punctuation and word formation in English. The contents page gives a complete list.

English Grammar Today is informed by a corpus of English called the *Cambridge International Corpus* (*CIC*) developed by Cambridge University Press. A corpus is a large collection of written and spoken language which is stored and processed by computers so that it can be used to describe a language and to serve as a basis for examples for learners. At the time of writing this corpus consists of over 1 billion words of English.

CIC also contains the *Cambridge Learner Corpus* which is a large collection of the language used by learners of English. The learner corpus is particularly helpful as it shows us the most common grammatical mistakes made by learners of English when they speak and write.

The *CIC* has been collected over many years and consists of real texts taken from everyday written and spoken English. The guidance is also informed by our own experience as teachers of English and by the experience of those with whom we have worked in the writing of this workbook.

This book can be used in class or by students working on their own. It is published together with a companion volume *English Grammar Today*, an A–Z reference book giving more detail and examples about the material covered in the workbook. The key at the back of this book provides the answers, grammar tips and cross references **EGT** to the relevant *English Grammar Today* entry.

The *English Grammar Today Workbook*:

- has a simple A–Z structure.
- uses real examples.
- can be used both in class and by learners working on their own.
- focuses on typical mistakes which learners of English make.
- gives you a lot of help with and practice in spoken English grammar.

Adjectives

1 **Underline the adjectives in each sentence. One sentence has no adjectives.**

1 They work very hard and are now enjoying a long holiday.

2 Time passes quickly.

3 She is always late for the school bus and she gets home late each evening too.

4 More and more daily newspapers can now be read online.

5 At his age it was a really hard mountain to climb.

6 The meal had been prepared really nicely and it tasted nice too.

2 **Put the adjective in brackets in the most likely place in each sentence.**

1 I like ∧ mushrooms. (wild) *wild*

2 In those rivers in Scotland all the salmon are ∧. (wild) *wild*

3 She's studying seventeenth century painting. (Dutch)

4 Are they Swedish or are they? (Dutch)

5 Her grandparents are very and go to church regularly. (religious)

6 In Thailand all the buildings are open to tourists. (religious)

7 Older people think that young people are less these days. (polite)

8 All the representatives of the company were very young men. (polite)

9 All the local people are very and have made me feel at home. (friendly)

10 Labradors make very loyal and pets. (friendly)

11 The detectives were very in their approach to the crime. (scientific)

12 All experiments on animals are forbidden. (scientific)

3 **Tick (✓) the correct sentence, a or b.**

1 **a** This isn't his only home. He owns two cottages in Ireland.
   b This home isn't only. He owns two cottages in Ireland.

2 **a** John was glad that he had passed the exam.
   b A glad John had passed the exam.

3 **a** This road is main. Take it. It'll be quicker.
   b Take this main road. It'll be quicker.

4 **a** His former business partner has bought a new house in Spain.
   b His business partner, who is former, has bought a new house in Spain.

5 **a** The ill child was sent to hospital immediately.
   b The child was ill and was sent to hospital immediately.

4 Complete the adjective with either *-ed* or *-ing*.

1 We went to the cinema but the film was really *boring*.

2 It was a really *tir*.......... train journey from New York to Chicago.

3 She doesn't like heights and she was *terrifi*.......... / *terrify*.......... when she went on the ski lift.

4 The weather at this time of year is *depress*.........., isn't it?

5 It's an *amaz*.......... book. It's all about a boat journey along the Amazon.

6 These are very *surpris*.......... results. We thought they would be a lot worse.

7 I feel *relax*.......... when I listen to this music.

8 There's an *interest*.......... article about digital cameras in the newspaper today.

9 The directions he gave us were really *confus*...........

10 They said that's the most *excit*.......... match they've seen for ages.

11 I was late for the interview and then went to the wrong company. It was really *embarrass*...........

12 The carnival was wonderful and I was completely *fascinat*.......... the whole time.

5 Tick (✓) the correct sentence, a or b.

1 **a** The asleep children are in the bedroom upstairs.
   b The children are asleep in the bedroom upstairs.

2 **a** Mark has alike sisters, hasn't he? They've both got lovely green eyes.
   b Mark's sisters are alike, aren't they? They've both got lovely green eyes.

3 **a** Rebecca has lots of friends at work but I think she feels an alone person.
   b Rebecca has lots of friends at work but I think she feels alone.

4 **a** Some people believe that there are alive creatures on the moon.
   b Some people believe that there are creatures on the moon that are alive.

5 **a** At 1 am the whole village was awake and still watching the fireworks.
   b At 1 am the whole awake village was still watching the fireworks.

6 Five of the sentences have mistakes with gradable and ungradable adjectives. Correct the mistakes and tick (✓) the correct sentences.

1 They live in a very detached house in the country.

2 Her concerts are always extremely popular.

3 They like absolutely Thai food.

4 It was very cold in the flat last night.

5 That's quite good coffee but I like it a lot stronger.

6 Our holiday was very wonderful.

7 They're now quite divorced.

8 We like reasonably organic vegetables.

7 Put the adjectives in brackets in the most likely order. Add *and* where appropriate.

1 She is a (romantic/English/famous) novelist.
She is a famous, English romantic novelist.

2 He owns an (vintage/white/enormous) car.

3 When they got married, his aunt gave them a (woollen/large/Chinese) rug and a (old/Italian/u-shaped/lovely) mirror.

4 They have just bought a (antique/lovely/rectangular/wooden) coffee table.

5 The (slim/beautiful) girl was wearing a (silk/blue/pink) dress.

6 She was remembering the hotel next to the (sandy/white/long) beach.

8 Rewrite the information in each item to make a single sentence.

1 The computer is powerful and fast. It's for the family.
It's a fast, powerful family computer.

2 It's a train. It's punctual. It's fast. It's smooth.

3 This phone is light. It's attractive. It's fashionable.

4 The jacket is black. It's warm and comfortable.

5 The washing machine is quiet and reliable. It's economical.

6 This armchair is classic and comfortable. It's leather.

9 Read the adverts for (*a*) a house and (*b*) a flat for sale. Put the notes into sentences to advertise the house and flat. The first one has been started for you. You may need to use a dictionary.

a

**House for sale:
Wednesbury village**
Detached/Victorian house. Lovely.
Situated in commuter village. Peaceful,
attractive village. Rear vegetable garden
large, well-kept. Five bedrooms, large,
newly-decorated. Spacious kitchen.
Homely. With dark oak cupboards
(English oak).

This is a lovely detached victorian house situated in an attractive, peaceful commuter village. It has ....

....

....

b

**Flat for sale:
Morkham Town Centre**
Beautiful, modern flat. Elegant. City
Centre. Two large bedrooms, centrally
heated. Stylish kitchen, spacious. New
TVs (flat-screen) in both living rooms.

....

....

....

10 Underline the correct adjective in each sentence. You may need to use a dictionary.

1 This new electric car is very *economic / economical*.

2 For her postgraduate degree she's decided to specialise in *economic / economical* policy.

3 She's a very famous *historical / historic* novelist.

4 Winning the motor racing world championship was a *historical / historic* achievement.

5 She was wearing a *classical / classic* white blouse and dark skirt and it was the right choice for the interview.

6 Don't you like *classic / classical* music?

11 Describe the people in this picture and the journey that you think they are about to take. Use at least **six** adjectives in your description.

....

....

....

....

....

Adjuncts (adverbials)

1 Underline the adjuncts in these sentences.

1 I hadn't visited my aunt <u>for six years</u>.

2 She realised in the end that she had made a serious mistake.

3 He hid the money under the bed.

4 At first nobody noticed that he had arrived.

5 We slowly began to understand what she was trying to tell us.

6 He lifted the lid very carefully and examined the contents of the box.

2 Decide whether the parts of the sentences in bold are adjuncts, postmodifiers or complements. Write A, P or C.

1 I bumped into my Maths teacher the other day **in the park**.   A

2 We went to the new Thai restaurant **in the shopping centre**. ....

3 I've put the clean towels **in the bathroom**. ....

4 She found an old coin **in the garden**. ....

5 I don't want to go to a party. I'm not **in the mood**. ....

6 That photo **in the silver frame** is a lovely one of my sister. ....

3 Five of the adjuncts in these sentences are in the wrong position. Correct the mistakes and tick (✓) the correct sentences.

1 She in the morning left the house early.

2 He plays very well the violin and the viola.

3 They suddenly realised that someone was following them in a car.

4 Always I take the bus to work.

5 The teacher told during the lesson the students to be quiet.

6 The government has, from time to time, changed its policy as regards universities.

7 I'll post tomorrow the letter.

8 In the end, you can only learn a language by practising it.

4 Complete each sentence using an appropriate preposition so that it is true for you.

1 I usually keep my English books in ....

2 I normally get up at .... during ....

3 I stay in bed a bit longer on/at ....

4 I often meet .... in/on/at ....

5 When I don't know a word in English, I usually ....

6 I usually go to .... after ....

7 I usually check my email before/after/in ....

8 I usually feel very tired at/after/in/on ....

Adverbs and adverb phrases

1a Underline the adverb in each sentence.

1 The little girl walked <u>carefully</u> to the edge of the river.

2 The new software performs well.

3 A face suddenly appeared at the window.

4 Can you swim fast?

5 I'm not afraid of hard work; I've always worked hard.

6 She was a friendly woman who warmly welcomed us.

7 The whole house was beautifully clean.

8 My uncle was a well-educated person.

9 Could you come here and help me?

10 I'll just run upstairs and get that book for you.

1b Move the adverbs in sentences 1, 3, 6, 9 and 10 to a different position without changing the meaning.

2 Fill in each gap with the adjective form or the adverb form of the words in brackets.

1 She always sings so .... (good)

2 The old woman smiled .... at everyone. (happy)

3 You look .... Is anything the matter? (sad)

4 He was a wonderful ballet dancer. He danced so .... (beautiful)

5 I think you behaved very .... last night. (bad)

6 The traffic was very .... so we arrived .... (slow, late)

3 Put the adverbs into the most appropriate position in each sentence. Sometimes more than one answer is possible.

1 I ∧ loved going to the theatre when I lived in New York. (always)
   always

2 Does she work on Saturdays? (usually)

3 My brother speaks Russian. (very well)

4 We saw a police car. (suddenly)

5 We'll get the six o'clock flight. (probably)

6 They had wanted a house near the beach. (always)

7 I have been feeling unwell. (recently)

8 She loves her parents. (dearly)

4 **Underline the adverb phrase in each sentence.**

1 You know <u>very well</u> what I'm trying to say.

2 Because of the fog, we drove extremely slowly.

3 It was silly of you to behave so badly.

4 The children were playing quite happily in the garden.

5 The teacher treated him rather unkindly, in my opinion.

6 Everything went absolutely smoothly.

7 I'll wait for you just outside.

8 It all happened fairly slowly.

9 The house didn't sell quickly enough, so they had financial problems.

10 Luckily for me, I didn't have to pay anything.

5 **Underline nine more adverbs in this extract from a personal diary. Write the type (*time, manner, place* or *frequency*) above the adverb.**

May 2010

20 *Thursday* We got up *early* that day and went downstairs,

time

excitedly awaiting the arrival of the carnival parade. There was already a

very large crowd in the village square, the place where people always went

on such occasions. A big, decorated lorry soon arrived, and a man in a red

costume ran hurriedly into the Town Hall. We waited eagerly, occasionally

glancing at the upstairs windows to see if any faces were visible there.

6 **Complete each sentence so that it is true for you. Use adverbs from the box.**

always	sometimes	~~normally~~	extremely	hardly	usually
ever	quite	slowly	never	fast	angrily	calmly

1 I normally get up late when i don't have to go to work .

2 When I finish work/school, I .

3 I like to walk/drive/cycle when .

4 Just before an exam, I usually feel .

5 I react when people .

6 I'm optimistic/pessimistic about .

7   Find and correct five more mistakes with adverbs in the text.

busily
The teacher ~~busyly~~ corrected the class tests. She counted up the marks very careful and wrote them on the list of names. The students had performed extremley well. Most of them had answered all the questions correct. That was because they had studied hardly. The teacher was real happy with the results.

8   Fill in each gap with the correct form of the words in brackets.

1   ....Luckily........ , we got home before the rain started. (lucky)

2   In English, *rise* can be .... confused with *raise*. (easy)

3   Why does she drive so ....? (fast)

4   People always get my name .... It's Jan, not Jane. (wrong)

5   The car was .... damaged, but ...., no one was injured. (bad, fortunate)

6   This camera works very ...., even without much light. (good)

9   Fill in each gap with a suitable adverb based on the adjectives in the box.

angry   excited   tearful   calm   sarcastic   ~~truthful~~

1   Tim spoke ......truthfully...... , 'I have to tell you. I cannot marry you. I don't love you.'

2   Alice shouted ...., 'Quick, quick! Look! Wow! Amazing!'

3   Oscar replied ...., 'No! And I'm sick of you all! Get out!'

4   Nuria reacted ...., 'Let's not worry. There's nothing we can do.'

5   'I shall miss you all. I am so sad to be leaving,' Tanya said ....

6   'It was really so kind of you to crash my car,' Rita said ....

10 Underline the correct adverb in each sentence.

1   I haven't seen Joe *ultimately* / *recently*. Is he not well?

2   You'll have to come and see our new house *some time* / *sometimes*.

3   I love Latin American music, *especially* / *specially* Brazilian.

4   I'm not sure who he is; *eventually* / *perhaps* he's one of the new teachers.

5   I searched everywhere for the key. I *lastly* / *finally* found it in an old box.

6   *Firstly* / *At first* I didn't like Madrid, but now I love it.

Clauses

1a Four of these are clauses, two are not. Tick (✓) the clauses.

1 Over the hills and far away.

2 That's right.

3 Time goes so quickly.

4 All the time in the world.

5 Her eyes were tired.

6 Let's go!

1b Make the items in 1a which are not clauses into clauses by adding words to them.

2 Decide how many clauses there are in each sentence.

1 They're from Devon but they moved to Manchester in the 1980s. ...2...

2 Because we're both working, there's no one in the house in the day. ....

3 Do you enjoy your job or do you find it stressful? ....

4 Isn't the oldest woman in the world living in Japan? ....

5 The suitcase wasn't that heavy so I took it as hand luggage. ....

6 Where is everybody? ....

3 In this essay some of the sentences are not complete. Change the punctuation or add to the sentences to make complete sentences.

Q3 Discuss ways that you could help the environment in your everyday life. There are a number of small things I could do to help the environment. For example, when I get up in the morning. I usually leave the tap running while I brush my tooth. If I don't do that anymore, Also, I use a new plastic bag every day. When I bring lunch to work. So using the same one more often. Finally, I buy a lot of fruit. Because I love fruit. I could try to buy fruit that is grown locally. Also fruit that is organic,	**Q3 Discuss ways that you could help the environment in your everyday life.** There are a number of small things I could do to help the environment. For example, when I get up in the morning. I usually leave the tap running while I brush my teeth.

4 **Put each sentence into the correct column.**

Declarative	Interrogative	Imperative	Exclamative
	1		

1 Shall I sit here?

2 This is the best lamb I've ever eaten.

3 Come here.

4 Do have another chocolate!

5 Don't worry.

6 She wasn't able to remember the name of the hotel.

7 What a wonderful smell!

8 His name is Ian.

9 How thoughtful you are!

10 They weren't joking.

11 Wasn't that strange!

12 Didn't they say the party was starting at 8 o'clock?

Affirmative and negative

5 **Complete the grid.**

Affirmative	Negative
1 This is easy.	This isn't easy.
Will they be coming with us?	2
Some people like walking for hours.	3
4	Can't I help you?
Go now.	5
Let's watch a film tonight.	6
7	Didn't they leave early?
8	Why aren't they selling the house?
9	Don't be there before 6.
Leave me alone.	10

Offers, invitations and suggestions

6 **Write an offer, invitation or suggestion using an imperative for each of the pictures. Use each word once only.**

~~cake~~ seat lunch dinner a break

1 offer: _Have some cake_

2 invitation: ....

3 suggestion: ....

4 suggestion: ....

5 invitation: ....

Exclamative clauses

7 Complete the exclamative clause for each situation with *what, how, aren't* or *can*. Use each word once only.

1 You've just received a bunch of flowers from your best friend.

.... a wonderful friend you are!

2 You meet an old friend in the street and you realise that you haven't seen each other for a year.

.... quickly time goes!

3 You're shopping with your friend and you see a fabulous pair of shoes.

Look at those ones!
.... they amazing!

4 You and your friend are watching a TV talent show. A new contestant sings for the first time and she is excellent.

Wow! .... she sing!

Main and subordinate clauses, finite and non-finite clauses

8a Mark the main clauses 'M' and the subordinate clauses 'S' in each sentence.

         S   M

  1 When we got to the station, the train had left.

  2 Buy some vegetables if you go to the market.

  3 Because they have a house in the country, they don't spend all of their time in the city.

  4 Before reading *Harry Potter*, I went to see the film.

  5 Having spent forty years in the army, he was very happy to retire.

  6 Although he was tired, he was so happy to have arrived safely in Rome.

8b Mark the subordinate clauses in 8a as finite or non-finite?

9a In each sentence, mark whether each clause is finite or non-finite.

           finite   finite

  1 This isn't my favourite room because it's very noisy.

  2 Being the youngest daughter, my parents still treat me like the baby!

  3 To make sure they got there early, they took the 7 am train.

  4 Helped by his friends, he collected over £1,000 for charity.

  5 Not having many friends, he felt rather lonely.

  6 In order to hire a care, we went to the airport the day after we arrived.

9b Rewrite the sentences using non-finite clauses and the appropriate punctuation.

  1 I'm a terrible cook so I usually don't have dinner parties.

      Being ....

  2 She sang at the Oscars ceremony to an audience of millions.

      Watched by ....

  3 I'm not very fit so I decided to go for a cycle after work in the evenings.

      Not being ....

  4 If you want to join the club, you just fill in a form online.

      In order to ....

Comparison

Comparative and superlative adjectives, (not) as ... as

1   Fill in each gap with the correct form of the adjective in brackets. Use the comparative and superlative forms and (not) as ... as ...

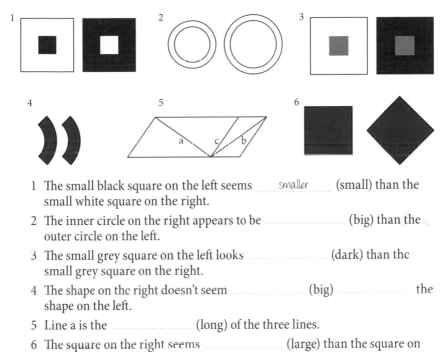

1   The small black square on the left seems ......*smaller*...... (small) than the small white square on the right.

2   The inner circle on the right appears to be .... (big) than the outer circle on the left.

3   The small grey square on the left looks .... (dark) than the small grey square on the right.

4   The shape on the right doesn't seem .... (big) .... the shape on the left.

5   Line a is the .... (long) of the three lines.

6   The square on the right seems .... (large) than the square on the left.

2   Fill in each gap using information from the table and the comparative or superlative form of the adjective in brackets.

Company	Destination	Price	Hotel	Journey time	Extras
Travelfirst	Paris	£256	★★★	2 hrs 20	breakfast included
Eurospeed	Prague	£309	★★★★	3 hrs 15	breakfast included
Rooms4U	Edinburgh	£159	★★★	1 hr 50	

We wanted to take a short city break in Europe so we searched on the Internet for some of (1) ......*the best*...... (good) offers. The trip to Edinburgh was (2) .... (cheap) but we had already been to Edinburgh several times so we decided not to go there. The journey to Paris was (3) .... (short) than the journey to Prague but the (4) .... (high) quality hotel was in Prague. The overall cost of the trip to Prague was (5) .... (expensive). Prague is (6) .... (far) away than Paris but the trip seemed to be (7) .... (good) value.

3a **You're signing up to a social networking site. You're asked some questions about yourself. Fill in the gaps with the correct form of the adjective in brackets and any other missing words.**

1 Do you have any .... (old) brothers or sisters?

2 Are you .... (happy) now .... when you were .... (young)?

3 Are you .... (busy) today .... you were yesterday?

4 What's .... (expensive) thing you've ever bought?

5 What's .... (interesting) book you've ever read?

6 What's .... (dangerous) thing you've ever done?

7 What's .... (tasty) meal you've ever made?

8 What's .... (nice) thing you've done today so far?

3b **Now answer the questions.**

Comparative and superlative adverbs

4 **Match 1–6 with an appropriate following sentence a–f. Complete the sentences with the comparative form of an adverb from the box.**

| far | badly | slowly | hard | well | ~~early~~ |

1 I was late for the meeting.   **a** He couldn't have done ....

2 I didn't do very well in my exams.   **b** I should have got up *earlier*

3 You got a speeding ticket?   **c** You're playing much ....

4 He got the slowest time in the race.   **d** You should have driven ....

5 You've really improved.   **e** I can't walk any ....

6 I'm so tired.   **f** I should have worked ....

5 **Correct the mistakes in these sentences.**

1 My oldest sister plays tennis better that me, but I can run more fast.

2 In my family, my son gets up the most early.

3 My younger brother cooks the worse of all of us. He's a terrible cook!

4 In the evenings my daughter arrives home more lately than her brother.

5 He speaks Spanish more fluent as Italian.

More, less, the most, the least

6a Look at the graph and fill in each gap in the newspaper article with *more, fewer, as, as much* and any other necessary words.

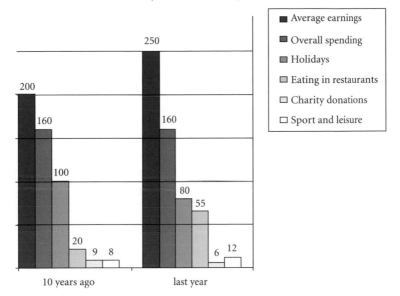

Sunday, February 26, 2011

Studies about how people in the UK live nowadays in comparison with how they lived ten years ago have shown an increase in average earnings, among other things. On average people earned (1)........................ last year (2)........................ they did ten years ago. Overall we spent about (3)........................ money last year as we did ten years ago. We took (4)........................ holidays last year (5)........................ we did ten years ago but we went out to restaurants (6)........................ . We didn't give (7)........................ money to charity (8)........................ we did ten years ago. We did (9)........................ sport (10)........................ .

6b Compare the differences in your life ten years ago and your life now.

....

....

....

7 **Fill in each gap and answer the question.**

Erin took four chocolates from a box. Maria took three more (1) ....
Erin. Davide took twice as many (2) .... Maria and one less
(3) .... Sinjan. Erin took two less (4) .... Rudi.

How many chocolates did each person take?

(5) Rudi .... Erin .... Davide ....
Maria .... Sinjan ....

Question: Who took (6) .... ? Answer: Erin

Question: Who took (7) .... ? Answer: Sinjan

As ... as, the same

8 **Look back to the pictures in exercise 1. Do you think the sentences are true or false? Rewrite the sentences giving your opinion. Use (not) as ... as, the same as and other comparative forms.**

1   I think the small black square on the left is as big as the small white square on the right.
I think the white square on the right looks bigger than the black square on the left.
I think the squares look the same as each other.

2   ....

3   ....

4   ....

5   ....

6   ....

Conditionals: *If, if only, provided, I'd rather, I wish*

1 Match the beginnings of sentences 1–10 with the most likely endings a–j.

1 ...f... 2 .... 3 .... 4 .... 5 .... 6 .... 7 .... 8 .... 9 .... 10 ....

1 If anyone had phoned for James,   **a** if you're travelsick.

2 If you want to grow vegetables,   **b** then she'd definitely help you.

3 Try these tablets   **c** we could still have been friends.

4 If he could help them,   **d** what would you do?

5 If she wasn't so busy,   **e** if she hadn't worked so hard.

6 If I were you,   **f** I would have told you.

7 If you get here early,   **g** I wouldn't go to Beijing in summer.

8 If he hadn't been so rude,   **h** there'll be a key under the mat.

9 If you lost that watch,   **i** you need to be very patient.

10 She wouldn't be famous today   **j** they'd be very grateful.

2 Find and correct the mistakes in each sentence.

1 If my grandfather were still alive, he will be 100 today.

2 If it rained, we swam every afternoon in the indoor pool.

3 If I would know her name, I tell you.

4 If I will have my mum's car tomorrow, I could give you all a lift.

5 I'd go by train rather than by car, if only the country has better trains.

6 I'll pass on your message if I will see them.

7 If she goes to the concert tomorrow, I go too.

8 If I would bring my laptop, would it possible to have it repaired?

3 Fill in each gap with the correct form of the verbs in brackets.

1 If we phone before 5 pm, they ...will deliver... the TV tomorrow. (deliver)

2 If the government raise taxes, more people .... the country. (leave)

3 If you've finished with the camera, I .... it back to Dave. (give)

4 If he .... more, he'd play the guitar a lot better. (practise)

5 If she didn't work so hard, she .... so tired. (not be)

6 If you took the car, you .... there in less than an hour. (get)

7 If she said how she felt, he .... very differently. (behave)

8 If she .... to Spain, she would've had better weather. (go)

9 If they'd repaired the roof properly, the storm .... so much damage. (not cause)

10 If they .... Thailand in 2002, they wouldn't be living there now. (not visit)

4 Fill in each gap with a word or phrase from the box. Sometimes more than one answer is possible.

> unless   in case   provided   providing
> as long as   so long as   ~~suppose~~

1   _suppose_   it rains, what shall we do?

2 We won't get there by midday .... we leave by 7 am at the latest.

3 I'll pack some sandwiches .... we get hungry.

4 We'd better take the mobile phone .... you need to check your texts.

5 .... the plane is late, will she be safe on her own?

6 .... they have proper travel insurance, they'll be fine.

7 .... there's a change of government, they are not going to set up a new company.

8 I'll buy extra food .... they bring their friends with them.

9 .... the weather gets better, they won't be doing the ferry crossing today.

10 .... the snow doesn't melt, we should be able to ski for most of next week.

5 Fill in each gap with *whether* or *if*. Where both *if* and *whether* can be used, write *whether/if*.

1 .... you call me tomorrow, I'll be able to tell you if you have been successful in the competition.

2 She didn't know .... or not she needed to take one more exam.

3 It depends on .... they behave themselves or not.

4 I wanted to know .... she was staying for two days or longer.

5 I don't think you should play with that injury but .... or not you do, it is up to you.

6 It's a question of .... she is fit enough to take part.

6 Fill in each gap with *otherwise, or else, if only* or *would rather/'d rather*. Sometimes more than one answer is possible.

1 We just met last week; .... we'd met earlier.

2 You'd better take an umbrella with you, ... you could get very wet.

3 Take the DVDs with you, ... you may never see them again!

4 .... you were honest with him, ... he could get the impression you were interested.

5 .... they didn't bring the dogs with them when they stay with us.

6 A: .... I were taller and more intelligent.
   B: Okay, but if you could choose only one, ... you .... be more intelligent or be taller?

7 Mark each sentence as formal (F) or informal (I).

1 If I were you, I'd book for seven days and you get two days free. I

2 If you'd like to come this way.

3 Few, if any, of the team wanted to play the match again.

4 Had you looked at the map, you would see that it's going to take ages to get there.

5 Had they contacted the manager when they arrived, he would have given them their membership cards.

6 They should rent a really luxurious house, if not a villa, in France.

7 He was extremely unpleasant, if not rude.

8 Can you help us to prepare the food? If so, here's the vegetables!

9 I'm sorry for interrupting the meeting. If you'd excuse me, I've got to go.

8 Write a one-line advertisement with a conditional *if* clause for each of the four products.

1 Chocolate: If you like chocolate, you'll fall in love with...

2 Car: ....

3 Hotel: ....

4 Computer game: ....

9 Complete each sentence so that it is true for you.

I wish I ..., if only ...

1 I wish I had ....

2 I wish my friends were ....

3 If only I could ....

4 If only I hadn't ....

5 I wish I had never ....

6 If only I ....

7 I wish my teachers ....

8 It's time I ....

Conjunctions

1 **Match the beginnings 1–12 with the most likely endings a–l. Then underline the conjunction.**

1 _f_ 2 .... 3 .... 4 .... 5 .... 6 .... 7 .... 8 .... 9 .... 10 .... 11 .... 12 ....

1 I like travelling,	**a** she can't come due to illness.
2 Although it rained all day,	**b** she felt much better.
3 We were very proud of her,	**c** before you sign anything.
4 As she told you,	**d** they still enjoyed visiting the gardens.
5 Please keep it tidy for us,	**e** he still loved playing computer games.
6 Always read the small print	**f** <u>but</u> I don't like airports.
7 While I'm pleased for them,	**g** though I may be a bit late.
8 After she told the truth,	**h** while we are away.
9 I'll see you at 7 this evening	**i** because she worked so hard to pass.
10 Since you couldn't come,	**j** or I'll be really cross.
11 Don't tell my sister	**k** we've invited your deputy.
12 Although he worked with computers all day,	**l** I still think they were very lucky to win the prize.

2 **Five of the sentences have mistakes with conjunctions. Correct the mistakes and tick (✓) the correct sentences.**

1 So I've been running most days this month and feel really fit.

2 I'm going to Beijing whereas I'd like to study Chinese medicine.

3 They didn't like their hotel room while they complained to the manager.

4 The paintings were first shown in an exhibition in Moscow in 1910, though few art critics provided positive reviews at the time.

5 He wanted to give up learning Russian because it's too hard so he can't do it.

6 Before telling us he had bought a new bike, he tried to sell us his old one.

7 A: Why didn't you like her? B: Since she is always too busy to talk to us.

8 After deciding to resign, she changed her mind at the last minute.

3 **Complete each sentence so that it is true for you.**

1 I want to .... in order to ....

2 Since I've been ...., I ....

3 When I'm bored, I ....

4 I'd like to visit ...., because ....

5 All my friends ...., whereas I ....

4 Fill in each gap with a conjunction from the box. Use one of the conjunctions twice.

even if   even though   either ... or   not only ... but also

1 .... he was ill that week, he continued to go to college every day.

2 .... you pay me back the money you owe me .... I'll contact the police.

3 .... they win the match on Saturday, they'll still be bottom of the league.

4 They .... visited London and New York .... took an even longer flight to Sydney.

5 .... you paid me a lot of money, I wouldn't go rock climbing.

5 Underline the correct conjunction. Underline more than one conjunction if more than one is correct.

1 *While / When / As* I understand how you feel, there's no need to be rude.

2 He was skiing in Austria *while / when / as* he broke his arm.

3 *Although / Since* she was injured, she continued to play the match.

4 *As / Because* it was getting dark, they decided to sit at home and watch TV.

5 *Even if / Even though* she retired early from the company, she still sees all her friends.

6 [from a newspaper] The prime minister has announced a new economic plan *cos / because* the elections are approaching.

7 She watched the film *while / since* texting her friend the whole time.

8 *Although / Though* she had jetlag, she still went to work the next day.

6 Five of the sentences have mistakes with conjunctions. Correct the mistakes using *or* or *but* to replace the incorrect conjunctions. Tick (✓) the correct sentence.

1 We'd better take the car and we shall be late.

2 Don't make me eat that chocolate cake or I'll get fat.

3 The restaurant was very crowded or we found a table.

4 I dropped that expensive vase on the floor as fortunately it didn't break.

5 Yesterday it was far too hot outside, since today the temperature is lower.

6 He doesn't smoke and eat fatty food.

7 Fill in each gap with the conjunctions from the box. You can use the same conjunction more than once. Sometimes more than one answer is possible.

although	but	as	not only ... but also	because
even though	either ... or	both ... and		

ASK **ANNIE**

Problem:
Dear Annie,
I love my boyfriend (1)................................... I find it difficult to talk to him about my personal feelings (2) .... he just asks too many questions. What should I do?

Thanks,
Samantha (aged 19)

Reply:
Dear Samantha,
I understand what you mean, (3) .... you should try hard to see your boyfriend's point of view (4) .... he just wants to be closer to you. (5) .... you find it difficult, it is perhaps best to give information about yourself gradually. (6) ....
will it make your relationship stronger, (7) .... it will make
(8) .... you (9) .... your boyfriend feel better.

Good luck,
Annie

8 Complete each sentence in your own words.
1 The theatre was offering cheap tickets in order to *get more people to see the play.*
2 We'd better go by train in order not to ....
3 He ate too much food so he ....
4 The film made us cry because ....
5 I'm buying a more powerful computer so that ....
6 We're not allowed to spend the money until we ....

9 Fill in each gap with a conjunction from the box. Use each word only once.

so that	so	~~although~~	until	in order to
and	whereas			

PISCES
20 Feb-20 March

(1) ....Although.......... you let your heart rule your head, you need to show more common sense at times, (2) .... you won't get into too much trouble. (3) .... some people are careful with money, people with your star sign are normally not and next week will see some possible financial changes in your life. (4) .... you need to plan your life more (5) .... things are back to normal and (6) .... to avoid too many disappointments (7) .... unpleasant surprises.

Determiners

1a The first determiner in the text is underlined. Underline ten more determiners.

> JOURNAL
>
> A recent study showed that two billion emails are sent each day, or two million messages every second. Most people find that they cannot keep up with this flood of communication and many people experience 'email stress', the feeling that they must answer all emails the moment they arrive.

1b Complete the questions with determiners, then answer the questions so that they are true for you.

1 How .... emails do you send, on average, per day?
2 Do you answer .... your emails the moment they arrive, or do you wait to answer some of them?
3 Do you send .... text messages? How .... per day?
4 When was the last time you sent .... letter?
5 How many hours per day do you spend on .... Internet?
6 Do you use any .... forms of electronic communication, for example, chat rooms, social networking sites?

2 Fill in each gap with *a* or *an*.

1 .... egg 2 .... bird 3 .... uncle 4 .... one-to-one lesson
5 .... university 6 .... hot day 7 .... MP3 file 8 .... hour
9 .... easy question 10 .... wheel

3 Fill in each gap with the definite article *the* where necessary. If *the* isn't necessary, write X.

1 .... sun has come out. Let's have lunch in .... garden.
2 .... Everest is the highest mountain in .... world.
3 He committed a serious crime and was in .... prison for five years.
4 Did you read it in .... newspaper or hear it on .... radio?
5 We spent a week near .... Lake Tahoe in California, then we went to .... Mojave Desert.
6 Have you ever been shopping in .... Oxford Street in London? It's one of the most famous streets in .... UK.
7 She did a lot of work for .... poor during her life.
8 .... M1 motorway in England was opened in 1959.
9 Which river is longer, ... Nile or .... Amazon?
10 We looked at .... moon through a telescope. It was beautiful.

4 There are six more mistakes with the definite article *the* in the text. Correct the mistakes by deleting three definite articles and adding three.

~~The~~ life is very expensive for students these days because the cost of living has increased. This is because economy is in a bad state at the moment. Minister of Education has promised to increase financial support for students. However, if economic situation does not improve, the things will not get better. The future is not looking good. The unemployment is high, so students will have fewer chances of getting the jobs when they graduate.

85

5 Fill in each gap with *some* or *any*.

1 A: Are there .... high mountains in the Netherlands?
   B: No, there aren't. The highest point is 321 metres above sea level.

2 A: Why are you drinking black coffee? Don't we have .... milk?
   B: I wanted it black. I didn't want .... milk.

3 A: Would you like .... tea? I've just made a pot.
   B: Mm, yes, please! I'd like .... sugar in it, if you don't mind.

4 A: Can you lend me .... money for the parking machine?
   B: Sure. I've got .... coins. How much do you need?

5 A: Were there .... people at the party that you knew?
   B: Yes, there were .... guys from work, but there weren't .... friends of ours.

6 Underline the correct determiner in each sentence.

1 The school has decided to change *it's* / *its* policy on the use of calculators during maths lessons.

2 We don't need *this* / *these* furniture anymore.

3 We spent very *few* / *little* money on our holiday this year.

4 The students finished *their* / *there* exams last week.

5 We're going to sell *our* / *ours* cars and buy two bicycles.

6 I don't like these shoes. The *others* / *other* shoes are better.

7 **Read the remarks then answer the questions.**

Richard: 'Neither boy had any money.'

 Joanna: 'None of the girls looked happy.'

~~Ramesh~~: 'Both men were wearing black.'

 Ulla: 'I saw some children playing in the street.'

Anoma: 'Half of the class seemed to be asleep!'

1 Who made an affirmative statement about two people? *Ramesh*

2 Who made a statement about 50% of the people in a group? . . . .

3 Who made an affirmative statement about a small, indefinite number of people? . . . .

4 Who made a negative statement about two people? . . . .

5 Who made a negative statement about more than two people? . . . .

8 **Fill in each gap with a determiner from the box. Use each word once only.**

both	~~each~~	all	every	none	one

1 The President congratulated the children and gave *each* of them a prize.

2 . . . . student knows that hard work is the key to success.

3 . . . . of his friends came to his wedding. He was very disappointed.

4 . . . . of these windows is broken. I wonder who broke it?

5 . . . . his brothers, Mark and Simon, became engineers.

6 . . . . her friends were away so she had no one to play with.

9 **Put the determiners in brackets in the correct position in each sentence.**

1 We don't have ⋀ large boxes. (enough) — *enough*

2 She gave me a wonderful present for my birthday. (such)

3 There were people who offered help to the police officer. (few)

4 Have you got money? (enough)

5 I have information, if it is of value to you. (any)

6 Let me get you coffee and biscuits. (another, some)

7 People came into the shop early this morning. (several)

8 My best friends have got married this year. (two)

9 Both parents came to the school meeting. (her)

10 One of the customers filled in a complaint form. (every)

10a In four of these sentences, you can use a determiner as a pronoun to avoid repeating a noun. Where you can use the determiner as a pronoun, cross out the second noun in bold as in the example.

1 Harry brought his tennis **racket** and Peter brought his ~~**racket**~~ too.
2 I don't want these **books**; I want those **books**.
3 This is not my **jacket**. That's my **jacket**, over there.
4 He didn't just burn some of the **books**, he burnt every **book**.
5 I don't need any more **pens**. I already have several **pens**.
6 I can't decide which of the two **sweaters** I like. Shall I buy both **sweaters**?
7 Mary-Jo showed us her **poem** but Lilian would not show us her **poem**.
8 Are you looking for your **baseball cap**? Is this one your **baseball cap**?

10b In the sentences where you didn't cross out the second noun, what changes could you make to avoid repeating the noun?

....
....
....
....

11 Complete each sentence so that it is true for you.

1 I never seem to have enough ....
2 The most important person in my life is ....
3 If I could learn any musical instrument, I'd choose ....
4 I'd love to buy some ....
5 I really need another ....
6 This year, I've bought very few ....

12 Complete the descriptions of the pictures using a determiner from the box and any other necessary words.

| none | neither | all | both | half | ~~two~~ |

1 There were three boys in the park. Two of them were wearing baseball caps.

2 .... is on the table; .... is on the floor.

3 There were three girls on the beach. .... wearing shoes.

4 There were two men in the office. .... were asleep.

5 The two women were sitting on the sofa. .... wearing glasses.

6 There were four boys in the street. .... carrying books.

13 Fill in each gap with *few, a few, little* or *a little*.

In a recent survey, young children seemed to have (1) .... knowledge of where the food they eat comes from.
Only (2) .... children knew that eggs came from chickens.
Very (3) .... of the children knew how spaghetti was made; some thought it grew in the ground, and (4) .... of the children thought it grew in trees or bushes. The bad news is that the same survey has been carried out (5) .... times in the last 30 years, but it seems the results get worse each time and there is (6) .... hope that things will improve. However, the good news is that if children spend (7) .... time each week learning about food, they quickly become interested and want to know more.

25

Discourse markers

1 Underline the discourse marker in each sentence.

1 So, why don't we order a takeaway?

2 We're going to meet at eight tomorrow morning and then we'll all walk to St Mark's Square together, okay?

3 Right, let's go.

4 Anyway, why don't we think about it for a day or two and then decide?

5 The restaurant was interesting … well, it wasn't great.

2 Fill in each gap using a word from the box. Sometimes more than one answer is possible.

actually	right	now	so	okay	fine

1 Let's begin. ...., I want to start by introducing Dr Harrod Moynes.

2 A: I'll pick you up at 8.45 and we'll get to the airport by 9.30.
B: .... I'll see you then.

3 We're here at last! ...., who has the key?

4 ...., if you look at the picture on your left, you'll see that it was donated to the hospital by the people of Westbury in 1910.

5 A: You're from London, aren't you?
B: No, ..., I'm from Oxford.

3 Underline the correct discourse markers in each situation. Underline more than one discourse marker if more than one is correct.

1 A teacher says at the beginning of a class:
Okay / Right / Anyway, I want you to open your book at page five.

2 The director of the company says at the end of a meeting:
Actually / Fine / Right, is there anything else we need to discuss?

3 Friends are talking on the phone and one says:
Sounds like you had a great time last night. I wish I could have been there. *Right / Anyway / Finally*, did I tell you that we've decided to move house?

4 A museum guide says:
If you look to your right, you will see the early nineteenth-century watercolours. *So / Actually / Fine*, this collection is new to the museum.

5 A waiter brings the menus and says:
Firstly / Actually / Okay, let me tell you that the special of the day is roast duck with sweet potatoes and the soup of the day is vegetable.

4 **Use the discourse markers in brackets to organise the sentences.**

1 Chop the onions. Fry them for five minutes. (and then, first of all)
First of all, chop the onions and then fry them for five minutes.

2 There are many reasons why this factory shouldn't be built. It will be bad for the environment. It will mean heavy traffic in the village. It will look ugly. (what's more, firstly, secondly)

3 I can't work late tonight. I have to babysit for my sister. I've worked late two evenings this week already. Why don't you ask Bill instead? (so, on top of that, for a start)

4 At least two teachers are ill every week. We have a list of substitutes whom we can call and we can usually find someone to substitute within half an hour. (so, in general)

5 It was a long night. We lost our keys and searched everywhere but couldn't find them. We had to phone Jason at 2 am because he has a spare key for the house. It was 3 am when we got to bed! (and then, to begin with, in the end)

5 **Complete each sentence with an appropriate ending.**

1 The restaurant was dark. **I mean** *I couldn't even read the menu.*

2 I have very little money left at the end of each month. **You see**

3 Everyone was happy with the marks for their essays. **In other words**

4 Cats are just so different to dogs. **You know what I mean**

5 I want to study Medicine at university, but **the thing is**

6 Underline the most appropriate discourse marker in each reply.

1 A: Can I borrow your pen for a minute?
B: *Absolutely / Exactly.* Go ahead.

2 A: She's the best teacher we have had so far.
B: *Probably / Definitely.* I totally agree with you.

3 A: The point is, he should have told us sooner.
B: *Exactly / Not really.* Then we could have found a solution.

4 A: Are you and Dave going to the surprise party for Barbara?
B: *Precisely / Probably.* We still haven't found a babysitter though.

5 A: Can we have the bill please?
B: *Certainly / Exactly.* I'll bring it right away.

7 The discourse markers in these sentences show attitude. Choose *a* or *b* to explain their meaning.

1 **Unfortunately**, he's decided to come with us.
a I'm happy about this.　　**b** I'm not happy about this.

2 We will, **obviously**, pay for this ourselves.
a It is clear.　　**b** It isn't clear.

3 It's going to be sunny, **I think.**
a I am sure.　　**b** I am not sure.

4 This is not an easy decision **if you ask me.**
a It's what I think.　　**b** It's what everybody thinks.

5 **Essentially**, we don't have enough money to continue the project.
a The main point is …　　**b** The final point is …

8 Use a discourse marker from the box to make the sentences less direct. Use each discourse marker once only.

just	sort of	arguably	perhaps	roughly

1 We should ask for permission.
2 There are 20 candles left in the box.
3 Can you close the door?
4 It's hot in here.
5 She was the best flute player of her generation.

9 **Choose the right response (a–e) for each situation. Use each response once only.**

1 You bang your finger with a hammer. ....

2 You find very old sandwiches in your bag. ....

3 You find out that you have passed your exams. ....

4 You drop you keys and they fall into a puddle of water. ....

5 Your friend tells you she has won £1,000. ....

a **Wow!**   b **Ouch!**   c **Oh no!**   d **Yuck!**   e **Hooray!**

10 **Fill in each gap in this graduation speech with a discourse marker from the box. Use each discourse marker one once only.**

in addition	in conclusion	secondly	on the one hand
thirdly	on the other hand	moreover	firstly

(1) ...., I would like to welcome you all here today for the graduation ceremony. (2) ...., I would like to congratulate all of those who have graduated today. And (3) ...., I would like to thank all of their families and friends who have come to celebrate with them. (4) ...., this is a very happy occasion but (5) ...., it is also a very sad occasion because it marks the end of your college days. (6) ...., it is the last time that all of you and all of us will be gathered together. (7) ...., it marks a big time of change in your life when you move from being a student to starting a career. But let's not be sad. This is a very happy day for everyone and your future paths lie ahead of you. (8) ...., remember that there are so many opportunities for you. There are so many things you can do, so "Seize the day!".

11 **Write an appropriate response for each situation.**

That's terrible!   That's amazing!   Oh really?

Exactly!   That's shame!

1 A: Jean slipped on the ice and broke her wrist.   B: ....

2 A: William's getting married.   B: ....

3 A: I'm afraid I can't meet you for lunch today.   B: ....

4 A: A man was found alive ten days after the earthquake!   B: ....

5 A: This decision isn't good for the company. We need to consider the
    direction we want to go in.   B: ....

12 **Underline the most appropriate response to each statement.**

1 A: Maggie has decided to leave university.
   B: *Oh really? / Right.*

2 A: Look at that rain. We're going to need raincoats and umbrellas!
   B: *Yeah. / Definitely.*

3 A: Grace won the art competition and got £10,000 as a prize.
   B: *That's amazing! / That's interesting.*

4 A: I've left my memory stick on the bus and all my files are on it!
   B: *Wow! / Oh no!*

5 A: Green tea is so good for you.
   B: *Absolutely. / Fine.*

13 **Decide which three responses are not appropriate and suggest
a more appropriate response. Tick (✓) the two appropriate responses.**

1 A: Cathy fell down the stairs and broke her leg.
   B: That's terrible. ....

2 A: Look, a pink snail's shell.
   B: That's amazing! ....

3 A: Depending on the species, centipedes can have from 30 to 200 legs.
   B: Wonderful. ....

4 A: I've broken my nail!
   B: Right. ....

5 A: Can you open the window, please?
   B: Oh really? ....

14 **Write a statement to match each of the responses.**

1 A: .... B: Oh really?

2 A: .... B: That's terrible.

3 A: .... B: Wonderful.

4 A: .... B: I see.

Ellipsis and substitution

1 **Remove a word from each sentence to make it more informal without changing its meaning.**

1 I was glad ~~that~~ he told me about her illness.

2 We went to the party and we danced all night.

3 I'm sorry that you didn't get the job.

4 They went to Malta and they had a wonderful holiday.

5 I remember the name of the author but I can't remember the title of the book.

6 He telephoned or he emailed all the people in his class.

7 On the same day, our car had a puncture and it ran out of petrol!

8 Is he afraid that he won't be able to use the video camera properly?

2 **Remove words from each sentence to make it less repetitive.**

1 She said she'd phone this morning but she hasn't ~~phoned~~ yet.

2 She thinks I criticise her too much but I don't criticise her too much.

3 I know the microwave's not working. When it is working, the green light comes on.

4 Salma can't swim but fortunately everyone else on the boat can swim.

5 Rumiko is a fan of the Tokyo Giants baseball team and her sister is a fan of the Giants too.

3a **The following texts all use ellipsis. Say in what context you would expect to find them.**

1 Speak a new language in one month ....

2 Man walks on moon. ....

3 Thinking about warm sun this winter? ....

4 Take 30g of brown rice and boil in a pan until cooked. ....

5 Single person looking for flat in North London area, near to underground station. ....

3b **Choose one of the contexts, 1–5, above and write a sentence using ellipsis.**

....

....

English Grammar Today Workbook

4 **Remove words from the replies to make them less repetitive without changing the meaning.**

1 A: Have another piece of cake.
 B: I'd better not ~~have another piece of cake~~. I'm on a diet.

2 A: Why don't they buy another car?
 B: They don't want to buy another car.

3 A: Did you ring Tom?
 B: No, sorry, I didn't ring Tom. I was too busy.

4 A: She could stay with us.
 B: Yes, she could stay with you.

5 A: Have you got time for a meeting later today?
 B: Yes, we have got time. Is six o'clock okay for you?

6 A: Are they getting married this summer?
 B: Yeah, they are getting married.

5 **Add words to each sentence to make it more formal.**

1 See Jack at the fair? *Did you see Jack at the fair?*

2 Know what I mean?

3 You ready yet?

4 Too late. The train's gone.

5 Careful when you light the fire.

6 Need any help with the shopping?

7 Lots of things to tell you about the people we met.

8 A: Tried phoning them?
 B: Yeah, but nobody at home.

6 **Where appropriate, remove pronouns from these sentences so that they sound more informal.**

1 I like your new coat. *Like your new coat.*

2 I wonder if she's feeling better.

3 I saw Jasmine last week. She said she was going to work in Mumbai for a month.

4 Okay, it sounds good.

5 Sorry, I don't agree.

6 We hope you arrived safely.

7 A: Where's the fruit juice?
 B: It should be in the fridge.

8 I expect it'll be crowded in the shops in town today.

7 **Rewrite these dialogues to make them more formal.**

1 A: Started to play chess, has he? Why chess?
B: Said he needed some mental exercise.
A: Problem is, it takes a long time to learn.

A: He has started to play chess, has he? Why did he choose chess?
B: He said he needed some mental exercise.
A: The problem is that it takes a long time to learn.

2 A: Wasn't happy, was he?
B: No, he was told he couldn't take the exam and got really cross.

A: ....

B: ....

3 A: Wrote to the bank to complain, did you?
B: Yes, and got a reply from the manager.
A: Shame you didn't do it earlier.

A: ....

B: ....

A: ....

4 A: Julie and Dave went to New Zealand, didn't they?
B: Yeah, went last week.

A: ....

B: ....

5 A: They didn't like the map we gave them.
B: Got confused, did they?
A: Yes, but good thing they had it or they might have got totally lost.

A: ....

B: ....

A: ....

8a **Use the chart below to complete the sentences with *so …* or *neither …* .**

Favourite sports

	Anne	Jim	Mark	Claire
Tennis	☺	☺	☹	☹
Football	☹	☺	☺	☺
Swimming	☺	☹	☹	☺

1 Anne likes tennis and .... *so does* .... Jim.

2 Jim doesn't like swimming and .... Mark.

3 Claire isn't keen on tennis and ....

4 Mark watches lots of football and .... Claire and Jim.

5 Claire is a good swimmer and .... Anne.

8b Write three sentences about yourself and people you know, comparing the sports you like and dislike.

....

....

....

8c Use the table of 'Favourite sports' in 8a to help complete these dialogues with the word in brackets and *so* or *not*.

1 Anne: Can we play tennis tomorrow?
   Jim: .... I hope so .... But I might have to work late at the office. (hope)

2 Anne: Would you like to go swimming this evening?
   Mark:............................. . I don't really like swimming. (afraid)

3 Claire: Do you think Anne will come to the football match?
   Jim:............................. . (expect)

4 Claire: Will you swim a lot on holiday?
   Anne:............................. . It depends on the weather, of course. (think)

9a Write a reply to this text message using ellipsis.

Text message
123 (1)   Abc

Just arrived. Really hot here.
How's weather there? Hotel
and food great so far.
Everything okay with you? Will
write again later.

Options   Close

....

....

....

....

....

....

9b Write a headline using the opening paragraph from this news story.

....

Women may be allowed to serve on a
submarine for the first time in the history of
the Royal Navy. The change follows
government pressure for full equal opportunities
for women in the armed forces.

10a Read the dialogue below in which two friends are deciding whether to go to a football match. It contains a number of examples of ellipsis.

A: How about the match on Saturday?
B: Don't know. It's in Manchester.
A: Too far?
B: Yeah and a bit too expensive.
A: Shall we watch it on TV instead?
B: Okay, Good idea. Your house or mine?
A: All right, mine. But you bring some food for us.
B: Pizzas okay?
A: Okay, great.

10b Two friends are planning a summer holiday. Write a brief dialogue (no more than ten lines) using at least two phrases from the box.

haven't been there	too expensive	don't know	good idea
not hot enough	did that last year	too far, isn't it?	

....

....

....

....

....

....

....

Future

Will, shall, be going to

1 **Fill in each gap with** *will, 'll, won't, shall,* **or** *shan't.*

1 I'll be in town around 10 am. .... you contact Alex or
.... I ?

2 I can tell you that England .... never win the World Cup.

3 Your parents .... be very happy if you don't ring them before
you go.

4 A: I don't think there .... be anything to eat at the party.
B: .... we eat first?

5 She .... be eighteen next month, ... she?

6 Tomorrow .... be cold and wet with strong winds from the west.

7 They're already late and .... have time to come with you
now, ... they?

8 A: Their train arrives at 12 am.
B: Okay, What time .... we leave?

2 **Fill in each gap with the correct form of** *will* **or** *(be) going to* **and an**
appropriate verb from the box. Both options are possible in some cases.

get	~~buy~~	be	close
watch	rain	decorate	spend

1 Tomorrow we're going to buy a new computer.

2 He needs some new glasses and .... his eyes tested next
Tuesday at 4 pm.

3 At last! She .... her bedroom this week.

4 It's getting very cold in here. I think I .... the windows.

5 Don't lend him any money. He .... it all.

6 Look at those dark clouds. It .... later this morning.

7 .... you .... at home or in the office tomorrow
morning?

8 I .... a film on TV. It's just starting, do you want to watch it too?

Present continuous (*I'm working tomorrow*), will, be going to

3 In each sentence, rewrite the verb in bold using the most appropriate future form; present continuous, *will* or *(be) going to.*

1 We've just bought Jane this antique watch. Do you think she **wears** it?

....

2 Two of our directors **go** to Beijing next Saturday.

....

3 [Mother, speaker B, talking about her young child]
A: She looks tired, doesn't she?
B: She's really exhausted; she **goes** to bed in a few minutes.

....

4 I **learn** some Spanish before my business trip to Argentina next month.

....

5 He's just been hit on the hand by a golf ball. It really **hurts** tomorrow.

....

6 Their theatre group **performs** a new play at 8 pm on Friday evening.

....

Present simple (*It leaves tomorrow*), be about to, be to

4 Tick (✓) the correct sentence, a or b. If both are equally likely, tick both.

1 **a** The referee is looking at his watch. The match starts.
b The referee is looking at his watch. The match is about to start.

2 **a** The train gets into Rome at 14.40.
b The train is about to get into Rome at 14.40.

3 **a** A new art gallery is about to open in the university in July.
b A new art gallery is to open in the university in July.

4 **a** Can you tidy the living room? Your aunt's about to arrive.
b Can you tidy the living room? Your aunt arrives.

5 **a** Hurry up! The ferry is just about to leave.
b Hurry up! The ferry is to leave.

6 **a** The Vietnamese president is to visit Singapore next month.
b The Vietnamese president visits Singapore next month.

7 **a** What time does your flight leave?
b What time is your flight about to leave?

Future continuous (*I will be working*), future perfect (*I will have worked here for ten years*)

5 Underline the most appropriate form in each sentence.

1 He's got a scholarship at the University of Stockholm and will *have studied / be studying* there for the next three years.

2 Good luck with your driving test tomorrow. We'll *have thought / be thinking* of you.

3 The latest government report shows that in 2020 90% of people will *be buying / have bought* goods online.

4 By the end of this month they will *have bought / be buying* a total of over 200 CDs and DVDs on line.

5 A: Will you *have read / be reading* the book by the end of August?
B: Actually, I'll *have finished / be finishing* it by the end of the week.

6 A: Can you ask him?
B: Yes, okay, but I won't *have seen / be seeing* him on Tuesday.

7 The band will *have performed / be performing* at the same time next Saturday.

8 This time next week we'll *be skiing / have skied* in Italy.

Future perfect, future perfect continuous (*I will have been working*)

6 Complete each sentence with the correct future perfect or future perfect continuous form of the verb in brackets.

1 [A hurricane has hit the island of Bermuda. Stephen and Alison are flying to Bermuda tomorrow.]
I think the hurricane ___will have finished___ by the time Stephen and Alison reach Bermuda. (finish)

2 [We moved house three years ago on June 13th.]
Can you believe it? We _____ in this house for three years on June 13th. (live)

3 [Jill is training for the New York marathon today. She runs five miles before she gets to work.]
Before she gets to work today, Jill _____ five miles. (run)

4 [The computers are very popular at that price and they are selling them fast.]
Unless you act quickly, they _____ all the computers. (sell)

5 [I'm washing both our cars while you are shopping.]
By the time you get back, I _____ both cars. (wash)

6 [He started writing his thesis four years ago next month.]
By next month, he _____ his thesis for four years. (write)

Future in the past

7a In this email, underline the five references to the future in the past.

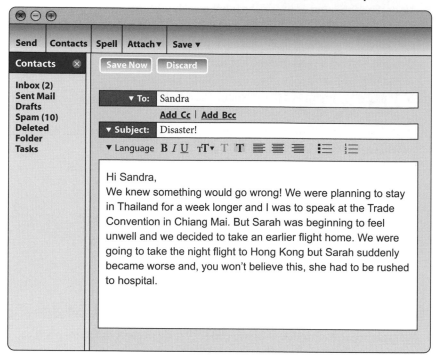

Hi Sandra,
We knew something would go wrong! We were planning to stay in Thailand for a week longer and I was to speak at the Trade Convention in Chiang Mai. But Sarah was beginning to feel unwell and we decided to take an earlier flight home. We were going to take the night flight to Hong Kong but Sarah suddenly became worse and, you won't believe this, she had to be rushed to hospital.

7b Fill in each gap using the verb in brackets to refer to the future in the past.

1 When we met last year, you .... to learn Chinese. (plan)

2 Geoff .... to London this morning but his car wouldn't start. (drive)

3 I .... due to speak at a conference in Warsaw but my flight was cancelled. (be)

4 It was the last performance of the play and I knew then that I .... never .... another performance like it. (see)

Future plans

8 You are about to travel to Russia and will follow the itinerary below. Write an email to a friend telling them what your future trip involves. Use the most appropriate phrases to refer to the future.

Itinerary: **Russian Capitals**

St Petersburg
°Moscow

Day	Activity
Day 1	Fly from London Heathrow to St. Petersburg. Meet guide. Go by private coach to your chosen hotel for four nights.
Day 2	A morning city tour to the Peter & Paul Fortress and Cathedral. *Special extra event (see below)
Day 3	A visit to the Hermitage Museum. And opportunity to explore the city independently.
Day 4	By train to Moscow with packed-lunch. Accompanied by guide. Transfer to your chosen hotel for three nights.
Day 5	City tour of Moscow, including the Novodevichy Convent.
Day 6	Optional morning visit to the Kremlin including the collections of the Armoury. Evening flight back to Heathrow.

*Private Ballet Performance Day 2: A gala ballet performance exclusively for our guests, featuring artists from the Mariinskiy (Kirov), Mussorgsky or other leading companies. Caviar during the interval.

. . . .

. . . .

. . . .

. . . .

. . . .

Hedges and downtoners

1 **Underline the hedge in each sentence.**

1 <u>I wondered if</u> I could borrow your tent?

2 We could possibly ask Gale to do it.

3 Maybe this isn't the best solution.

4 There's sort of an urgent need to get this report finished today.

5 I feel if they work harder, their sales figures will improve.

6 We reckon you need to improve the quality of the food rather then lower the price.

7 There's just a problem with the contract. Kay is sorting it out.

2 **Fill in each gap with an appropriate hedge from the box to make each sentence less direct. Sometimes more than one answer is possible.**

It's possible	Maybe	Would you mind
We are likely	We feel	

1 .... this isn't the best way of organising the room.

2 .... you need to reduce the price. It's too high.

3 .... turning the air-conditioning on?

4 .... that you got the infection while you were travelling.

5 .... to run out of money soon.

3 **Underline the downtoners in these sentences.**

1 I'm feeling <u>a bit</u> cold. Could you turn up the heating, please?

2 She may be slightly annoyed when we tell her that we can't go to dinner with her.

3 We could only just see the band on the stage. We were so far back in the stadium.

4 We need a tiny bit more salt in this.

5 He's barely eighteen years old. It seems so young to go sailing around the world alone.

6 The music is kind of loud.

English Grammar Today Workbook

4 Fill in each gap with an appropriate downtoner from the box. Sometimes more than one answer is possible.

| a bit | hardly | only just | slightly | somewhat |

1 8 pm is .... late for me.

2 The lecture was .... difficult to understand.

3 There is .... enough money in the account.

4 Can we afford to pay him .... more?

5 It's .... fair to ask Liam to drive me to the airport.

5 Tick (✓) the most direct sentence, a or b.

1 **a** We were wondering if you could help us dig our garden?
   b Could you help us dig our garden?

2 **a** It'll cost £100 to get there on the train.
   b I reckon it'll cost £100 to get there by train.

3 **a** Will you write down your name here, please?
   b Would you write down your name here, please?

4 **a** They will ask us to send more information.
   b They are likely to ask us to send more information.

5 **a** This could be the best solution to our problem.
   b This is the best solution to our problem.

6 Underline the correct downtoner in each sentence.

1 She was *a little bit / barely* four years old at the time.

2 We could see from their faces that they were *slightly / only just* annoyed that we were late.

3 His expression changed *barely / somewhat* when I told him the price; he thought it was far too costly.

4 We had *somewhat / only just* woken up when we heard the terrible noise.

5 I admit I was *a tiny bit / hardly* scared when the lights went out.

7 Write what you would say in each situation using a hedge.

1 You and your friend are having a party on Saturday night and you hope your brother will make some of the party food.
   We're having a party on Saturday night and we were hoping you would make some of the food.

2 Your friend is at your house for lunch. She has had a bowl of soup and you offer her some more.
   You say to her: ....

3 On a guided tour of a castle, the tour guide wants the tour group to follow her up to the tower.
   She says: ....

4 At the reception desk of a hotel, the receptionist wants to know the guest's name.

He says: ....

5 You are a waiter, the people at your table don't look like they are ready to order.

You say: ....

6 You are in a friend's house and you are feeling too warm.

You say: ....

8 **Rose is a young reporter and she has to interview a famous rock star called 'Mojo'. Look at her notebook and write the questions that she might ask. Make them sound more polite by using two questions instead of one.**

> Can I ask you about…?   What about …?   How about …?
> Do you mind if I ask you about…?

- *favourite city to play in?*
- *what do friends call him?*
- *another album before the end of the year?*
- *favourite album?*
- *relationship with other band members?*
- *next tour?*

can I ask you about touring? what's your favourite city to play in? ....

....

....

....

....

....

Imperatives

1 Tick (✓) the eight sentences which are imperatives.

1 Be careful when you open the door.

2 That's too loud!

3 Enjoy your trip.

4 Let's all sit down.

5 Don't forget to turn off the computer.

6 Please call again soon.

7 Doesn't he know their names?

8 You wait here.

9 Just give me a call.

10 Somebody clean the floor.

2 Write an imperative for each situation. More than one answer is possible.

1 A woman has slipped on the ice and you think she has broken her leg.

You say: ....

2  You're the teacher, the students in your classroom are all standing up when you come in.

You say: ....

3  Your best friend is leaving tomorrow on a three-month trip to The Netherlands.

You say: ....

4 Someone is trying to open a window in the office but they're turning the handle the wrong way.

You say: ....

5 You're planning to go to the theatre with a group of people. You send your friend a text message asking him to come.

You say: ....

3a **Decide which four imperatives are direct.**

1 Be quiet.

2 You stand up.

3 Just ask the lady at reception.

4 Turn off the radio.

5 Don't forget your toothbrush.

6 Let's start.

3b **Make the four direct imperatives less direct.**

. . . .

. . . .

4 **Underline the correct form in each sentence.**

1 The parcel has arrived but *let's don't / let's not* open it until Jack gets home.

2 This party is just getting started; *you don't / let's not* leave now!

3 A: Gary asked me to go to the cinema but I think I'll tell him that I'm busy.
   B: Martha, *don't / you don't*! You'll have a great time and Gary is a nice guy.

4 And finally *let's don't / don't let's* end this meeting without giving our
   colleague, Michael, our very best wishes in his new role as team manager.

5 The notice said '*Do not / Don't let's* use the lift in the event of a fire'.

6 A: How about we take a break now? B: Yes, *let's / take*.

5 **Fill in each gap with a verb from the box to make an offer or invitation
using an imperative.**

go	be	have	come	try	call	stay

1 There's more couscous left. . . . . on! . . . . some more.

2 My new apartment is in the city centre. Please . . . . and
   . . . . with me soon. It'll be fun!

3 . . . . one of these delicious chocolates.

4 Don't . . . . afraid to ask for help. You know my phone number;
   just . . . . me any time you need advice.

6a **Decide which three imperatives are formal.**

1 Do have a seat.

2 Don't let's say anything about this to Kevin yet.

3 Help yourself to some more dessert.

4 Let's not start too early in the morning.

5 Let us not forget to thank those who worked so hard on the project.

6b **Rewrite the formal imperatives so that they are more informal.**

. . . .

7 **Tick the more emphatic sentence.**

1 **a** Turn off the light, please. **b** Turn off the light, please, will you?
2 **a** You stay here. **b** Stay here please.
3 **a** Send me a post card, won't you? **b** Send me a postcard.
4 **a** Somebody call the police! **b** Let's call the police.
5 **a** Turn the music down, if you wouldn't mind? **b** Turn it down, will you?

8 **Rewrite these invitations as imperatives.**

1 Would you like to stay with us when you come to New York?
stay with us when you come to New York.

2 Why don't you come to the nightclub with us?

3 Do you want to try these muffins that Jamie made?

4 Why not leave your car at home and travel with us?

5 You must call to see me in my new office.

6 We could go to a restaurant this evening, if you like.

9 **The responses in these conversations are imperatives. Three of them might be heard as impolite. Change the responses to make them less direct.**

1 A: What time is it?
  B: Ask someone else. I don't have a watch.
2 A: Could you tell me how to get to Holman House?
  B: Don't ask me. I'm not from here.
3 A: I have no pen!
  B: You use mine and I'll use this pencil.
4 A: Can you hear the fire alarm going off?
  B: Everybody leave the room now.

Infinitives

1 **Three of the sentences have mistakes with infinitives. Correct the mistakes and tick (✓) the correct sentences.**

1 He promised to lock the door.

2 I can't to reach the top shelf.

3 We don't use that knife for to cut the bread.

4 To get to the shop, you have to turn left at the traffic lights.

5 Did you remember to phone your father?

6 He wanted find a good job in New York.

2 **Underline the correct form in each sentence.**

1 She might *to want* / *want* to talk to you.

2 He asked *to talk* / *talk* to the manager.

3 Have you decided *to sell* / *sell* your house?

4 She failed *to find* / *find* the key of the car.

5 *To be* / *Be* a nurse has always been her ambition.

6 The teacher didn't let us *to use* / *use* a dictionary in the exam.

7 Our parents made us *to tidy* / *tidy* our room every week.

8 We like *to take* / *take* a break at 11.30.

3 **Kathy is going to Australia for a year. Her friend Lisa lives in Australia. Add *to* where necessary and write X where *to* isn't necessary.**

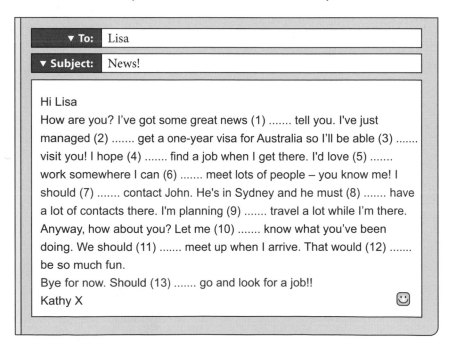

▼ To:	Lisa
▼ Subject:	News!

Hi Lisa

How are you? I've got some great news (1) .... tell you. I've just managed (2) .... get a one-year visa for Australia so I'll be able (3) .... visit you! I hope (4) .... find a job when I get there. I'd love (5) .... work somewhere I can (6) .... meet lots of people – you know me! I should (7) .... contact John. He's in Sydney and he must (8) .... have a lot of contacts there. I'm planning (9) .... travel a lot while I'm there. Anyway, how about you? Let me (10) .... know what you've been doing. We should (11) .... meet up when I arrive. That would (12) .... be so much fun.

Bye for now. Should (13) .... go and look for a job!!

Kathy X   ☺

Modality

Ability

1 **Rewrite the underlined words using _can, can't, could_ or _couldn't_.**

1 I <u>don't know how to</u> cook. I can't cook.

2 I <u>know how to</u> speak three languages. ....

3 When I was a teenager, I <u>knew how to</u> play chess but now I've forgotten the rules. ....

4 <u>Do</u> you <u>know how to</u> ride a horse? ....

5 A: <u>Don't</u> you <u>know how to</u> swim? ....
   B: I <u>know how to</u> now but I <u>didn't know how</u> until I was fourteen. ....

6 She <u>doesn't know how to</u> write text messages. ....

2 **Decide whether we can use _can, could_ or _be able to_ in each sentence. Tick (✓) one or more boxes and write the correct form(s) of the verb(s).**

	can / can't	could / couldn't	be able to / not be able to
1 She could / was able to read by the age of four.		✓	✓
2 A: I find his voice irritating and he talks too much. B: Yes, I .... see what you mean.			
3 I fell in the river but I .... swim to the bank.			
4 A: When you were a child, could you speak French as well as English? B: Yes. I ...., I was good at both.			
5 She said she might .... help us next week.			
6 I'm sorry, I .... join you for lunch tomorrow. Maybe some other day?			

Conclusions, certainty and possibility

3 Match each sentence to either A, B, or C.

A I am certain.   **B** I think it's likely.   **C** I think it's possible.

1 She won't be travelling with us.   A

2 We might be moving house.

3 The printer must be out of ink.

4 She could be nervous about the interview next week.

5 She can't be tired; she slept for nine hours last night.

6 It should cost around £100.

4 Fill in each gap with the most appropriate modal verb from the box. Use each verb once only.

> must   will   should   might   could   shall

1 We .... go to Norway for our holiday; we haven't decided yet.

2 Next year .... be the 500th anniversary of the university.

3 It's only 100 kilometres from here, so you .... be able to do the journey in two hours.

4 So you're Anna Logan. You .... be Jim Logan's wife. Nice to meet you.

5 This decision .... affect the company very badly.

6 I .... begin this talk by telling you a little about my work.

Obligation and necessity

5 Rewrite the phrases in bold without changing the meaning, using one of the items from the box. Use each item once only.

> must   have to   need to   should
> ought to   needn't   ~~don't need to~~

1 **You're not obliged to** get up early tomorrow.

You don't need to get up early tomorrow.

2 **The right thing for us to do would be to** help with the clean-up in the park.

....

3 **It's not necessary for you to** tell anyone about this.

....

4 I simply **feel a personal obligation to** call Kate today.

....

5 **Is it necessary for her to** study so much?

....

6 **Would it be a good idea if** we offer to babysit?

....

7 **I have no choice about living** in an apartment – I can't afford a house.

....

Modality: other verbs

6 Fill in each gap with a verb from the box. Sometimes more than one answer is possible.

> promise   seem   sound   tend   think

1 She ..... *promised* ..... me that she'd be home by 8 pm.
2 I .... his mother's name is Louise but I'm not sure.
3 It .... like yesterday that we arrived but we've been here a week.
4 She .... to work late most evenings. She says she works best after 6 o'clock.
5 You're going to Florida, so I hear. That .... like a nice idea.

7 Underline the correct verb in each sentence below.

1 It *appears / believes* that there are problems with the project.
2 We *feel / know* that there's something wrong with Lou but we're not sure.
3 Sheila *reckons / supposes* that no one is going to come to the party!
4 From what I *gather / feel*, the company is doing very badly.
5 They *appear / suppose* that the dog just found another home.
6 It *looks / expects* like there might be rain.

Conclusions, certainty and possibility

8 Match each sentence to either A or B.
A I believe this is true.   **B** I believe this is a possibility.
1 Lack of exercise can cause stress.   A
2 On a clear day, the mountains may be seen from here.   ....
3 The pain could be as a result of using the computer too much. ....
4 Finding a good manager can be difficult.   ....
5 It could be difficult to solve this crime.   ....
6 There might not be enough water in the jug.   ....

Ability

9 Write sentences about yourself using *can* or *be able to*.

1 .... make an omelette   4 .... play a musical instrument

2 .... speak Russian   5 .... ride a motorbike

3 .... save photos from a mobile to a PC

10 Write sentences about yourself using *could, couldn't, was able to, wasn't able to*.

When I was ten …

1 .... ride a bike   4 .... make cakes

2 .... use a PC   5 .... speak English

3 .... make a phone call

Possibility

11a Rewrite this paragraph so that the verbs in bold express less certainty.

Friday, March 11, 2011

could become

Cloning (1) **will soon become** the answer to the problem of baldness in both men and women because there (2) **will soon be** a way to clone hair. Millions of men and women suffer from this problem, but cloning (3) **will solve** this and men (4) **will not have to** go bald any more if they do not want to.

The idea behind this was recently tested on human beings by a team of British researchers, and the treatment (5) **works** in most cases. The researchers estimate that the technology (6) **will be** available within the next five years and that many men and women (7) **will benefit** from the treatment.

11b Write a short paragraph about a technological advance or change and the influence it could or will have on people's lives. Use modal verbs to express different degrees of certainty. Use the ideas in the box.

space travel   e-books   online learning   electric cars
drugs and medicines to keep people young   online shopping
climate change

....

....

....

....

....

English Grammar Today Workbook

Obligation and necessity

12 Decide whether these sentences have strong (S), weak (W) or no (N) obligation.

1 She mustn't open the present until her birthday. .....S....

2 We needn't lock the door. ....

3 We have to do the washing up. ....

4 They need to score two goals, at least. ....

5 You don't need to get dressed up for the party. ....

6 You should be more careful. ....

7 You don't have to take off your shoes. ....

8 They ought to start the concert earlier. ....

13 Write one sentence about yourself for each item on the list below. Choose from the following verbs. Use as many different verbs as you can.

must	have to	need to	should	ought to
needn't	don't need to	don't have to		

1 backup all my files every week   5 go to the dentist for a checkup

2 be in bed by 11 o'clock   6 take a holiday

3 get up earlier   7 drive to work

4 email my friends more often   8 work harder on my English

1 ....

2 ....

3 ....

4 ....

5 ....

6 ....

7 ....

8 ....

Modal verbs: *can, could, may, might, be able to*

1 **Fill in each gap with** *can, can't* **or** *could, couldn't*. **Sometimes more than one answer is possible.**

1 ..Can.. you speak Russian? We have a Russian visitor coming tomorrow who ...can't.. speak English.

2 When I was a child, I could stand on my head.

3 ..Can.. you help me with these boxes? I need to take them to the garage.

4 ..Could.. you read before you were five years old? According to the experts, most children .can.. learn to read before they start school if they get the right help from an adult.

5 ....Can you hear that noise? I wonder where it's coming from? ..Could.. it be a problem with the engine?

6 There .could. be intelligent creatures on other planets. We just don't know.

7 It .can.. be very hard to guess the pronunciation of English words from the spelling.

8 I .could.. pick you up from the airport next week if you like.

2 **Match the columns to make correct sentences. Use the words in the left-hand column once only. Sometimes more than one answer is possible.**

1 May   you read these bus times for me? I don't have my glasses.

2 Could   it help if I came a little earlier tomorrow?

3 Might   you ride a bike when you were five?

4 Can   I help you, sir?

3 **Tick (✓) the most appropriate explanation of the sentence, a or b.**

1 She could be Jim's sister.
  a It's possible she is Jim's sister, but I don't know.
  b I know she is Jim's sister.

2 It can be very cold in Stockholm in January.
  a It's possible that it is cold in Stockholm in January, but I don't know.
  b It's a fact that it is often cold in Stockholm in January.

3 You may find you don't need a coat – the weather's quite warm in June.
  a It's possible you won't need a coat; I have no idea.
  b It's possible you won't need a coat; I think you probably won't need one.

4 You could have warned me about the road works! It took me three hours to get here!
  a I wish you had warned me.   **b** It's possible that you warned me.

5 They might be away. They're not answering the phone.
  a I wish they were away.   **b** It's possible they're away.

English Grammar Today Workbook

6 You might ask me the next time you want to use my computer.
   a I think you should ask me.   **b** It's possible you'll ask me.

7 I can see what you mean when you say he's like his father.
   a It is possible I can understand.   **b** I do understand.

8 Seats at the stadium can cost up to €250.
   a I think that seats cost up to €250.   **b** I know that seats cost up to €250.

4 **Correct the mistakes with modal verbs in these sentences.**

1 Can your brother to play the piano?

2 The robbers stole half a million pounds but the police could capture them within a few hours.

3 A: May you help me put chairs out for the meeting? B: Yes, no problem.

4 It's snowing in New York, so her flight can be delayed. Let's hope not.

5 Were you able get in touch with Harry yesterday?

6 There are a number of things you can not take on board the plane with you.

5 **Complete each sentence so that it is true for you.**

1 When I was a child, I could ....

2 By the end of this year, I'll be able ....

3 One day I might ....

4 Tomorrow I may ....

5 If I .... , my English could get better.

6 I can't .... but I can ....

6 **Rewrite the sentences using the words in brackets and any other necessary words.**

1 The best idea for us is to go home. (as well)
We might as well go home ....

2 She fell off the boat into the river but she managed to swim to the bank. (able)
She ....

3 It's possible you're right, but I still think we should be careful. (may well)
You ....

4 It's possible that human beings will travel to distant planets one day. (could)
....

5 Will it be convenient for you to pick Georgie up from school tomorrow? (able)
....

7 Make the conversations more formal or less formal, as indicated. Where there is more than one possible answer, indicate which is the most formal.

1 Can I make a suggestion?

more formal: .... ?

2 You might talk to Professor White. He is very helpful.

less formal: ....

3 Can I help you to sort these papers out?

more formal: .... ?

4 Can you meet us for lunch tomorrow?

more formal: .... ?

5 Might I take your coat, madam?

less formal: .... ?

6 I'm sorry, I'm not able to help you.

less formal: ....

8 Write what you would say in each situation using one of the words or phrases from the box.

can   could   may   might   may/might as well   be able to

1 A friend is carrying two heavy suitcases. Offer to carry one of them.

Can I carry one of your suitcases for you? ....

2 Ask a colleague if it's possible for him to stay at work late to help you plan a presentation.

.... ?

3 Ask a friend about their ability to speak any other languages.

.... ?

4 Ask your boss permission to leave work early today.

.... ?

5 Suggest to your flatmate that it would be a good idea to stay at home this evening since the weather is so bad.

....

6 Tell a friend to take sun cream with them because people often get sunburnt at this time of year.

....

Modal verbs: *must, have to, have got to, need*

1a Fill in each gap with the correct form of *must* or *have to*. In some cases both are possible.

1 I .... remember to call Pete.

2 The travel agent says that we .... go via Paris. We don't have a choice.

3 What time .... (you) get to the station?

4 The health centre insists that all the children in the class .... have an injection.

5 .... (you) leave the house early every day?

6 She .... be home by 10 pm.

7 The door's very heavy. You .... push to open it.

1b Fill in each gap with the negative form of *must* or *have to*.

1 In the examination room students .... use a dictionary.

2 You .... become a member but tickets are cheaper for members.

3 A: It's raining. B: Good. I .... water the garden.

4 .... (you) be there by six o'clock?

5 It's Paola's birthday next Wednesday. You .... let me forget.

2 Match statements 1–4 with a–d. Then choose the most appropriate modal verb in a–d. Sometimes more than one answer is possible.

1 It cost $200.

2 Please keep your voice down.

3 Are you free on Friday?

4 My headache's worse.

a You *mustn't / don't have to / haven't got to* shout.

b I don't know. I *must / 'll have to / 've got to* check my diary.

c You *must / 'll have to / 've got to* go to bed

d But I said it *must / had to* be cheap.

3 Fill in each gap to refer to the past or the future. Use the correct forms of *must* or *have to* with the verb in brackets.

1 Kieran was away last weekend. He .... (go) and see his mother.

2 The train was cancelled so we .... (hire) a car.

3 You .... (get up) early tomorrow if you want to see the sunrise.

4 Please use his bike but you .... (let) him have it back by Monday.

5 Why .... (you apologise) for something you didn't do?

4 **Fill in each gap with the correct word or phrase from the box.**

don't need	doesn't need	needs
needn't	needn't have	need

1 I .... to make a hair appointment. My hair's getting too long.

2 We .... worried. They didn't miss the train.

3 You .... rush. We've got plenty of time.

4 Tell Flo she .... to wait for me. I'll see her later.

5 The cake .... to be kept in the fridge. It's got cream in it.

6 We .... a tent. We've got one, thanks.

5 **Look at these rules at a public swimming pool. Write full sentences to explain to someone what the rules are. Use *must, have to* and *need to*.**

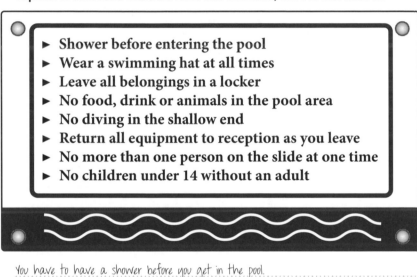

► **Shower before entering the pool**
► **Wear a swimming hat at all times**
► **Leave all belongings in a locker**
► **No food, drink or animals in the pool area**
► **No diving in the shallow end**
► **Return all equipment to reception as you leave**
► **No more than one person on the slide at one time**
► **No children under 14 without an adult**

You have to have a shower before you get in the pool.

....

....

....

6 **Write what you would say in each situation using *must* or *have to*.**

1 Your friend is waiting for the results of exams. She must be very nervous.

2 You open your front door and go in but five minutes later you can't find your keys. ....

3 Your brother phones. He didn't get the job he wanted. ....

4 You get home. There's water dripping from the ceiling. ....

5 You're in a traffic jam. It isn't usually busy at this time. ....

6 You get home. No one is in. ....

7 Tick (✓) the most informal sentence, a, b or c.

1 **a** Do I have to pay now?
    b Have I got to pay now?
    c Must I pay now?

2 **a** She's got to be the best for the job, hasn't she?
    b She has to be the best for the job, doesn't she?
    c She must be the best for the job, mustn't she?

3 **a** Have you to meet them at the airport?
    b Have you got to meet them at the airport?
    c Must you meet them at the airport?

4 **a** Need I explain it in more detail?
    b Do I need to explain it in more detail?
    c Have I to explain it in more detail?

8 **Correct the mistakes with modal verbs in these sentences.**

1 They'll have got to hurry up if they want to get there by 7.30.

2 I must work late last night as I had a report to finish.

3 Does she must talk so loudly?

4 There don't must be any noise in here. People are trying to work.

5 You've to must get that letter to the post today.

6 She don't need to come for very long.

7 We didn't need bring food. There was a lot there already.

8 You must to come and have dinner soon.

9 You needn't a coat. It's not cold.

9 **Match sentences 1–6 with a–f and decide which express obligation and which express conclusions.**

1 *e* 2 .... 3 .... 4 .... 5 .... 6 ....

1 He's got to be her brother.   **a** Jana's got an important phone call.

2 He's got to be in work at lunchtime.   **b** I'll do it later.

3 You must be very pleased.   **c** He has to answer the phones.

4 You must be very quiet.   **d** Perhaps she's his girlfriend.

5 She needn't necessarily be his wife.   **e** Look at how similar they are.

6 She needn't do the washing up now.   **f** You've done brilliantly.

Modal verbs: *should* and *ought to*

1a Fill in each gap with *should* or *shouldn't* and a verb from the box.

eat	be able to	choose	~~be~~	make up	wait
keep	try	include			

Getting your five portions a day

Most people know that we (1) _should be_ eating more fruit and veg. But most of us aren't eating enough. Did you know that we (2) .... at least five portions of fruit and vegetables every day? Fruit and vegetables are good sources of many vitamins and minerals, and are very low in fat, yet most of us (3) .... more of them in our everyday diet. Fruit and veg (4) .... about a third of the food you eat each day. You (5) .... to one thing. You (6) .... a variety. If you count your portions each day you (7) .... increase the amount you eat quite easily. When you feel like a snack, you (8) .... a biscuit or a packet of crisps. Instead, try to choose an apple, a banana or perhaps even some dried fruit. You (9) .... until tomorrow. Start today.

30

1b Go through the text again and using *ought to* and *ought not to*.

2 Read the text. Is any of the information new to you? Make some suggestions to a friend about the ideal way to prepare and cook vegetables.

Getting the most out of fruit and veg

We lose some vitamins and minerals from fruit and veg when we prepare or cook them. Here are some tips on how to get the best from them.
Eat fresh fruit and veg as soon as you can rather than storing it for a long time. Or use frozen fruit and vegetables instead.
Don't overcook fruit and veg. You could use a steamer or a microwave.
Use as little water as possible to cook fruit and veg. Then use the cooking water in a soup because you'll keep some of the lost vitamins and minerals.
Don't leave any vegetables open to the air, light or heat after you have cut them up. Cover and chill them but don't leave them in water.
Avoid adding fat or rich sauces to vegetables or sugar to fruit. Keep it natural.

30

3 Write a suggestion using *should* or *ought to* for each picture.

1

2

3

4

5

6

1 There should be fewer people on the trampoline. *or* There shouldn't be so many people on the trampoline.

2

3

4

5

6

4 Nine of the sentences have mistakes with modal verbs. Correct the mistakes and tick (✓) the correct sentence.

1 Shouldn't you to go now?

2 Do we ought to tell them we're going to be late?

3 She ought to drive more slowly, shouldn't she?

4 They don't ought to have stayed so late.

5 The guidebook says we would get a taxi from the airport.

6 It's up to you to decide what would be done.

7 They should bought more computers for the classrooms.

8 I sould finish now because it's getting late.

9 The computer should be fixed weeks ago.

10 He should have better advice when he was training.

5 Write what you would say in each situation using *should* or *ought to*. Sometimes more than one answer is possible.

1 You expect Linda to arrive soon.
Linda should be here soon. or Linda ought to arrive soon.

2 You have a meeting this afternoon. You tell your colleague that you don't expect the meeting to take longer than half an hour.
It ....

3 It's often difficult to park in your road but you can normally find a parking space somewhere nearby.
You ....

4 The journey took two hours and normally it only takes one hour.
It ....

5 The weather forecast predicted a sunny day but it's raining.
It ....

6 A friend came for dinner and brought you a lovely bunch of flowers.
You ....

7 Your plans have changed. You don't know if your friend Flora knows. You wonder whether to phone her.
Should .... ?

8 You stayed up late last night and you're finding it hard to get up now.
I ....

9 Your neighbour didn't lock his garage door. His bike was stolen.
He ....

10 You come home late. Nobody knew where you were. Your flatmate asks why you didn't leave a note or tell someone where you were going.
I ....

6 Make each sentence more formal or less formal, as indicated.

1 Do not hesitate to contact us should you have any difficulty finding the information you require.
less formal: Please contact us if you have any problem finding what you need.

2 Should you wish to cancel the agreement, you have 14 days to do so.
less formal: ....

3 If you need the emergency services in the UK, dial 999.
more formal: ....

4 I should very much like to come with you. Thank you.
less formal: ....

5 I would think that an hour would be plenty of time.
more formal: ....

6 Ought we to tell someone that we're leaving?
less formal: ....

English Grammar Today Workbook

Modal verbs: *will, shall* and *would*

Will

1 Fill in each gap with *will, will not, 'll* or *won't*.

1 Passengers with luggage .... need to check in at desks 5-8.

2 I .... be able to give you a lift if you like.

3 It's not going to rain, is it? I .... need a coat, will I?

4 A: .... she be okay on her own? B: Yes. I think so.

5 A: Don't buy me an expensive present, ... you. B: Okay, I won't.

6 A: Do you think she'll get the job? B: Yes, I think she ....

7 There .... be any shops open now. It's too late.

8 The management .... accept responsibility for items lost or stolen.

2 Use the most likely form, *will* or *'ll*, to make a request, suggestion, decision, prediction or offer for each situation.

1 You arrange to meet a friend outside the cinema at 6 pm.
I'll meet you at 6 outside the cinema.

2 A waiter asks you what you'd like. You ask for a black coffee.

3 You're cold. The door is open. You ask someone near the door to close it.

4 The phone rings. You're quite sure that it's your sister, Cath.

5 You find the noise your son is making annoying. You ask him to stop.

6 You promise to phone your mother tomorrow.

Will, shall, would

3 Match each of the questions and sentences, 1–9, with the most likely category a–h. Use one of the categories twice.

1 Shall I do that for you? d
2 Would you turn down the music a bit?
3 Will you text me when you're leaving?
4 Shall we get the later train?
5 I won't come again if you talk to me like that.
6 I'll always be there for you.
7 What shall we do with the old television?
8 You will go. You have to.
9 I'll have the chicken please.

a command
b promise
c threat
d offer
e request
f asking for advice
g decision
h suggestion

4 Helen is organising an evening to raise money for a local charity. Yesterday she had a meeting with some people who offered to help her. Here's a summary of the notes from the meeting.

What	Who	Comments
Food & drink	Aman to buy drinks Hamish to organise food	Hamish suggested cheese, biscuits, grapes.
Tickets & ticket sales	Carlo	Carlo to design tickets. He can print them at work.
Quiz	Katie to write questions.	Her sister, Jo, also offered to help.
Music	Ask 'The Bridge' – local band. Frank to ask them if they're free.	Must get a licence: Lara offered to get it.
Setting up and clearing up	Helen	Helen asked everyone to help with this.

Using the information in the table, write what each person said. Use *shall, will* and *'ll* where possible.

Aman: I'll buy the drinks. *or* shall I buy the drinks?

Hamish: ....

Carlo: ....

Katie: ....

Jo: ....

Frank: ....

Lara: ....

Helen: ....

5 **Nine of the sentences have mistakes with modal verbs. Correct the mistakes and tick (✓) the correct sentence.**

1 I'll must finish some work before I go home.

2 I explain to you how to get there.

3 I do my best to get the job.

4 I hope he shall reply to my e-mail.

5 We shan't be back until Saturday.

6 When you will arrive at Lausanne station, take the exit to the left.

7 We'll let you know when the meeting will be arranged.

8 It will be a great idea to have a new computer in here.

9 A: You'll make dinner, won't you? B: Yes, I'll.

10 If you visited us, we shall be delighted.

Will and *would*

6a **Change the words in bold to make each sentence more or less formal, or more or less direct, as indicated.**

1 **Will** you sign here please?

   more formal: would you sign here please?

2 The food was terrible. I think I **shall** write and complain.

   less formal: ....

3 We**'ll** see each other on Friday, **won't** we?

   more formal: ....

4 **Would** you bring us the bill when you're ready?

   more direct: ....

6b **Make each sentence less direct.**

1 I suggest that you come back later.

   ....

2 I advise you to wear boots if you've got them. The ground is quite uneven.

   ....

3 I recommend Cyprus as a holiday destination.

   ....

Modal verbs: *would, would like, would rather*

1 **Answer each question so that it is true for you. Use *I'd* ...**

1 If you were an animal, what animal would you be and why?
I'd be a dog because dogs sleep, eat and go out for walks.

2 If you could drink anything now, what would you drink and who with?

3 If you could have any food now, what would it be and where?

4 If you could meet any famous person, dead or alive, who would it be? Why?

5 If you could be anywhere now, where would you be and what would you be doing?

6 If you could go on holiday now, where would you go and who with?

2 **Underline the correct alternative in each sentence.**

1 We'd like *making / to make* a reservation for Saturday.

2 I'm going to the shops. *Would / Do* you like anything?

3 I *like / 'd like* to make an appointment please.

4 Gina *would like / likes* to go everywhere on her bike. She says she gets there faster than by car.

5 *Do / Would* the children like sausages for dinner tonight?

6 A: I'm meeting Linda later. Would you like to come?
B: Yes, I'd really *like. / like to.*

3a **Write a sentence with *would like to have* ... for each situation.**

1 I wanted to watch my son's football match but I was late.
I'd like to have watched the match but I was late.

2 I wanted to learn the piano when I was young but I didn't get the chance.

3 I wanted to ask more questions at the meeting but we didn't have time.

4 Your sister wanted to be a doctor but she didn't get the grades.

5 We wanted to go skiing last year but it was too expensive.

English Grammar Today Workbook

3b Think of things that you've wanted to do but couldn't. Write three
sentences using *I'd like to have ...*

1 ....

2 ....

3 ....

Would rather and *would prefer*

4a For a magazine article about lifestyles, we asked a group of people who
work together about their likes and dislikes. What questions did we ask
them? Use *Would you rather ...?*

		Millie	Roland	Shara	Aran
1	**a** be poor and happy **b** be rich and unhappy	a	b	a	a
2	**a** have fruit for breakfast **b** a cooked breakfast	a***	a	b	a
3	**a** start work early and finish early **b** start late and finish in the evening	a	b***	b	a
4	**a** read a book **b** watch tv	b	b	a	b
5	**a** jump into a pool of freezing water **b** do a parachute jump	b	a	a	a

1 *would you rather be poor and happy than rich and unhappy?* ....

2 ....

3 ....

4 ....

5 ....

4b Summarise the results using *would rather* or *would prefer to*. Where there are asterisks *** indicating a strong preference, use *would much rather* or *would much prefer to*.

1 Millie, Shara and Aran would all prefer to be poor and happy than rich and unhappy. Roland would rather be rich!

2 Millie ....

3 Millie and Aran .... but Roland ....

4 ....

5 ....

4c Now answer the questions in the table for yourself.

1 ....

2 ....

3 ....

4 ....

5 ....

5 Tick (✓) the correct sentence, a or b, for each situation. Sometimes both are possible.

1 A friend has invited you to dinner. She doesn't want you there before 8 pm.
   a She'd rather we didn't arrive before 8. **b** She'd rather not arrive before 8.

2 Your son is going out for the evening. You don't want to go out.
   a I'd rather not go out tonight.　　　**b** I'd rather you didn't go out tonight.

3 You're going out to eat somewhere. You don't really mind where you go but you'd prefer not to have a burger.
   a I'd rather not have a burger.　　　**b** I'd rather we didn't have a burger.

4 You told a friend something that you didn't want them to tell anyone else. You find out that they have told someone else.
   a I'd rather you hadn't told anyone.　　**b** I'd rather not tell anyone.

Modality: expressions with *be*

1 Fill in each gap using *be about to*, *be likely to* and *be due to*.

Norbeth Museum
opening 23rd May

1 It..........rain in the next few hours.

2 The Norbeth museum ....open on 23rd May.

3 The plane..........land.

	ARRIVALS	
FLIGHT	**FROM**	**TIME**
XG106	Rome	13:25
FL208	Dublin	13:30
NA146	Tokyo	13:34

4 I can't talk now. We..........have dinner.

5 There..........be long delays because of the fog.

6 The Dublin flight ....arrive at 13:30.

2 Rewrite the sentences using the verb *be* and the words in brackets.

1 I intended to phone you when you phoned me! (about)

I was about to phone you when you phoned me! ....

2 Jim will be late. He always is! (bound)

....

3 You should send your CV with your application. (supposed)

....

4 *Zendo* will become the biggest maker of sports goods in Europe. (set)

....

5 She intended to apply for the job but she changed her mind. (going)

....

6 She couldn't finish her report in time for the annual meeting. (able)

....

7 It's a bad plan and it will fail. (certain)

....

8 The meeting was arranged to start at 3 pm, but it didn't start till 3.30. (to)

....

3 **Use the words in brackets with the correct form of *be* to ask each question.**

1 What time / your train / arrive? (due to) *what time is your train due to arrive?*

2 Which room / we / go to for the next class? (supposed to)

3 everyone / use the photocopier, or just the staff? (allowed to)

4 we / sign these forms? (meant to)

5 people / vote for the President or did they have a free choice? (forced to)

6 we / make contact with people from other planets this century? (likely to)

4 **Write what you would say in each situation, using a phrase from the box.**

due to	likely to	about to	meant to	allowed to

1 A friend phones you a minute before you go into class.
You say: *I can't talk now. I'm about to go into class.*

2 You want to know if a friend will probably be in the library tomorrow.
You ask: _____ ?

3 You want to know if your friend has to take any exams this term.
You ask: _____ ?

4 You want to know if you can use the computer lab during the lunch break.
You ask: _____ ?

5 Your teacher gives you a dictionary. You want to know if it's intended to be
used in class or only for homework. You ask: _____ ?

5 **Use the verb in brackets and name something that ...**

1 ... you can't do at the place where you work or study. (be allowed)
We're not allowed to bring food into class.

2 ... you should have done recently but you didn't. (be supposed)

3 ... you will probably do during the next few months. (be likely)

4 ... you will certainly do today or tomorrow. (be sure)

5 ... you think will definitely happen in your country. (bound)

English Grammar Today Workbook

Modality: tense

1a Which of these modal verbs can refer to past time? Tick (✓) the boxes.

can		would		should		might	
must		may		will		could	

1b Mark the verbs in bold to indicate if they refer to the past (P), present (Pr) or future (F).

1 We **must** meet some time next week. *(F marked above must)*

2 Dave wanted to come but he **couldn't** make it because of the traffic.

3 You **should have** asked Nora – she **would've** helped you with the recipe.

4 I **can't** imagine anything worse than living in a big city.

5 He **may** go to university next year. He hasn't decided yet.

6 **I'll** often go for a jog before breakfast. I love it.

2 Underline the correct modal verb.

1 Yesterday, we thought we *will / would* have a picnic by the river, but we didn't go in the end because we thought it *may / might* rain.

2 If I'd known you were arriving, I *could / can* have come to collect you.

3 She asked me if I *will / would* go with her yesterday to the hospital, but I *can't / couldn't* as I was too busy.

4 Because I'd lost my ticket I *must / had to* pay again before I *could / can* get into the exhibition.

5 Experts agree that children *can / could* generally learn languages faster than adults. However, if adults have the right motivation, they *would / will* learn just as quickly as children.

3 Change each sentence to refer to past time.

1 Doing three exams in one day **must be** a very tiring experience. *(must have been written above)*

2 I **should be** in London, but because of the snow, they cancelled the show.

3 In the mornings, **I'll** normally go online and read the news, then **I'll** answer a few emails.

4 We've **had to** wait a long time before getting our money back.

5 **Are you able to** help out in some way to organise the school show?

6 We **ought to** get in touch with her immediately.

4 **Complete the indirect speech reports. There may be more than one possible answer.**

1 "I can swim faster than my sister."
He said he _____ could swim faster than his sister _____.

2 "I used to go to work by bus but now I drive."
She said she _____.

3 "We shall need more money."
They said that they _____.

4 "I may have sent it to the wrong address."
She said she _____.

5 "You may use the office computer."
She said I _____.

6 "The package must be delivered by five o'clock."
He said the package _____.

5 **Complete each sentence so that it is true for you.**

1 If I hadn't studied English, I might have _____.
2 If I'd had more time last year, I would have _____.
3 I should have _____ but I didn't.
4 When I was a child, I could _____.
5 I used to _____ but I don't any more.
6 Soon I'll be able to _____.

Negation

1a Underline any negative words in these sentences and decide if the sentences are TRUE or FALSE.

1 Camels <u>don't</u> store water in their humps.

2 Crocodiles don't cry.

3 Elephants aren't the only animal that can't jump.

4 The Great Wall of China is not the only man-made structure you can see from space with the human eye.

5 There is no gravity in space.

6 Shakespeare didn't write his plays. Someone else wrote them, not him.

7 Elephants never forget.

1b Read the answers to find out if you were right. Fill in each gap with a word from the box. Sometimes more than one answer is possible.

unlikely	doesn't	can't	nothing	won't
not	aren't	no	never	either	un-	didn't
couldn't	~~isn't~~	wasn't	none		

1 TRUE: It _____isn't_____ the hump that allows a camel to survive without water but it's true that most other animals .... survive as long as camels. The hump is .... more than a lump of fat which provides them with the same energy as three weeks of food.

2 TRUE: When crocodiles eat, their eyes produce water. They're .... really crying.

3 TRUE: Rhinos and hippos .... able to jump ....

4 TRUE: Even roads and sometimes vehicles can be seen from space, ... aided, without the help of a telescope. Some people think that the Great Wall of China, the pyramids and Las Vegas can be seen from the moon but actually .... of these are visible so far way.

5 FALSE: Gravity is everywhere, even in space. The effect of gravity gets weaker with distance, but it .... disappears.

6 WE DON'T KNOW: Some people say that Shakespeare .... write his plays because he .... properly educated, and he .... have experienced the many things he wrote about.

7 TRUE: Elephants are .... to travel alone but when a group gets too big, the eldest daughter .... stay with her pack. She moves away and starts a new group, but she .... forget her roots. One researcher witnessed a mother and daughter elephant who seemed to know each other after 23 years of separation.

2 Rewrite each sentence/question to make it negative. Sometimes more than one answer is possible. Think about the differences in meaning.

1 Are you feeling a bit tired? .... *Aren't you feeling a bit tired?* ....

2 Take an umbrella. ....

3 Have we met before? ....

4 Might he be late? ....

5 There are some useful books in the library on the subject. ....

6 Some of my friends like cooking. ....

7 Jules and Petra will be coming. ....

8 Something happened when I rang the bell. ....

9 I hope you're going to ask for more money. ....

10 To have asked Julio for his help would have been difficult. ....

3 Use the words in brackets to make each sentence more emphatic, more polite or more formal, as indicated.

1 There's no need to speak to him like that. (whatsoever)
More emphatic: *There's no need whatsoever to speak to him like that.* ....

2 If you're not interested, let me know. (in the least bit)
More emphatic: ....

3 She didn't say anything to me. (at all)
More emphatic: ....

4 I didn't think I'd get the job. (not for a moment)
More emphatic: ....

5 She didn't often ask for advice. (rarely)
More formal: ....

6 A: Do you mind if we sit here?
B: No. (not in the least)
More polite: ....

Nouns

1a Underline 10 more nouns in this text. Do not underline the pronouns.

How to boil an <u>egg</u>

Take one fresh egg and make a small hole in the shell with a pin. Place it in a pan of cold water. Heat the water till it boils; let the egg continue to boil for 3–4 minutes. Eat it with a little salt.

1b Read the text again and find:

1 two uncountable nouns: .... and ....

2 a plural noun: ....

2 Fill in each gap with the plural form of the noun in brackets.

1 I saw two ....*men*........ entering the building. (man)

2 She went to the dentist to have her .... fixed. (tooth)

3 Some .... were playing in the street. (child)

4 There were some .... in the field. (sheep)

5 I met two .... yesterday who know you. (woman)

6 Are you scared of ....? (mouse)

7 My .... are aching! (foot)

8 We saw some very brightly-coloured .... in the lake. (fish)

3 Underline eight more compound nouns in this text.

In most countries, men suffer more <u>heart attacks</u> than women. However, a survey in 2009 suggested that women were closing the gender gap. As women's lifestyles changed, more of them consumed fast food and junk food, causing a rise in the number of cases of obesity*. Higher blood pressure and higher cholesterol among women resulted in more heart attacks. "This is not just another health scare," said a scientist. "It is a wake-up call for all women."

*being very overweight

4a Form compound nouns by adding a word from the box to a word below.

opener	room	keeper	way	house	site	screen

shop.................... run.................... web.................... wind....................

bottle.................... bath.................... green....................

4b Which of the compound nouns in 4a do you associate with:

1 the Internet? ....   5 a car? ....

2 buying things? ....   6 a kitchen? ....

3 an airport? ....   7 having a shower? ....

4 growing plants? ....

5a Label the items in the pictures.

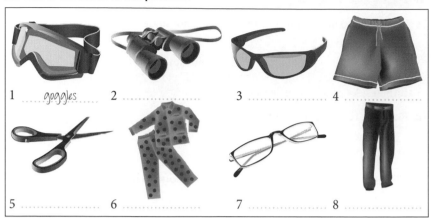

1 .....goggles..... 2 .... 3 .... 4 ....

5 .... 6 .... 7 .... 8 ....

5b Use the nouns in 5a to complete the sentences.

1 Do you always wear .....goggles..... when you swim?

2 The children have new .... They look so cute at bedtime.

3 Can I borrow your ....? I'd like to cut out this job advert.

4 If you want to see the wildlife, don't forget your ....

5 You should wear .... on the beach. The sun is very strong.

6 I need some smart .... to go with my new jacket.

7 I need to buy some new .... for the summer. I like it when my legs get tanned.

8 I can't read this small print. I think I need ....

6 These sentences all contain collective nouns (group words) in bold. Complete each sentence with an appropriate plural noun.

1 To find the cause of the problem, the government has appointed a **team** of experts (or scientists or researchers).

2 It was a bad place to have a picnic. We were attacked by **swarms** of ....

3 We saw a **flock** of .... near the river.

4 On her birthday, I took her a **bunch** of ....

5 So that everyone knew what they were allowed to do and not allowed to do, the committee drew up a **set** of ....

6 We looked into the field and saw a **herd** of ....

7 Fill in each gap with a noun form of the verb in brackets.

1 She spent all her .....savings..... on a new car. (save)

2 .... on your new job! (congratulate)

3 It took me a long time to get used to my new .... (surround)

4 Every year, he has to pay almost 30% of his .... in tax. (earn)

5 Don't leave any personal .... in the meeting room during lunchtime. It's not safe. (belong)

6 Do you have any particular .... as regards food? (dislike)

8 Underline the correct verb form in each sentence. If both verb forms are possible, underline both.

1 Physics *were* / *was* my favourite subject at school.

2 The news *is* / *are* on TV at six o'clock.

3 The government *is* / *are* hoping that the economy will improve soon.

4 Aerobics *is* / *are* great fun. You should come along to our class!

5 The audience *seems* / *seem* to be really enjoying the concert.

6 The team *was* / *were* not ready for the final and played very badly.

9 Make the nouns in bold in this text more gender neutral.

Ever since she was a little girl, my younger sister Sylvia wanted to be a police
officer
~~woman~~ and my brother Dan always wanted to be a **fireman**. I wonder if it was

a love of uniforms? But Sylvia, unlike some little girls of her age, never said

she wanted to work for an airline as an **air hostess**; it was always the police.

My older sister, Emma, always dreamt of being an **actress**. She studied drama

during the day and worked as a **waitress** at a local restaurant in the evenings to

pay for her education. I was only ever interested in being a teacher and I finally

became a secondary school **headmaster**. One way or another, we all achieved

our ambitions. Sylvia was very successful; she joined the police and is now

Chairman of the National Police Federation.

10 Fill in each gap with the correct preposition.

1 This year will be my third attempt ...*at*... passing my law exams.

2 What was the reason .... his strange behaviour?

3 There has been a sharp increase .... the price of gold this year.

4 I would love to do research .... the causes of climate change.

5 There's an exhibition .... African art at the local museum.

6 I'd love to be a member .... your drama club. Can I join?

7 She was a great politician. She saw the need .... change and made it happen.

8 I'm a newcomer .... this type of software. Can you explain it to me?

9 He did an excellent translation of some English poems .... Spanish.

10 The visit .... The Art Institute was the highlight of our trip to Chicago.

11 If the nouns in bold need a complement, fill in the gap with a complement from the box. If the noun doesn't need a complement, write X.

| of loneliness | ~~that she is French~~ | of frustration | in temperature |

1 The **fact** _that she is French_ means she can get a job anywhere in the European Union.

2 The **plan** .... seemed crazy to me.

3 There was a **rise** .... and the liquid changed colour.

4 We all felt a **sense** .... because the plan had not worked.

5 He wrote a song that won a .... **prize**.

6 A **feeling** .... came over me as I looked at the empty landscape.

12 Look around you in the room or place where you are. Make a list of the names of ten things you can see. Then label each noun according to its type (countable, uncountable, plural only, compound, piece word).

phone (countable); sunglasses (plural only) ....

....

....

....

....

Nouns: countable and uncountable nouns

1a Write the uncountable nouns connected with travelling which these pictures represent.

(two answers) (two answers)

1 _information_ 2 .... 3 .... 4 ....

1b Give two countable examples of each uncountable noun in 5a.

1 _information:_ train times / maps 3 ....

2 .... 4 ....

2 Fill in each gap using the correct word from the brackets.

1 I love .... in general but I hate long ....! (journey, travel)

2 A: Have you got any Japanese ....?
   B: Yes, I've got some 1000-yen .... (currency, note)

3 A: Do you have a lot of ....?
   B: No, just one .... (suitcase, luggage)

4 A: Have you booked the ....? B: Yes, I've booked a small .... near the beach. (hotel, accommodation)

5 We need .... about trains to Lisbon. Is there a .... on the internet? (timetable, information)

3a Put the nouns from the box into two groups, countable and uncountable.

chair	equipment	furniture	tool	rice
progress	bread	news	advice	question
orange	soap	wallet	piano	

countable	uncountable
chair	

83

3b Seven of the sentences have mistakes with countable and uncountable nouns. Correct the mistakes and tick (✓) the three correct sentences.

1 Have you made any progresses with your essay?

2 The plumber has left some tools on the bathroom floor.

3 I cooked much rice. Would you like some?

4 Some of these furnitures are very old.

5 There is a soap in the cabinet.

6 This website sells sports equipments. I bought a tennis racket from there.

7 I have an interesting news for you.

8 We bought some new chairs.

9 Would you like an orange?

10 My parents always give me good advices.

4 Tick (✓) the sentence which correctly describes each picture.

1

a She gave me some chocolate.

b She gave me some chocolates.

2

a I need a paper.

b I need some paper.

3

a There was glass on the floor.

b There was a glass on the floor.

4

a It's the complete work of Shakespeare.

b It's the complete works of Shakespeare.

5

a Have some cake!

b Have a cake!

6

a I've spilt my juice. Get some cloth, quick!

b I've spilt my juice. Get a cloth, quick!

5 If the nouns in bold need a piece word, fill in the gap with a piece word from the box + *of*. If no piece word is necessary, write X.

loaf	piece	bar	flash	~~bit~~	item

1 I had a .... *bit of* .... **luck** the other day. I won a competition in a magazine.

2 Suddenly there was a .... **lightning** and a loud rumble of thunder.

3 When we were in Las Vegas, we took a .... **trip** to the Grand Canyon.

4 I bought a .... **chocolate** and broke it into four big pieces, one for each of us.

5 When you're in town, will you buy a .... **bread**, please?

6 We had a great .... **time** in Estonia; we really enjoyed it.

7 She told me an interesting .... **news**.

8 I bought a .... **furniture** on the internet yesterday. It's a long dining table.

6 Underline the correct option and complete the sentences with your own ideas.

1 Some friends and I recently had *a* / *a lot of* fun: we dressed in chicken costumes and collected money for charity in the town centre .

2 We had *beautiful weather* / *a beautiful weather* when ....

....

3 This year, I have increased my *knowledge* / *knowledges* of ....

4 I have some *experiences* / *experience* of working ....

5 I would like to write a *poetry* / *poem* about ....

6 Our teacher sometimes gives us *homeworks* / *homework* where we have to

....

7 In my life, I have made several *trip* / *trips* to ....

8 If I was a scientist in a university, I would like to do some *research* / *researches* into ....

Objects: direct and indirect objects

1 Underline the direct object in each sentence. If there is no direct object, write 'none' at the end of the sentence.

1 I love oranges.
2 He bought a French-English dictionary.
3 Whenever I see an ice-cream seller, I buy a big strawberry cone.
4 The guitar is my favourite musical instrument.
5 Do you want more coffee?
6 I'm feeling hungry. What time is dinner?
7 She hates me – she always ignores me at parties.
8 Laurie took me to the station on his motorbike.

2 Underline six more direct objects and circle five more indirect objects in this email.

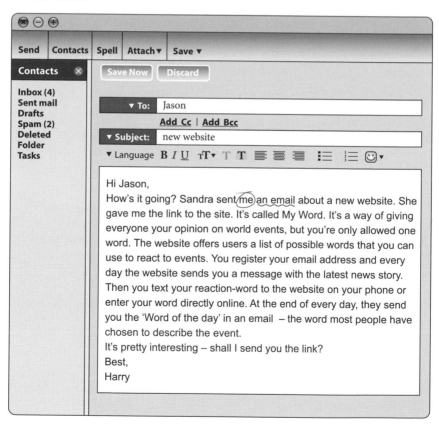

Send | Contacts | Spell | Attach ▼ | Save ▼

Contacts ✖   Save Now   Discard

Inbox (4)
Sent mail
Drafts
Spam (2)
Deleted
Folder
Tasks

▼ To: Jason

Add Cc | Add Bcc

▼ Subject: new website

▼ Language   B I U ᴛT▼ T T ≡ ≡ ≡ ≔ ≔ ☺▼

Hi Jason,
How's it going? Sandra sent me an email about a new website. She gave me the link to the site. It's called My Word. It's a way of giving everyone your opinion on world events, but you're only allowed one word. The website offers users a list of possible words that you can use to react to events. You register your email address and every day the website sends you a message with the latest news story. Then you text your reaction-word to the website on your phone or enter your word directly online. At the end of every day, they send you the 'Word of the day' in an email – the word most people have chosen to describe the event.
It's pretty interesting – shall I send you the link?
Best,
Harry

English Grammar Today Workbook

3 Rewrite each sentence using an indirect object without a preposition.

1 She gave an expensive present **to her husband** on his birthday.
She gave her husband an expensive present on his birthday.

2 Martin bought a computer **for his daughter** when she passed her exams.

3 We owe a lot of money **to the bank**.

4 Come over tomorrow and I'll cook a Chinese meal **for you all**.

5 I'm going to visit Peter in hospital. I'll take some chocolates **for him**.

6 My friend Carolina taught the words of a Spanish song **to me**.

4 Write one sentence to describe each of these situations. Use direct and indirect objects.

1 Gary went to see his aunt. He took some flowers with him.
Gary took his aunt some flowers.

2 Hugh invited his classmates to his house. He cooked a wonderful Japanese meal.

3 Luke didn't want to lie to me. So he told the truth.

4 It was our wedding anniversary. Our son bought some chocolates.

5 Kevin needed somewhere to stay. So I offered the spare room in my flat.

6 I couldn't get Arlo on the phone. So I sent an email.

7 Alan liked Jane very much. So he sent a Valentine's Day card.

8 Rita was thirsty. So I fetched a glass of water.

5 Write a sentence to describe each picture. Use direct and indirect objects
and an appropriate form of a verb from the box.

bring	read	show	buy	make	sing

1 children – cake – their dad

2 Jane – a folk song – us

3 Sylvia – bedtime story – her daughter

4 Tim – bicycle – his wife – for her birthday

5 Richard – a bunch of flowers – Megan

6 little boy – drawing – everyone

1 ....
2 ....
3 ....
4 ....
5 ....
6 ....

6 Complete each sentence with a direct and indirect object so that it's true
for you.

1 I sent ....
2 I once owed ....
3 I showed ....
4 I always give ....
5 I would never lend ....

English Grammar Today Workbook

Passive

1 **Fill in each gap to make a passive sentence using the verb in brackets.**

1 Portuguese ......_is spoken_...... in Brazil. (speak)

2 The laptops .... in Taiwan. (manufacture)

3 *Anna Karenina* .... by Tolstoy. (write)

4 As she walked into the building, she realised that she .... (watch)

5 The interview with the president .... now. (televise)

6 Will you .... to their wedding? (invite)

7 The soup should .... but not .... (heat, boil)

8 Last year the winners .... a silver cup. (give)

9 The flat upstairs must .... before people can live there. (decorate)

10 Haven't you .... by the nurse yet? (see)

2a **Fill in each gap with a passive phrase from the box. Use each phrase once only.**

had been given	was sent	would be shown
wasn't being helped	could be seen	had been told
had been treated	would be given	

Consumer reviews

GRIEVES GYM

I went to the gym for the first time last week. I (1) .... to arrive at 9 am, when I (2) .... how to use the equipment. When I got there, no instructors (3) .... anywhere and I (4) .... no information about what to do. I waited for ages. It was obvious that I (5) .... and one of the reception staff apologised to me and said a full explanation (6) .... to me. In the end I went home very angry and sent an email to the gym complaining about the way I (7) .... The next day I (8) .... a large bunch of flowers by the gym manager, as well as a letter of apology and one month's free membership!

2b **Identify the types of passive forms in 1–8 above: past simple passive, past continuous passive, past perfect passive, modal simple passive.**

1 ....   5 ....

2 ....   6 ....

3 ....   7 ....

4 ....   8 ....

3 Four of these sentences have mistakes with *get* + passive and *get/have something done*. Correct the mistakes and tick (✓) the correct sentences.

1 He **got himself injured** while playing football.

2 The company closed and all the workers **had themselves sacked**.

3 We **had our washing machine repaired** this afternoon.

4 Yesterday **my hair got cut**. I love it.

5 My mobile **got stolen**.

6 They always **got their holidays paid for** by his parents.

7 I **had the window broken**.

8 I **had the car clean** as well while it was at the garage.

4 Here is an extract from a dialogue. Rewrite the underlined sections as active voice forms. Use the words in brackets as subjects of the sentences.

A: Can you believe how much <u>footballers are paid</u> these days? (they …)

B: No, but it er explains why <u>they are always getting criticised</u> in the papers. (the papers)

A: They've all got big expensive cars and houses and stuff too.

B: I suppose <u>they don't want to be ignored</u>, do they? (they don't want people …)

A: Oh well, I'm just jealous. I know <u>I'll never be paid</u> that much by my boss. (my boss)

A: Can you believe how much they pay footballers these days?

B: ....

A: ....

B: ....

A: ....

5 Rewrite these newspaper headlines as full passive sentences.

1

Mexico agrees new hotel plans

2

European leaders agree climate change deal

New hotel plans have been agreed by Mexico.

3

Flood damages 500 homes

4

Major bank announces 200 job losses

....

6 Fill in each gap with the passive form of the verb in brackets. Use a passive + *by* where appropriate.

Kids' paintings to be shown

A painting which (1) .... (create) local children

(2) .... (unveil) tomorrow in Independent Street Park,

Radford, at 11 am.

Six park seats also (3).............................. (make) and (4).............................. (paint)

children and young people from local primary and secondary schools.

Teachers said the children enjoyed (5).............................. (ask) to help the

local community.

---

7 The following science experiment has been written by a nine-year-old child in the active voice but it should be written in the passive voice. Rewrite the text in the passive voice.

We cleared the desk and covered it with newspaper. We made a volcano out of clay. We used red clay around the top of the volcano to make it look like lava. We made a hole at the top of the volcano and added 1 teaspoon of baking soda. Then, we put in a few drops of red food colouring and a few drops of washing-up liquid. We poured in some vinegar and stood back!

The desk was cleared

....

....

8 Match the beginnings of sentences 1–6 with the most likely endings a–f. Fill in each gap using *by*, *with* or *in*.

1 I slipped and fell

2 The shops were crowded

3 Her victory at the TV awards was marked

4 He has been invited to a dinner party

5 She looked really ill

6 I dreamt that I was

a .... one of the company directors.

b and was covered .... spots.

c attacked .... giant spiders.

d .... a special DVD of the TV show.

e and got splashed .... mud.

f .... people doing Christmas shopping.

9 **Decide whether each sentence is more formal (F) or more informal (I).**

1 You've got to get yourself a new kitchen fitted.

2 If you are to be selected, you need to have a good interview.

3 Here's a spare key, in case you get locked out.

4 Changes to the primary school system are expected to be debated.

10 **Fill in each gap to make a passive sentence using the word in brackets.**

1 It _was decided_ to postpone his visit. (decide)

2 It .... that the population of the United Kingdom will rise to 70 million by 2020. (estimate)

3 He .... to have committed several robberies in the area. (believe)

4 The meeting still hasn't finished so no decision .... yet. (make)

5 I .... to report to reception in the main building at 10 am. (tell)

11 **Rewrite each sentence in the passive voice using the modal verb in bold. Use the word in brackets as the subject of the sentence.**

1 She looks in pain so they **must** have given her an injection. (She)
   She looks in pain so she must have been given an injection.

2 You **can** make bookings up to seven days before the event. (Bookings)

3 It's hospital policy, I suppose, so they **might** not allow us to see her. (We)

4 We rang the bell but there was no answer. We tried again in case they **couldn't** hear us. (We)

5 What I said to her **must** have hurt her. (She)

12 **Write the context where you would expect to read or hear each sentence.**

1 Your call is in a queue and will be answered as soon as possible. ....

2 Rooms must be vacated before 11 am. ....

3 To be continued. ....

4 Your water supply may be discontinued if the amount below is not paid by July 31. ....

5 Not to be opened, except in an emergency. ....

6 Your account with us will be closed immediately. ....

Past: past simple, past continuous and present perfect simple

Past simple (*I talked*)

1a Match sentences 1–5 with a–e and underline the past forms.

1 .... 2 .... 3 .... 4 .... 5 ....

1 She had a bump in the car.
2 I didn't go to work on Tuesday.
3 We went swimming on Saturdays.
4 He looked very tired.
5 They usually travelled by train.

a He needed a holiday.
b We always had chips afterwards.
c They didn't like flying.
d I had a day off.
e She was okay but they took her to hospital anyway.

1b Which pairs of sentences refer to something that happened more than once?

....

2a Did you know …? Fill in each gap with the past simple form of the verb in brackets and add a number or date from the box.

45 billion	1982	1800	1153
million	120	1900	200

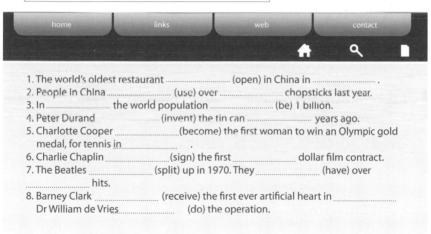

1. The world's oldest restaurant .... (open) in China in ....
2. People in China .... (use) over .... chopsticks last year.
3. In .... the world population .... (be) 1 billion.
4. Peter Durand .... (invent) the tin can .... years ago.
5. Charlotte Cooper ....(become) the first woman to win an Olympic gold medal, for tennis in ....
6. Charlie Chaplin .... (sign) the first .... dollar film contract.
7. The Beatles .... (split) up in 1970. They .... (have) over .... hits.
8. Barney Clark .... (receive) the first ever artificial heart in ....
   Dr William de Vries .... (do) the operation.

2b Identify the regular and irregular verb forms in the sentences above.

....

3 **Find and correct the mistake in each of these sentences.**

1 I work at least 45 hours last week.

2 He did go to the match on Saturday?

3 We didn't ate in restaurants when I was young.

4 The telephone ringed and she picked it up.

5 You wasn't at the party.

6 I got my exam results. I fail two of them.

Past continuous (*She was playing*)

4 **Fill in each gap with the past continuous form of the verb in brackets.**

1 When ⟨i was teaching⟩ (I/teach) in France, I lived in the school.

2 You know the girl .... (he/tell) you about. Well she's over there.

3 .... (we/chat) and Tim interrupted. He's so rude.

4 .... (I/try) to get to sleep but it was raining really heavily.

5 Why .... (you/run)? Were you late?

6 .... (he/not/listen) to you. I could tell from his face.

7 Who .... (drive) when the police stopped you?

8 .... (I/not/lie) when I said I was at work last night.

5 **Use your own ideas to add background information to each situation using the past continuous.**

1 He ⟨was playing football⟩ when he was hit in the face by the ball.

2 The baby .... and then it started to smile.

3 She fell over as ....

4 .... and the smoke alarm went off.

5 .... so I took my umbrella.

6 .... so I turned the TV off.

Past simple or past continuous? (*He walked* or *He was walking*?)

6 **Fill in each gap using the verb in brackets. Use one past continuous form and one past simple form in each sentence.**

1 As we ⟨were getting⟩ (get) nearer, we ⟨heard⟩ (hear) the crowd shouting from the stadium.

2 They .... (not/laugh) when they .... (see) the state of the house.

3 The phone .... (ring) just as I .... (fall) asleep.

4 No one .... (watch) so she .... (take) another piece of cake.

5 She .... (tell) me a joke and she .... (start) to laugh.

6 We .... (do) the gardening and .... (find) some animal bones.

7 **Correct the six mistakes with the past simple and the past continuous.**

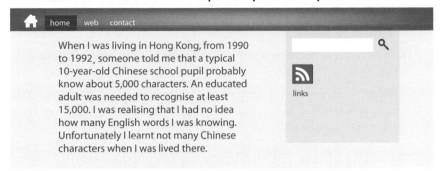

When I was living in Hong Kong, from 1990 to 1992, someone told me that a typical 10-year-old Chinese school pupil probably know about 5,000 characters. An educated adult was needed to recognise at least 15,000. I was realising that I had no idea how many English words I was knowing. Unfortunately I learnt not many Chinese characters when I was lived there.

links

Past simple or present perfect simple? (*They ate* or *They've eaten*?)

8 **Underline the correct form in each sentence.**

1 My uncle *broke / has broken* his arm about six months ago.

2 When they were younger they *have walked / walked* to school.

3 I *haven't felt / didn't feel* very well last weekend.

4 We watched a film while we *waited / have waited* for our flight.

5 That bread *didn't taste / hasn't tasted* very fresh when I bought it.

6 *Have you seen / Did you see* him? He didn't see you.

9 **Choose the correct sentence, a or b, to follow sentences 1–6. In some cases both may be possible.**

1 There was a good programme on the TV last night.
  a Did you see it?   **b** Have you seen it?

2 It's 11 o'clock already.
  a I've had such a busy morning so far.   **b** I had such a busy morning so far.

3 I went for a coffee with Rachel last Thursday.
  a I didn't see her since.   **b** I haven't seen her since.

4 He'll be in Berlin until Friday.
  a He's gone there for a conference.   **b** He went there for a conference.

5 I'm waiting for Paul to give me the report.
  a He still didn't do it.   **b** He still hasn't done it.

6 Ouch! My finger really hurts.
  a I don't think I've broken it though.   **b** I don't think I broke it though.

Past perfect simple and past perfect continuous

Past perfect simple (*He'd seen it before*)

1 **Fill in each gap with the past perfect simple form of the verb in brackets.**

Did you know …?

1 Mozart __had composed__ (compose) his first pieces of music by the age of 5.

2 Tiger Woods.................................already.............................(start) to play golf by the age of 2.

3 Kim Ung-yong, a Korean boy,...........................(learn) to speak German, English and Japanese by the time he was 4.

4 William Sidis, an American child genius,...........................(write) four books by the time he was 7.

5 The actress Tatum O'Neal...........................already ....(win) an Oscar by the age of 10.

2 **Serge went to work and left this note for his flatmate, Tom. Look at the picture and write which jobs Tom had done and not done by the time Serge came home.**

Can you clear up a bit? Bill and Ahmet are coming round for dinner, remember? Here's a list of things to do!

- Take the bread out of the oven.
- Fold the clothes. Take them upstairs.
- Do the washing up. Feed the dog.
- Empty the rubbish. Wash the floor.
- Clean the windows.
- Throw out the flowers.
- Don't forget to turn off the lights before you go out and get the shopping.

See you later. Serge

He'd taken the bread out of the oven.

....

....

....

3 **Combine the two sentences using the word in brackets. Use the past perfect simple for the event which happened first.**

1 She recovered from her illness. Anna went back to work. (when)
   when she'd recovered from her illness, Anna went back to work.

2 I went to the party. Dad told me not to go. (even though)

3 They didn't do any preparation. They both passed the exam. (but)

4 I ate a big breakfast. I went to the gym. (after)

5 I went to bed early. I had a tiring day. (because)

6 June went to the hospital. She promised to visit Linda. (as)

4 **Use the past perfect simple of the main verb to report each statement. Change the pronouns if necessary.**

1 'I didn't go to the meeting.'
   Ahmed said that *he hadn't been to the meeting* .

2 'We wanted to see that film but it was too late.'
   Helen said that

3 'I left my credit card in the shop.'
   Paul realised that

4 'The service wasn't great and the food was cold.'
   They complained that

Past perfect continuous (*She'd been talking about him*)

5 **Underline the past perfect continuous forms.**

Andrés finally sat down in his own kitchen, happy to be home. At last, here he was. He'd been waiting for this moment for a long time. He didn't know if it was morning or evening. He'd been travelling for 48 hours, bus, train, plane, train again and then a taxi. He didn't know if he wanted to eat or just go to bed. He'd been feeling quite hungry when he got off the plane despite the fact that he'd been snacking throughout the journey. Jen phoned about half an hour after he'd got off the plane. She was wondering if she could come and see him. She'd been working all day and was on her way home. They hadn't seen each other for over a year. He had been really looking forward to seeing her. The doorbell rang.

6 Use the pictures to write what had been happening the moment before each situation 1–6. Use the past perfect continuous.

fix bike   paint wall   clear up broken glass

make bread   cry   not feel well

1 Izumi had grease on her hands. .... *She had been fixing her bike.*
2 Sal's trousers had white paint on them. ....
3 Greg had cut his finger. ....
4 Frankie had flour on his apron. ....
5 Agnes' face was red and she looked upset. ....
6 Paul was in bed. ....

Past perfect simple or past perfect continuous?

7 Underline the correct form of the verb. Sometimes more than one answer is possible.

1 We were shocked after we'd *heard / been hearing* the news. We couldn't believe it.
2 I'd *tasted / been tasting the soup.* I added some lemon juice. It needed more flavour.
3 Mary and Gill had *been knowing / known* each other since they were three.
4 I'd *read / been reading* all the Harry Potter books before the films came out.
5 Gary had always *been hating / hated* his job so he decided to leave.

Past simple, past continuous, past perfect simple or past perfect continuous

8 Correct the mistakes in these sentences.

1 It was the best film I ever saw.
2 If we saw you, we would have said hello.
3 Tim had been stolen from the company for years and eventually he lost his job.
4 They hadn't been hearing anything strange during that night.
5 She had watched TV when the lights went out.

9a Fill in each gap using the most appropriate past tense form of the verb. Sometimes more than one answer is possible.

My time in Berlin

It was late at night on 9 November 1989. I (1) _was sitting_ (sit) in my apartment in West Berlin. I (2)............................ (play) cards for a few hours with some friends but we were tired and (3)............................ (decide) to turn the TV on. There was a news headline that two East German citizens (4)............................ (cross) into West Berlin without restrictions. We (5)............................ (live) just a few kilometres from the border with East Germany. People (6)............................ (talk) about it for weeks, but we (7)............................ (know) if any of it was true. Early the next morning, we (8)............................ (jump) on the underground train to go to the wall. Normally the journey to the wall only (9)............................ (take) 20 minutes, but the news (10)............................ (spread) quickly and thousands of people (11)............................ (try) to get there too.

At first people (12) .... (not/believe) it but soon everyone (13)............................ (realise) that something incredible (14)............................ (happen). After we (15)............................ (travel) for more than an hour, we arrived. There was chaos as crowds of people (16)............................ (gather) around the border crossing. Then I realised that it was true – the night before they (17)............................ (raise) the barrier and East Berliners (18)............................ (walk) through. As they came into West Berlin everyone (19) .... (cheer). Then people (20)............................ (start) to break down the concrete wall with axes. Later I (21)............................ (go) across the border into East Berlin. I was lucky enough to be there at such an important historic moment. I'll never forget it.

9b Think of an important or surprising thing that has happened to you. Describe the event, the background to the event and what happened after it. Use the past simple, past continuous, past perfect simple and past perfect continuous.

....
....
....
....
....

Possession

1 **Six of these sentences have mistakes. Correct each mistake and tick (✓) the correct sentences.**

1 Where is the childrens' clothing department?

2 The boy's bikes are in the garden shed.

3 I agree with the old saying that a dog is man's best friend.

4 The mens' changing room at the pool is closed because they are painting it.

5 Lillian's favourite author is Anita Shreve.

6 Ben Nevis is Britains' highest mountain.

7 The workers' pay has been increased since the strike.

8 Rhys's sister is called Emily.

9 Brendan's mothers' friend owns the house that we stayed in.

10 In the end, it was the governments' decision.

2 **Rewrite each sentence using 's.**

1 The car belonged to John.
   It was .... John's car ....

2 She borrowed a jacket which belonged to her sister.
   She borrowed her ....

3 Richard and my mother are brother and sister.
   Richard is my ....

4 Ellen owns the laptop but she has lent it to me for a week.
   I've borrowed ....

5 Fluffy is the name of the dog which belongs to Linda and Owen.
   Fluffy is the name of ....

6 Westminster Abbey is one of the oldest buildings in London.
   Westminster Abbey is one of ....

3 **Tick (✓) the correct sentence, a or b.**

1 **a** I've only had one hour's sleep.   **b** I've only had one hours' sleep.

2 **a** Have you read todays' paper?   **b** Have you read today's paper?

3 **a** My house is five minutes' walk from here.
   b My house is five minute's walk from here.

4 **a** There is at least another week's work to do on the house.
   b There is at least another weeks' work to do on the house.

5 **a** She never wears last year's fashion.
   b She never wears last years' fashion.

4   John and Lisa live in Edinburgh and have two children, Ivan (16 years old) and Jacob (12). Write eight sentences using *'s* and three sentences using *s'*.

	John	Lisa	Ivan	Jacob
Favourite food	pasta	steak	fish and chips	fish and chips
Favourite holiday destination	Morocco	Barcelona	Kenya	skiing in the Alps
Favourite film	*Pulp Fiction*	*Pulp Fiction*	*Lord of the Rings*	*Harry Potter*
Favourite hobby	hiking	hiking	football	computer games
Favourite music	rock	classical	hip-hop	pop

John's favourite food is pasta. The boys' favourite films are Lord of the Rings and Harry Potter.

....

....

....

....

5   Rewrite each sentence using *of* and a possessive pronoun (e.g. *mine, hers*).

1   Martin is my colleague.   Martin is a colleague of mine.
2   Kevin and I are close friends. ....
3   Paul is one of her uncles. ....
4   Mrs Lovett is our neighbour. ....
5   Jason is one of Maria's brothers. ....
6   John Whyte is one of their cousins. ....

6   Tick (✓) the correct sentence, a or b.

1   **a** The doorway of the oldest building in the town is very unusual.
     b The oldest building in the town's doorway is very unusual.

2   **a** The organisation's name was *Earth Care*.
     b The name of the organisation was *Earth Care*.

3   **a** The leg of the horse was cut.   **b** The horse's leg was cut.

4   **a** Spain's most famous dish is paella.
     b The most famous dish of Spain is paella.

5   **a** Elderly people's memories of the past are very interesting.
     b The memories of the past of elderly people are very interesting.

Prepositions

1 Underline the correct prepositions in the text.

A Nervous Flier

My aunt loved America and planned to travel (1) *across / over* the country by train from Chicago to Seattle and then (2) *at / to* San Francisco, which is (3) *with / on* the west coast, 200 miles south of Seattle. But first there was the flight! The take-off made her very nervous and it took ages before we were (4) *above / over* the clouds. She kept putting her hands (5) *over / along* her eyes. She sat (6) *by / against* the window and wouldn't move. Finally, (7) *by / after* a couple of hours, she got up and walked (8) *through / across / along* the aisle and once the plane had flown (9) *through / over* the Pacific, she

became more relaxed. However, when the plane was landing (10) *between / among* two mountains and (11) *over / along* a large stretch of water, she got very nervous again. After we landed, she became very excited and pushed (12) *along / through* a crowd of people to see her daughter, my cousin, who was waiting (13) *beside / next to* the bank and (14) *before / in front of* the arrivals gate. But my cousin had a real shock (15) *for / about* her mother. She had her new husband with her and she hadn't told my aunt (16) *about / with* him!

2a Fill in each gap with a preposition from the box. You can use each one more than once. Sometimes more than one answer is possible.

in	into	at	on	by	until	during	for

They lived (1) .... Italy (2) .... three years, studying (3) .... a college (4) .... the centre of Milan. They decided to rent a big house (5) .... the mountains (6) .... a very beautiful village. They travelled (7) .... Milan most days (8) .... train. (9) .... the three years they were (10) .... Italy, they spent time (11) .... the opera, enjoyed many evenings (12) .... the theatre, got used to crossing the city (13) .... tram and, (14) .... long summer evenings, they enjoyed sitting (15) .... their balcony, which overlooked the mountains. They are now back (16) .... America but cannot wait (17) .... the end of March when they return. (18) .... June they have exams and they then have (19) .... the end of the year to decide their future.

2b Write a short text (no more than four sentences) about any plans you have to work or travel. Use at least three prepositions.

....

....

3 **Fill in each gap with a preposition. Sometimes more than one answer is possible.**

1 They will meet you .... the bus station just .... 10 am.

2 Where's Joan's office? It's .... the end of the corridor, on the left.

3 A: He's lost the headphones .... his MP3 player.
   B: That's them .... his briefcase, isn't it?

4 We're going .... Wales for our holidays this year. We've rented a cottage .... the south coast.

5 They told us to stand .... a queue but we had to really push to get a seat .... the bus.

6 They live .... 15, Meadow Lane. It's .... the centre of the city.

7 .... 2020 over 2 billion people will be using English as a first or foreign language.

8 Can you write your name .... the first page of the book? It's a present .... Jack.

9 This book should be returned to the library .... the last day of May.

10 I've got maths homework to do. Can we wait .... later?

4 **Underline the correct prepositions.**

1 They were so bored that they all walked out *in / during* the lecture.

2 We like going for long walks with our friends *during / in* winter.

3 I'm so sorry I'm late. I'll meet you *in / during* half an hour and I can stay *in / for* at least another hour or two.

4 She has been learning Spanish *for / since* five years.

5 He's been waiting for you *for / since* nearly two hours. He says that it feels like he's been here *since / for* yesterday.

6 A: Can I borrow your bike? B: Okay, but *by / till* when?

7 He finally found his phone *between / among* a pile of clothes on his bed

8 The state of Georgia is *between / among* South Carolina and Alabama.

9 She lives two floors *below / under* our apartment.

10 He was so careful when he travelled that he hid his money *below / under* his shirt.

5a **The prepositions in the box are all used in fixed expressions. Put them into groups to show their meaning.**

by plane	on purpose	at breakfast	in a hurry	on business
at lunch	in love	by train	in the evening	in pain
in private	out of the office	by accident	on foot	in secret
on Sunday	by mistake	out of danger	by chance	on holiday

means of travel by plane	circumstances or the way things happen by chance, in private

a particular day or part of a particular day at lunch	being somewhere else on holiday

5b Write a short paragraph using at least *three* of the following fixed
expressions: *in a hurry, by train, by plane, in love, in the evening.*

....

....

6 Write sentences about the picture using at least eight of the prepositions.

along	across	outside	in front of	over	towards
outside	in	below	onto	opposite	on

....

....

....

....

Prepositions with nouns, verbs and adjectives

7 **Fill in each gap with a preposition. If no preposition is necessary, write X.**

1 I'm not interested .... football.

2 Can we discuss .... your results?

3 We completely agree .... you.

4 Have you seen the advertisement .... the job in Vienna?

5 That's absolutely typical .... them.

6 A: Did you enjoy the film?
   B: Yes, it was great, thanks. It was .... life in Brazil in the 1930s.

7 She is responsible .... all their travel to and .... Egypt.

8 One of the children is very ill and needs to be looked ....

9 Congratulations .... passing your driving test.

10 What's the matter .... their dog?

11 He married .... Julie and his sister is married .... Julie's brother.

12 Can you pay .... the taxi?

13 The population .... India will increase in the next few decades.

14 We are all very proud .... what she has achieved.

15 It depends .... what she says.

8 **Complete each sentence by adding a preposition and the correct form of the verb in brackets.**

1 We are really looking forward _to meeting_ her. (meet)

2 She's been thinking .... her job. (change)

3 He accused them .... his watch. (steal)

4 I am very interested .... with you. (work)

5 He's relying .... to retire at the end of the year. (be able)

6 They're both worried .... their luggage. (lose)

7 The team are very good .... matches in hot conditions. (win)

8 It's a new machine .... coffee. (make)

9a **Complete each sentence with the object form of the pronoun in brackets, the correct preposition and the correct form of the verb in brackets.**

1 His teachers suspected (he) _him of cheating_ (cheat) in the exam.

2 The traffic jams prevented (they) .... (get) to the meeting on time.

3 That reminds (I) .... (walk) in the mountains in Switzerland.

9b **Complete each sentence with the object form of the pronoun in brackets and the correct preposition.**

1 Please thank (she) .... her help with the gardening.

2 We want to congratulate (you) .... the birth of your son.

3 They threatened (we) .... legal action.

10 Write an appropriate response from the box for each statement.
Sometimes more than one answer is possible.

Who's it by?	What's it about?	Who with?
Who for?	Where was she coming from?	
What for?	Where to?	Who to?

1 They're going on holiday. _____where to?_____

2 It took her ages to get here. ....

3 Laura's coming round tonight. ....

4 This package has just arrived in the office. ....

5 I've just finished the best book I've read in ages. ....

6 She gave all her CDs away. ....

7 I went to the cinema last night. ....

11 Look at this horoscope and underline the five prepositions in the text.
Then write a horoscope for Scorpio using one or two sentences and at
least three prepositions.

LEO
24th July – 23rd August

Whatever your feelings are towards someone you live or work alongside, it is essential that you are honest with them. Over the next few days, take advantage of all your opportunities, be honest, and you will be successful in everything you do.

SCORPIO
24th October – 22nd November

....

....

....

....

....

Present perfect simple and present perfect continuous

Present perfect simple (*I've started*)

1 Describe each picture using the present perfect simple.

1  2  3

4  5  6

1 he/make/a cake *He's made a cake.* ....

2 they/break/a window ....

3 I/just/run/10 km ....

4 he/eat/too much ....

5 they/win/the game ....

6 he/just/come back ....

2 Fill in the gaps in each sentence with the present perfect simple form of a verb from the box, and *for* or *since*.

want	be	live	do	know	work	seem

1 Katie .... *has done* .... the same job .... *for* .... ten years.

2 His mother .... on holiday .... last Sunday.

3 They .... in that house .... 1965.

4 We .... each other .... a long time.

5 Helen and Cath .... together .... a while.

6 Dad .... much happier .... he left his job.

7 They .... to buy a bigger house .... the children were born.

3 **Use the words to write sentences (1–5) or questions (6–8) in the present perfect.**

1 I / always / hate / ironing   *I've always hated ironing.*

2 Martha / have / three different jobs / since school ....

3 we / already / book / the flights and hotels ....

4 he / still /not find / a job ....

5 I / not have / breakfast / yet ....

6 they / finish / already ? ....

7 you / not / do / your homework / yet ? ....

8 How long / she / live there ? ....

4a **We asked 20 people some questions about their internet use. Use the information from the table to fill in each gap. Use the present perfect.**

Have you used the internet to …?	never	once	often
do food shopping	4	7	9
sell something	9	8	3
read the news	5	1	14
buy a train ticket	1	12	7
book a holiday	10	5	5
send a gift to someone	8	7	5

Seven people (1) *have done*   their food shopping only once on the internet.
Only one person (2).................... never..................a train ticket online.
Seven of the people (3)....................a gift to someone once using the internet.
14 people (4)....................often....................the news online. Ten of the
people (5)....................never....................a holiday on the internet. Only
one person (6)....................the news online only once.

4b **Now use the information to write five more sentences.**

Five people have never read the news online.

....

....

....

4c **Now answer each question so that it is true for you.**

I've never booked a holiday on the internet.

....

....

....

5 Think about your own experiences. Use the ideas in the box and write sentences about yourself using the present perfect.

> best job   most exciting city   tastiest food   worst film
> most surprising thing   best book

The most exciting city I've visited is New York. *or* New York is the most exciting city I've visited.

....

....

Present perfect continuous (*We've been waiting*)

6 Fill in each gap with the present perfect continuous form of the verb.

1 Carlo's not very well. He's *been sleeping* (sleep) most of the day.

2 Where have you been? I .... (worry) about you.

3 We're not sure where to go on holiday. We .... (think) about Iceland.

4 It's okay. I .... (not/wait) very long.

5 I .... (answer) the phone all morning. It hasn't stopped ringing.

6 Dora .... (apply) for all sorts of jobs but she hasn't got one yet.

7 We .... (not/make) much progress. We're still stuck on question 2.

8 She's very good at the piano even though she .... (not/play) for long.

9 It's a lovely house. How long .... (they/live) there?

10 He's told you all about his family problems. What else .... (he/tell) you about?

7 Read the situations and write an appropriate sentence or question using the present perfect continuous. Use a verb from the box below.

> rain   work   ~~clean~~   practise   play   travel

1 The windows are shining. You're carrying a ladder and a bucket. You're a bit wet.
   You say: *I've been cleaning the windows.*

2 Today is Tuesday. It started to rain three days ago. It's still raining.
   You say: It ....

3 Your friends are travelling around South America. They arrived in South America six weeks ago.
   You say: They ....

4 It's Sunday evening. You meet your neighbour. Unusually, she's in her work clothes and she's carrying her briefcase.

You ask: Have .... ?

5 You come back home at lunchtime and your son is playing games on the computer. He was playing games when you left the house this morning.

He says: I ....

6 You can hear a friend playing the piano. It sounds much better than the last time you heard her playing.

You ask: Have .... ?

Present perfect simple or present perfect continuous?

8   Match each sentence, 1–10, with the appropriate following sentence, a or b. Which pair of sentences 1–10 have an identical meaning?

1	I've been trying to find out train times.	**a** I've given up. I can't find any information at all.
2	I've tried to find out train times.	**b** My internet connection has just gone down. I'll try again later.
3	Have you been reading this book?	**a** Yes, I'm really enjoying it.
4	Have you read this book?	**b** Yes, I didn't like it much.
5	Have you looked at all the holiday photos?	**a** No, we haven't finished yet.
6	Have you been looking at all the holiday photos?	**b** Yes, but we still haven't finished.
7	He's been thinking about leaving his job.	**a** He's decided to stay because he needs the money at the moment.
8	He's thought about leaving his job.	**b** He wants to do something completely different.
9	Most of the teachers have worked here for more than five years.	**a** Three of them are retiring next year.
10	Most of the teachers have been working here for more than five years.	**b** They're all very experienced.

English Grammar Today Workbook

Present simple and present continuous

Present simple (*I talk*)

1 **Fill in each gap with the present simple form of the verb in brackets.**

1 A housefly .... (live) for 25 days.

2 Your heart .... (beat) about 101,000 times a day.

3 On average, we .... (speak) almost 5,000 words a day

4 How many bones .... a human head .... (contain)?

5 An African elephant .... (not/have) many teeth. In fact, it only
.... (have) four.

6 We .... (not/see) with our eyes. We .... (see) with
our brains.

7 Bees .... (visit) 4 million flowers to make one kilo of honey.

8 The average American .... (watch) 140 hours of TV a month.

9 Six times twelve .... (make) seventy-two. (6×12 = 72)

10 Bats .... (not/sleep) upside-down, do they?

11 How many hours of sleep .... a typical 6 year-old
.... (need)?

12 A dog .... (not/drink) water if it .... (not/be) thirsty.

2 **Correct the mistake in each sentence.**

1 Jack never replys to my emails.

2 The advert do not say anything about the price.

3 A person who travelling a lot, learning a lot of things.

4 His mother does'nt want to change her car. She likes the one she has.

5 One of my friends always go to school by car.

6 He doesn't washes his hair often enough.

7 Don't it cost anything to park here?

8 How long it takes to get to Paris?

3 **Use the words to write sentences about some people's daily lives. Use the
present simple form of the verbs. Then match each sentence with a person
from the box below.**

| teenager   ~~vegetarian~~   cyclist   doctor   teacher   baby |
| trainee chef   ski instructor |

1 never / I / meat / eat   I never eat meat. (vegetarian)

2 night / in / the / cry / he / sometimes ....

3 usually / she / class / 12 / each / in / have ....

4 she / before / at / 10 o'clock / not get up / weekends ....

5 much / not work / I / the / in / summer ....

6 you / ride / always / breakfast / before? ....

7 it / where / hurt? ....

8 you / bread / make / how? ....

4 Fill in each gap using the correct form of the verb in brackets.

Review

The book of the film

James Cameron (1)................ (return) to film-making after a twelve year break.

Academy Award-winning writer and director of *Titanic* and the *Terminator* series, was making the film *Avatar* for over ten years. The film (2)................ (follow) the story of Jake, an ex-marine who (3)................ (not/know) whether to support his fellow humans on earth or the aliens who (4)................ (live) on the planet of Pandora.

The Art of James Cameron's Avatar is a book that (5)................ (tell) the story behind this epic 3-D action adventure. The book (6)................ (explore) the art used by the creative team to bring Cameron's vision to life.

Designers, animators, costume designers and creature makers (7)................ (talk) about how they bring together their talents to make this film. It (8)................ (have) more than 100 exclusive full-colour images. It (9)................ (include) sketches, paintings, drawings and film stills. It (10)................ (interview) the actors and (11)................ (give) many of the stories of the makers of the film. *The Art of James Cameron's Avatar* (12)................ (reveal) the process behind the creation of set designs for the film.

It (13)................ (bring) readers behind the scenes of the amazing film. (14)................ (you/think) that you'd like to buy this book?

5 You've made this cake using the recipe. Tell a friend how to make it. Use the pictures and the correct present simple forms of the verbs in the box. Use ordering words (*first, then, and, now, next*).

whisk

sieve

Ingredients	Equipment
250g soft butter	2 bowls
250g sugar	cake tin
4 eggs	whisk
250g flour	wooden spoon
	large metal spoon
	sieve

Cooking time 20 mins

* sift the flour means to put it through the sieve to make it finer and add air.

turn on	put	pour	mix	break	whisk	add
mix	*sift	stir				

First you turn on the oven to 180°C. Then ....

....

....

....

....

Present continuous (*She's talking*)

6 Fill in each gap with the present continuous form of the verb in brackets.

1 I .... (work) in London every day this week.

2 Will you hurry up! We .... (wait) for you.

3 They've been in America for three weeks but they .... (come) back today.

4 Why .... Claire .... (cry)?

5 What speed .... he .... (travel) at?

6 Why .... you .... (be) so horrible?

7 I .... (not/complain). I think the food is delicious.

8 .... she .... (not/live) with her sister any more?

9 We .... (not/move). We've decided to stay in this house.

10 I .... (not/try) to change your mind.

7 **Last year a company called Infrad introduced some policies to save energy. Write a report of the changes that the company is making now and the plans that they have for the next few months. Use the present continuous.**

The Infrad Green Code

Changes we are already making	Immediate plans for the next six months
✳ Use less paper.	✳ January – install solar panels on the roof of the company building.
✳ Don't print documents unless you have to.	✳ Look for ways to use less water.
✳ Switch off lights when leaving a room.	✳ Use alternative energy supplies.
✳ Turn off computers when not in use.	✳ March 21st – have a 'no cars' day.
✳ Separate rubbish into glass, paper and plastic.	✳ Winter – lower temperature of heating by 1°C.
✳ Recycle more.	
✳ Don't charge mobile phones unless it's necessary.	

We're already using less paper in the office now and we're installing solar panels in January.

....

....

....

....

English Grammar Today Workbook

Present simple and present continuous

8 Read the puzzle then underline the present simple forms and circle the present continuous forms.

A fast train leaves London for Brighton at 3.45 pm. At the same time, a slow train departs from Brighton for London. The fast train is travelling at 140 km per hour and the slow train is going at 90 km per hour. The fast train doesn't stop at any stations. The slow train stops at two stations. The slow train is carrying passengers and mail. When they meet, which train is further from London?

Answer: Neither. When the two trains pass each other, they are exactly the same distance from London. It doesn't matter which way you're going.

36

9 Underline the correct alternative. Sometimes both answers are possible.

1 You want some milk in your coffee.
Do you think / Are you thinking this milk is okay to drink? It's *smelling / smells* strange to me.

2 You can hear a language that you don't understand. You make a guess.
I think they *speak / 're speaking* Hungarian.

3 An extract from a formal letter
I'm *attaching / attach* a cheque for the work you have carried out.

4 Talking about fear
Spiders *don't frighten / aren't frightening* me.

5 You walk into a room.
It's *seeming / seems* a bit dark in here. Can I put the light on?

6 You're describing a friend.
She *laughs / 's laughing* a lot.

7 You're going to a party. You need directions.
You could ask Jane. She's *knowing / knows* where it is.

10a Decide if each sentence refers to regular actions, actions happening now or future actions. Tick (✓) the correct box.

	regular	now	future
1 I cook and he does the washing up.			
2 You're being extremely difficult			
3 She's always complaining.			
4 The train doesn't get in until after midnight.			
5 I understand what you're saying.			
6 I respect your views but I don't agree with them.			

10b For questions 1–4, change the verbs in the present simple to the present continuous and the verbs in the present continuous to the present simple. Do the meanings change? Tick the correct box for each and write why you can't change the verbs in 5 and 6.

	regular	now	future
1 I'm cooking and he's doing the washing up.		✓	
2			
3			
4			
5			
6			

11 Think about your life and write about both the temporary and permanent things.

> work   family   home   friends
> food   holidays   free time

Friends often come for dinner. I work at home. We often go camping for our holidays.

....

....

....

....

English Grammar Today Workbook

Pronouns

Personal and possessive pronouns (*she, us, his, mine*)

1 Fill in each gap with a personal or possessive pronoun.

1 A: I need to speak with Gill? Is __she__ here? B: Yes, that's __her__ in black.

2 Erik and Alf are younger than ...., but I'm a lot wiser than ....!

3 Where are we in this photo? Oh, there we are. Look at the two of .... standing at the back.

4 A: Are these shoes your sister's? B: No, they're not ....

5 A: I don't fancy going to the cinema. I'm too tired. B: .... too.

6 A: Do you know the headteacher's name? B: Yes, ... 's Brian Taylor.

7 If anyone phones for Anita, can you ask .... to leave a message.

8 .... always put the price of petrol up in the summer, don't ....?

9 .... says in the paper here that .... need to apply early for tickets.

10 They were late. He said he couldn't wait any longer so he left without ....

2 Underline the correct word in each sentence.

1 Is that our new boss? I hear that he's a good friend of *you / yours*.

2 Someone's taken my suitcase by mistake and I have *their / theirs*.

3 A: Shall we take a car? B: Yes, let's take *mine / our*.

4 Russian is our native language so it's easy for us but *it / one* takes a lot of practice to learn to speak a language like *ours / its*.

5 A: Was there a voicemail message? B: Yes, *it / she* was Jean.

6 My phone's not working again. Can I borrow *your / yours*?

7 A: Did you bring your swimming costumes?
B: Both of *we / us* have forgotten *ours / ones*.

8 He can't lend you that camera. It's not *his / its*.

Reflexive and reciprocal pronouns (*myself, yourself, each other*)

3 Seven of these sentences have mistakes with pronouns. Correct the mistakes and tick (✓) the correct sentences.

1 I hurt me while playing football.

2 She wants to buy herself a new flat in the centre of town.

3 They have taught themselves to write in Mandarin Chinese.

4 She's gone to South America by hers.

5 We'd better hurry ourselves.

6 I know it's difficult but you'll have to help each other.

7 They email themselves every week.

8 If you don't use it for three hours, the computer switches itself off.

9 They got on very well and put each other numbers in their phones.

10 She's always laughing at herself.

11 Are you both painting the house yourself?

12 Are they playing badminton by ourselves or do they want us to join them?

Pronouns: *one, some*

4 **Fill in each gap with *none, ones, one* or *some*.**

A: Can I get you both a coffee?

B: Thanks. I'll just have a small (1) ....

C: A large (2) .... for me, please.

A: How about cakes? There's strawberry and chocolate.

C: I'll have four chocolate (3) .... I'll take (4) .... home with me.

B: I'm on a diet. (5) .... for me thanks.

A: Sorry about this but someone has just taken the last cakes. Can you believe it? But the assistant has just gone to get (6) .... more.

Indefinite pronouns (*everyone, someone, nothing, everything*)

5a **You arrive very late at an airport and miss your flight home. Fill in each gap with an indefinite pronoun.**

You can't phone (1) *anyone* because (2) .... has stolen your phone. You're angry and need to tell (3) .... how you feel. You're hungry and want (4) .... to eat but all the shops are closed and (5) .... has gone home and there's (6) .... to ask. You're very tired and need to find (7) .... to sleep but there's (8) .... in the airport and there's (9) .... to do. (10) .... is dark and cold and it's six hours before the next flight. You decide that things can only get better from now.

5b **Continue the story. Write three sentences, using indefinite pronouns.**

Eventually, I found somewhere to sleep ....

....

....

Demonstrative pronouns (*this, that, these*)

6 **Underline the correct words. Sometimes both answers are possible.**

1 *This / It* is how it happened. My phone rang and it was the police.

2 Listen to *this / that*. I've got some interesting news for you.

3 The strawberries are over there. Are *these / those* what you want?

4 There have been a number of floods in the region and experts have suggested that *these / those* are due to climate change: *This / That* is why we need action now.

5 A: She feels a bit sick. B: Oh, why's *that / this*?

6 Economic History: *This / that* is the study of social and economic change.

7 A: He says he's lost his watch. B: I'm afraid *this / that* is his problem.

8 It's a lovely day and we've done absolutely nothing. We should have more days like *this / these*.

9 Look, watch me. Do it like *this / that*, not like *this / that*.

10 [a telephone call] Hello, *this / that* is Charles. Who's *this / that*?

7 Match 1–6 with a–f and fill in each gap with *one* or *ones*.

1 Would you like a drink?

2 Do you want me to get you some peppers?

3 Help yourself to the chocolates.

4 The DVDs we saw last week were awful.

5 What sort of job would she like best?

6 Can you fetch the photos?

a I'll just have this ...., thanks.

b .... with the chance to travel round the world.

c But these are definitely good ....

d Yes, a couple of green .... please.

e I've got ...., thanks.

f Which ....? Do you mean the boat trip ....?

8 Rewrite the sentences in brackets without repeating the noun in bold.

1 I haven't got any toothpaste. (Can you get me **toothpaste** from the supermarket?) *can you get me some from the supermarket?*

2 These shoes are really tight. (I must get new **shoes**.)

3 This map doesn't show us where to go. (I've got another **map** in my bag.)

4 Need an umbrella? (Why don't you take this **umbrella**?)

5 I haven't got any money. (Sorry, I can't lend you **money**.)

6 A: Do you have any leaflets on visits to Oxford? (B: We don't have **leaflets** today but we will have **leaflets** tomorrow.)

9a Replace the nouns in bold in this text with appropriate pronouns.

Television was invented in the 1920s by John Logie Baird. **Television** has become more popular than ever. **Television** can be entertaining, informative and educational. There is a dark side though – people can get addicted to **television** and some people have three or more in their houses. People spend hours in front of **televisions** and can become lazy. How much time do you spend in front of **your television**?

9b Give your opinion about television using at least three pronouns.

....

10a A picture for a holiday company shows a beach and a blue sea. Why is the pronoun *you* is used?

10b Here are two different one-line advertisements for a new car. Which one do you prefer? Why?

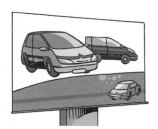

Relative and interrogative pronouns (*who, which, how* etc)

11 General Knowledge Quiz. Write the questions for these answers 1–10.

1 *what is Camembert?*
Camembert is a famous French cheese.

2 ....
The Taj Mahal is in India.

3 ....
The Second World War ended in 1945.

4 ....
Shakespeare wrote *All's Well That Ends Well*.

5 ....
The New York Stock Exchange is on Wall Street in New York.

6 ....
The Eiffel Tower is the tallest building in Paris.

7 ....
The film that won the 2009 Oscar for best film was *Slumdog Millionaire*.

8 ....
The man who first walked on the moon was Neil Armstrong.

Punctuation

Capital letters (A, B)

1 **Put capital letters into these sentences where necessary.**

1 Well, I'm busy on monday so why don't we meet on tuesday next week.

2 my brother john has just moved to thailand from hong kong but at the moment he and professor hammond are staying at the peninsular hotel and are meeting their chinese friends this evening.

3 She's an expert on italian history and has just sent details of her research to the new york times newspaper.

Commas (,) and question marks (?)

2 **Five of these sentences have punctuation mistakes. Correct the mistakes by adding commas and question marks. Tick (✓) the correct sentences.**

1 It's a big city. It's a busy exciting dangerous place.

2 She's a kind helpful and intelligent girl.

3 We travelled through Chile Brazil Argentina and Paraguay. Eduardo our guide stayed with us for the whole journey.

4 You haven't got the job but we'll keep your details for future vacancies.

5 Because the sea was so rough the ferry for Dublin wasn't able to leave.

6 Come and see us when you next visit Athens.

7 Glasgow was the city that was selected to be the world capital of culture.

8 A: Okay so we'll see you outside the cinema in town shall we.
   B: Thanks for asking but I can't tonight. Perhaps next week.

Colons (:) and semi-colons (;)

3 **Put either a colon or semi-colon in each sentence.**

1 There are four main reasons for the fall of the Roman Empire economic, social, political and military.

2 Her new book is called *Everyday English Cookery A Guide for Beginners*.

3 English is widely used in public life in S.E. Asia in Singapore it is the language of education and government.

4 The road works will cause problems in the city centre, of course it is the only way to start to solve the transport crisis.

Quotation marks (" ") and exclamation marks (!)

4 **Three of these sentences have punctuation mistakes. Correct the mistakes and tick (✓) the correct sentences.**

1 'I hope I get this answer right,' she said to herself.

2 He asked 'what are the dates for the concert'?

3 They said, "Where can we find a good Italian restaurant near here?".

4 'Don't try to go back to work too soon,' the doctor said, 'even if you have taken all the tablets.'

5 Gosh. That sounds very dangerous. Now listen to me. This is important.

6 Oh no. Please don't ask me to talk to the whole class. I get really nervous.

Contractions (*I'm*) and apostrophes (')

5 **Correct the mistakes with contractions and apostrophes in each sentence.**

1 They dont like driving long distances.

2 Isnt that his headteacher?

3 Whod like some more salad?

4 Orange's for sale.

5 You mustnt tell anyone.

6 Theyve seen the film already so theyre not coming with us.

7 Who's jacket is this? It's not mine. It must be your's.

8 The committee has made it's decision.

Numerals and internet punctuation

6 **Write the spoken phrases in bold as numerals or in their written form. Use abbreviations for units of measurement.**

1 Date of birth. **August seventeenth, nineteen seventy seven.** 17/8/1977

2 **Two thousand three hundred and fifty**

3 **Eight point five**

4 He runs **three thousand metres** every weekend.

5 It weighs **ten kilograms.**

6 The bank opens at **nine thirty am** and closes at **five pm.**

7 You can contact them on their website; **www dot the swimming club dash humus dot org**

8 My email is **jane dot cooper at cambuni dot co dot uk**

General punctuation

7 **Punctuate this sentence.**

have you seen that film you know no country for old men that won an oscar for best film in march 2008

Questions

1   Match the questions 1–6 with their answers a–f.

1 You're going to cook for ten people?
2 Is it a big multinational?
3 Which house is yours?

4 He's your brother, isn't he?
5 Do we turn it to the left or to the right?
6 Does this belong to Brian?

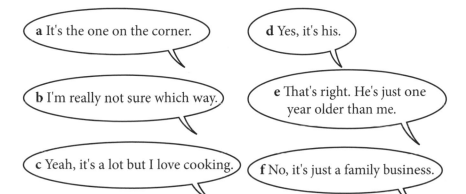

a It's the one on the corner.

d Yes, it's his.

b I'm really not sure which way.

e That's right. He's just one year older than me.

c Yeah, it's a lot but I love cooking.

f No, it's just a family business.

2   Sort the questions below into the grid.

1 *Yes–no* question	
2 Alternative question	
3 Echo question	
4 Two-step question	
5 *Wh*-question	
6 Statement questions	
7 Question tags	
8 Follow-up questions	a Didn't they?

a A: They didn't go on holiday last year. B: Didn't they?
b Can I ask you about your childhood? Was it happy?
c This is the letter you wanted me to post?
d You're the person who has the key, aren't you?
e Would you like tea or coffee?
f What age is her husband?
g Have you finished with the scissors?
h A: I'm not feeling well. B: You're not feeling well?

3 Write an appropriate question to match Keiko's answers.

1 A: ....
   B: I'm from Japan.

2 A: ....
   B: No, I live in Osaka.

3 A: ....
   B: It can take six hours by car but the
   Shinkansen train only takes two and a half
   hours. You can also fly from Tokyo to Osaka
   and that takes an hour and a half.

4 A: ....
   B: At the moment, I'm working in a marketing company.

5 A: ....
   B: I'm happy working there for now but I'd like to start my own events
   management company. I'd like to specialise in organising parties.

4 Imagine what the first speaker said before each statement question.
Sometimes more than one answer is possible.

1 A: Oh no! I've lost my key and it's the only one.   B: It's the only key?

2 A: ....   B: We can't go?

3 A: ....   B: The road is closed?

4 A: ....   B: This is the last one?

5 A: ....   B: No one is going?

5 Write a statement question to show surprise in response to each of the
sentences. Sometimes more than one answer is possible.

1 A: [two friends are looking at a photo] The one with sunglasses is my uncle.
   B: ....

2 A: Okay, everybody, I've made a cake for the party.
   B: ....

3 A: I'm going to learn how to play the guitar.
   B: ....

4 A: Oliver has decided to leave college.
   B: ....

5 A: I've passed my driving test.
   B: ....

6 **Use the two phrases to form an alternative question.**

1 go for a walk / watch a DVD

would you like to go for a walk or watch a DVD?

2 light on / off

3 go out on New Year's Eve / stay in

4 Swedish / Norwegian

5 shop open / closed

6 with sugar / without

7 **Change each of the statements into a *yes-no* question.**

1 You wore hippy clothes in the 1970s. Did you wear hippy clothes in the 1970s?

2 You cycle at the weekend.

3 There's a new lock on the door.

4 We're going to have to sell the car.

5 They won't be home by dinner time.

6 She might be jealous.

8 **Write an appropriate *yes-no* question to match each answer.**

1 A: Does it open jars and bottles?
  B: No, it only opens cans.

2 A: ....?
  B: Yes, and it can record movies as well.

3 A: ....?
  B: No, because I can't use the Internet on it.

4 A: ....?
  B: Yes, it actually could sleep five but it wouldn't be very comfortable.

5 A: ....?
  B: No, it's my sister's. She lent it to me.

9 **Add one more question to make a two-step question.**

1 Are you hungry? .... *would you like some lunch?* .... (lunch)

2 Where's the nearest cash machine? .... (near here)

3 What job do you do in the hotel? .... (reception)

4 Where are the car keys? .... (seen them)

5 Where shall I leave the boxes? .... (floor)

10a **Write the full form of these short questions.**

1 A: Going out tonight? B: Hopefully!

....

2 A: I have to go to town this afternoon. B: What for?

....

3 A: You seen the latest Bond film? B: No, not yet.

....

4 A: This the right way to do it? B: I think so.

....

5 A: I'm not buying her a birthday present. B: Why not?

....

10b **Write the short informal form of these questions.**

1 Have you seen my blue pen? ....

2 Is this the way to the bathroom? ....

3 A: I'm going out tonight with Colm. B: Where are you going to? ....

4 A: Amy's going on holiday with a friend. B: Who is she going on holiday with? ....

5 Are you driving to Birmingham? ....

11 **For each echo question, imagine what the first speaker said.**

1 A: *I've given up my job.* .... B: You've done what?

2 A: .... B: You paid her how much?

3 A: .... B: She shouted at who?

4 A: .... B: They went where?

5 A: .... B: He said what?

6 A: .... B: They did what?

12 Imagine you are saying these sentences but you can't remember something or you are not sure of something. Reword them using a question in each one.

1 I saw a great film last week. I can't remember its name.

I saw a great film last week. what was it called?

2 Her birthday is next week. I can't remember which day.

3 Carmen's married to ... Tell me what her husband's name is.

4 There's a little café somewhere around here. I'm not sure where it is.

5 They have two daughters. One is called Liz and I can't remember the other one's name.

13 Fill in each gap with the correct *wh*-word from the box. Use each word only once.

| who | which | whom | what | whose |

1 .... phoned just now?

2 To .... it may concern, I wish to complain about the service in your restaurant.

3 .... road is the least busy in the morning?

4 .... was the name of the perfume you were wearing yesterday?

5 .... keys are these?

14 Decide if each interrogative pronoun (*wh*-word) is being used as a subject or an object. Write S (subject) or O (object).

1 What caused the fire? 4 Who phoned the police?

2 Who did she tell? 5 Which pen works?

3 Which car did you buy?

Questions: *how* and *what … like?*

1   **Fill in each gap with *how* and, if necessary, a word from the box.**

far	old	about	long	often	much	many	lovely

1 .... 's your mother? I heard she wasn't very well.

2 .... do you go to the gym?

3 A: .... did she give you? B: 20 euros

4 .... more chairs do we need?

5 .... are their children now?

6 .... is it to the station from here?

7 .... have you two known each other?

8 .... stopping for a coffee?

9 I don't know .... she manages to do it all.

10 .... to see you!

2   **Match 1–8 with the responses a–h.**

1 ..*g*.. 2 .... 3 .... 4 .... 5 .... 6 .... 7 .... 8 ....

1 What's Bruno like?   **a** Great. Really spacious.

2 How's Cleo today?   **b** Oh, how is he?

3 What does Guy look like?   **c** What does he like?

4 What's the weather like?   **d** No, what's he like?

5 Do you know Stephan?   **e** He's tall with dark hair.

6 I'm looking for a CD for Jim.   **f** Cold but dry.

7 I saw Claude yesterday.   **g** He's lovely. A bit shy.

8 How's the new house?   **h** Much better.

3   **Write an appropriate response or question for each situation. Use *how, how about …?* or *what … like?***

1 Your friend tells you she's won a holiday to Barbados.   *How fantastic!* ....

2 You suggest to friends that you go for a walk tomorrow. ....

3 A friend asks you if you saw a drama on TV last night. You didn't but you want to know about it. ....

4 Your partner comes home from work. Ask them about their day. ....

5 Your cousin tells you about a friend who has lost his job. ....

6 You haven't met your new boss yet but your colleague has just met her. You ask your colleague's opinion of her. ....

Questions: *wh*-questions

1 **Match the questions with the answers in the dialogue.**

1 ....g.... 2 .... 3 .... 4 .... 5 .... 6 .... 7 ....

1 Where are we eating?   **a** Six of us, I think.

2 Which one?   **b** You are!

3 When did you make the booking?   **c** It's Jan's birthday.

4 What time are we meeting?   **d** Yesterday.

5 Why are you taking flowers?   **e** The one on Duke St.

6 How many of us are going?   **f** Seven, at the main entrance.

7 Who's paying?   **g** At the nice Greek restaurant in town.

2 **Use the information in the table below to complete and answer the questions. Fill in each gap with a word from the box.**

| Who | What | Which | How | Why | When | Where |

	Languages studied					Travel plans
Name	*French*	*Russian*	*German*	*Portuguese*	*Chinese*	*Month: place*
Jaime	✓	✓				
Leo	✓	✓	✓			April: Paris
Camille	✓		✓			
Fabricio				✓		Feb: Brazil
Fidelma		✓	✓			
Sofia		✓			✓	May: Shanghai, IT conference

1 ...who... is learning French but not German or Portuguese? ...Jaime...

2 .... person is learning German but not Russian or Portuguese? ....

3 .... many languages is Leo studying? ....

4 .... language is the most popular? ....

5 .... people are studying two languages? ....

6 .... is Fabricio going in February? ....

7 .... is studying one language? ....

8 .... is Sofia learning Chinese? ....

9 .... is Leo going to France? ....

10 .... is Sofia going to do in Shanghai? ....

3 Make questions from these words using the correct question word. Sometimes more than one answer is possible.

1 A: you / work? .... *where do you work?* ....
B: In the café, on the corner.

2 A: they / laugh? ....
B: I told them a joke.

3 A: cook / yesterday? ....
B: I did. It's your turn today.

4 A: do / the washing up in your house? ....
B: We've got a dishwasher.

5 A: eat / all the cake? ....
B: Not me. I expect it was the children.

6 A: coat / be this? ....
B: It looks like Lara's.

7 A: you / open the window? ....
B: You have to push it quite hard.

8 A: colour / you / prefer? ....
B: I like the blue better.

9 A: you / come to see us next? ....
B: I'm hoping to come in the new year.

4 Read the text and write *wh*-questions for the answers 1–8.

Virgin launches plans for trips to space

The founder of Virgin Atlantic Airlines, Richard Branson, has announced plans for the world's first passenger rocket into space. The rocket, Virgin Galactic SpaceShipTwo, can take six passengers into space. The journey lasts just two hours. It's not cheap though. It costs each person around €130,000. 300 people have already signed up. Sir Richard and his family are in the first group to make the trip when the rocket plane is ready.

Each seat has two large windows next to it – one at the side and one overhead to give passengers a great view of space. During the flight passengers experience a strange feeling that their bodies do not weigh anything before the spacecraft re-enters Earth's atmosphere. The first flights leave from New Mexico, in America, but Sir Richard hopes to have flights from all over the world.

1 who is Richard Branson?
   He's the founder of Virgin Atlantic Airlines.

2 ....
   He's just announced plans for the world's first passenger rocket into space.

3 ....
   Virgin Galactic SpaceShipTwo

4 ....
   Two hours

5 ....
   About €130,000 per person

6 ....
   Richard Branson's family

7 ....
   So that passengers get a great view of space.

8 ....
   New Mexico

5 Think of someone you admire but do not know. You have the opportunity to interview them for a magazine. Write five questions you would ask them.

Relative clauses

1a Fill in each gap with a relative pronoun (*who, whose, which* or *that*). Sometimes more than one answer is possible.

1 Physics is the science .... I find hardest to understand.

2 I'd like to say thanks to everyone .... helped me.

3 The accountant, ... job is to make the figures add up, made a simple mistake.

4 Climate change is an issue .... everyone is talking about.

5 The film, ... cost $27 million to make, stars several well-known actors.

6 There's a girl .... I work with .... comes from Canada originally.

7 He picked up a small white stone, ... he handed to her.

8 This is my friend Jo, ... daughter is in the same class as mine.

1b In which sentences can you leave out the relative pronoun? ....

2 Write definitions for the words on the left using information from the table.

1 a botanist	a shape		parents have died.
2 a surgeon	a doctor	who	has five sides.
3 a pentagon	a child	whose	you use to open tins or cans.
4 an orphan	a tool	that	you buy for less money than you expected.
5 a tin opener	a place	which	protects your computer.
6 a spa	an object	where	studies plants and flowers.
7 anti-virus software	a scientist		
			you go to relax, often in water.
8 a bargain	a program		performs operations.

1 A botanist is a scientist who studies plants and flowers.

2 ....

3 ....

4 ....

5 ....

6 ....

7 ....

8 ....

English Grammar Today Workbook

3 Describe these people and things in your own words using relative clauses. Use words from the box if you need help.

> ~~sunflower: seeds, petals~~   carpenter: work, wood   bee: insect, honey
> protractor: measure, angles   paper clip: attach, paper

1
2
3
4
5

1 A sunflower is a large flower which has yellow petals. *or* A sunflower has seeds which are made into sunflower oil.
2 ....
3 ....
4 ....
5 ....

4a Tick (✓) the true statement, a or b.

1 The doctors, who worked in Britain for 6 months, didn't have a problem with their English.
   a Some of the doctors worked in Britain for 6 months. The doctors who worked didn't have a problem.
   b All of the doctors worked in Britain for 6 months.

2 The students only enjoyed the weekend activities which they did with their friends.
   a All of the weekend activities were with their friends.
   b Some of the weekend activities were with the students' friends. The students didn't enjoy the other activities.

3 Candidates who got over 80% in the final exam went to medical school.
  a All the candidates got over 80% and went to medical school.
  b Some of the candidates got over 80%. These candidates went to medical school.

4 He's very like his brother who lives in London.
  a He has one brother. His brother lives in London. He is similar to his brother.
  b He has more than one brother. One of them lives in London.

5 I sat down at the table which was right in front of me.
  a There was only one table. It was right in front of me.
  b There was more than one table. I sat down at the nearest table.

6 The house has two large bedrooms, which are bright and spacious.
  a There are two bedrooms. Both of them are bright and spacious.
  b Two of the bedrooms in the house are bright and spacious.

4b Which of the relative pronouns in the main statements 1–6 could you replace with *that*?

4c Which of the relative clauses gives extra, not essential, information?

4d Rewrite each sentence (1–6) so that it matches the other meaning, a or b.

1 *a only the doctors that worked in Britain for 6 months didn't have a problem.*

2

3

4

5

6

5 Combine the sentences using a relative clause to create one sentence. Use the relative pronouns *who, whose, where, which, that*.

1 Kate's brother Nico is at university in Berlin. He is 19.
Kate's brother Nico, who is 19, is at university in Berlin. or Kate's brother Nico, who is at university in Berlin, is 19.

2 Each person has to ask a question. The questions have to be about capital cities around the world.

3 This is Norma. Her husband works with Jen.

4 Not far away from here, there's a great organic supermarket. I often go there to buy vegetables.

5 The courses are three days long. The courses cost £300.

6 Gina decided not to go out because she was too tired. It's understandable that she decided not to go.

6 **Correct the mistakes in each of the sentences. Think about the punctuation as well as the words.**

1 The Trevelan Hotel, that is set on the cliffs above two wonderful beaches, is a great place to go for a short break.

2 She's the person whom runs the French club at school.

3 That's the book which I'm reading it at the moment.

4 They get on very well which makes things easier.

5 She repeated Miguel's words, he had said to her a few minutes before.

6 We know the sources of energy which they are environmentally-friendly.

7 Another thing what we need to talk about is the holiday.

8 The main character in the book, who's name is Antonia, is an archaeologist.

9 We've got a great new employee who she has just joined the company.

10 It was one of the best films that I've ever seen it.

11 I have a friend his parents named him after a famous film star.

7 **Rewrite the conversation so that it sounds more informal and natural.**

A: There was something else about which I wanted to talk you.
B: What's that?
A: You know the girl to whom you were talking at lunch?
B: Yeah. Elena, she's the one with whose sister I went to school. Why?
A: She's the woman with whom I used to work – the one with whom I had the big argument.
B: What about?
A: She said I'd stolen company property, which was completely untrue.

A: *There was something else (which) I wanted to talk to you about.*

B: ....

A: ....

B: ....

A: ....

B: ....

A: ....

8 Think of some words in your language (for example professions, people or objects) that you don't know the word for in English, then write five questions to find out what the words are.

What's the word for... What do you call ...	... a person (who / that)... ? ... a thing (which / that)... ? ... a place where ... ?

what do you call a person who designs buildings?

9 Use the information below to write a short description of the holiday destination. Use relative clauses where appropriate.

Blackrock is a 5 star holiday destination. Blackrock is at the heart of the Pembrokeshire National Park in Wales. It is designed to inspire and connect with the surrounding environment.

FEATURES

Accommodation	Facilities
a mix of timber lodges, studios and cottages	sports club open every day
set on a tranquil hill around a traditional village	large indoor sports hall
unique and luxurious	outdoor play facilities
designed to be comfortable	badminton, volleyball and tennis
studios and cottages built from sustainably-sourced wood	viewing area for spectators who want to watch not play
built in a traditional Welsh style	health and beauty Spa
	shops
	beaches
	pubs and restaurants

Friendly experienced staff, always happy to answer your questions.

Blackrock, which is a 5 star holiday destination, in wales.

Reported speech

1 Rewrite each sentence as indirect or direct speech, as indicated.

Direct speech	Indirect speech
"I didn't call Moya", said Tina	1 Tina said she hadn't called Moya.
"Stop making so much noise while I'm studying", Bryan told Heidi.	2
He said, "It is a terrible film".	3
4	She said that the train leaves at 7.10 every morning.
"You need help," we told her.	5

2 Complete the grid with rules for backshift changes.

present simple → past simple
present continuous →
present perfect simple →
present perfect continuous →
past simple →
past continuous →
future (*will*) →
past perfect →

3a Use the most appropriate reporting verb 1–5 for a–e using the correct punctuation.

a Well, my name is Terrence but everyone calls me Terry.

d I'll never do that again.

b The food is cold.

e Is there a bookshop near here?

c Stop talking.

1 (She ordered) "stop talking," she ordered.

2 (He asked) .... 4 (He complained) ....

3 (She promised) .... 5 (He explained) ....

3b Rewrite the sentences from 3a as reported speech.

1 she ordered us to stop talking .... 4 ....

2 .... 5 ....

3 ....

4 **Correct the punctuation mistake in each sentence.**

1 "We're all feeling ill" he said.

2 Grace thought; "I don't want to tell him the real reason why I want to leave."

3 'Are you all ready'? she yelled.

4 "Oh no" they said when they heard the news.

5 I said: 'let's decide tomorrow.'

6 He asked me what I wanted?

5 **Five of the sentences have mistakes with *ask*, *say* and *tell*. Correct the mistakes and tick (✓) the correct sentences.**

1 'Don't ring the bell when you call. Just knock gently on the door,' she said us.

2 All of a sudden he told her he was leaving.

3 She said me that she hadn't been feeling well.

4 They told me, "What do you think you will be doing five years from now?"

5 'Congratulations!' she said to me when I came into the room.

6 My mother tell me never to walk home alone.

6a **Rewrite the direct speech as indirect speech.**

1 "Don't go in there!" she warned.
She warned us not to go in there.

2 "I'll never speak to you again if you tell anyone," he threatened.
He threatened ....

3 "I copied my essay from the internet," she confessed.
She confessed ....

4 "We want to know the truth," they demanded.
They demanded ....

5 "You have to let us in," we protested.
They protested ....

6 "You must fill in the form using a black pen," she instructed.
She instructed ....

6b **Rewrite the dialogues as indirect speech using the verbs in brackets.**

1 Giovanna: Have you driven alone before?
Jack: No, this is the first time without an instructor.

(*ask, admit*) Giovanna asked Jack whether he'd driven alone before and he admitted that it was his first time without an instructor.

2 Fernando: It may cost too much.
Luis: That's true.
Frances: Actually, I don't agree.

(*suggest, agree, disagree*) ....
....

3 Emily: Our room is too warm and the air conditioning isn't working.
   Hotel manager: I'm sorry, I'll see what I can do.

   (*complain, say*) ....

   ....

4 Kevin: Renting a car will cost too much.
   Agata: There are four of us so it won't.
   Kim: I agree with Agata.

   (*think, argue, agree*) ....

   ....

5 Kate: Have you seen Tania?
   Bill: I haven't seen her since this morning.

   (*ask, reply*) ....

   ....

7 Rewrite each sentence as indirect or direct speech, as indicated.

Direct speech	Indirect speech
We asked, "Is this the only cinema in town?"	1 we asked if / whether this was the only cinema in town.
2	The student inquired whether Prof. Vaughan was in his office.
'What time is the last train?' wondered Nathan.	3
4	I suggested that we might take a break.
5	He commented that it was a wonderful restaurant.
'Don't wake the baby', he whispered.	6
'Get in line!', they ordered us.	7

8 These sentences have mistakes with backshift changes. Find and correct the mistakes.

1 Olivia is going to be late this morning. I phoned her last night and she said she is feeling tired.
2 They thought we have sent them the report before then.
3 I asked if they went to *Il Bacio's Pizzeria* and she said that they had.
4 James said they have been walking past the station at that time.

5 I thought the movie will start at 8 o'clock.

6 She asked him what he has been doing.

7 They said they aren't hungry because they had eaten earlier.

9 You and your colleagues have been talking about holidays. Change what your colleagues said into reported speech to tell your partner.

1 Anna: "I went to Spain a year ago on a walking holiday but I'm planning something more exciting next year."

Anna said that she went to spain last year on a walking holiday but she's planning something more exciting next year.

2 Dave: "I hate airports and I love hiking so my ideal holiday is walking for miles every day."

Dave said ....

3 Liz: "I've decided to save up for big holiday next January."

Liz said ....

4 Richard: "My wife and I have been doing house exchanges for the last four years. It's worked out really well."

Richard said ....

5 Ian: "We're going camping this year in France with the kids."

Ian said ....

6 Melissa: "I've been going to Italy for the last three summers but next year I am going to do something different."

Melissa said ....

7 Tony: "We swapped our house with a couple from San Francisco for two weeks last year and it worked out really well."

Tony said ....

8 Ronan: "We've gone on skiing holidays in the past but not with the kids."

Ronan said ....

9 Jamie: "I can't afford to go on holiday since I bought my house."

Jamie said ....

10 Tom: "I like to stay in Britain."

Tom said ....

English Grammar Today Workbook

10 Kelly is organising a party at her house, which she shares with her college friends Maria, Linda and Toshiko. She also talked to her friends Marco and Renata. Fill in each gap in the email to her friend Yuko.

Maria: *Shall I bring some friends from work?*

Marco: *Can we hire a DJ?*

Toshiko: *We should all make some party food.*

Linda: *We must invite Paul and his friends.*

Renata: *A fancy dress party would be a good idea. I might dress up as a witch.*

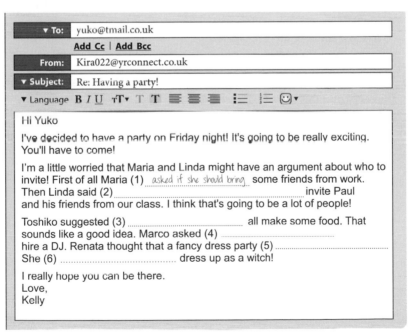

▼ To:	yuko@tmail.co.uk
	Add Cc | **Add Bcc**
From:	Kira022@yrconnect.co.uk
▼ Subject:	Re: Having a party!

▼ Language **B** *I* U ꞏT▾ T **T** ≡ ≡ ≡ ≔ ≣ ☺▾

Hi Yuko

I've decided to have a party on Friday night! It's going to be really exciting. You'll have to come!

I'm a little worried that Maria and Linda might have an argument about who to invite! First of all Maria (1) _asked if she should bring_ some friends from work. Then Linda said (2) _____ invite Paul and his friends from our class. I think that's going to be a lot of people!

Toshiko suggested (3) _____ all make some food. That sounds like a good idea. Marco asked (4) _____ hire a DJ. Renata thought that a fancy dress party (5) _____ She (6) _____ dress up as a witch!

I really hope you can be there.
Love,
Kelly

Speech acts

1 **Match each sentence 1–7 with the most appropriate speech act.**

1 Hurry up and get dressed. command   warning

2 Add some flour to the butter and stir.   suggestion

3 Jane, would you like some more coffee?   request

4 I'll be there at 8 to pick you up.   offer

5 Could we leave our car at your house while we   promise
are on holiday?

6 Why don't you use different software? That   ~~command~~
one's not very good for photographs.

7 Caution: wet paint!   instruction

Commands and instructions

2 **Tick the less direct command, a or b?**

1 **a** Get me McFines' number, Maria. I need it urgently.
   b Can I ask you to get me McFines' number, please, Maria? I need it
urgently.

2 **a** Send us the contract immediately.
   b We'd like you to send us the contract immediately.

3 **a** Call me a taxi, please.   **b** Will you call me a taxi, please?

4 **a** I'd be grateful if you closed the door quietly, please.
   b Close the door quietly, please.

5 **a** You must take off your shoes.   **b** Take off your shoes, please.

3a **Fill in each gap in this recipe with a word from the box. Use each word once
only. You may need to use a dictionary.**

fry	~~chop~~	add	leave	grate	heat	beat

Making a cheese and onion omelette

(1) _chop_ an onion and (2) _____ three eggs. (3) _____ some oil in a frying pan and (4) _____ the onions until they are brown and then (5) _____ the eggs. (6) _____ some cheese onto the omlette and (7) _____ the frying pan on a low heat for three or four minutes.

3b **Write instructions for the quickest thing that you can cook.**

....

....

Offers and invitations

4 Decide whether each of the following is an offer or an invitation.

	offer	invitation
1 Would you like a biscuit?		
2 Do you want to come and join us?		
3 Can I get you a chair?		
4 You'll have to have dinner with us some evening.		
5 Do sit down, Mr Graham.		
6 How may I help you?		

5a Fill in each gap using a verb from the box. Use each verb once only.

shall	would	want	can	let

1 .... me carry your suitcase.   4 .... you like me to book a taxi for you?

2 .... I empty the dishwasher? 5 .... I do anything to help?

3 .... some breakfast?

5b Write an offer and an invitation based on each picture.

1

2

3

4

5

Offer	Invitation
1 Can I carry your bags?	Would you like to go shopping with me?
2	
3	
4	
5	

6 Fill in each gap with an appropriate reply, *yes*, *no*, or *thanks*. Sometimes more than one answer is possible. Only use one word each time.

1 A: Do you want to have lunch with us?

B: .... That'd be lovely.

2 A: Would you like to come to the cinema with us tonight?

B: ...., please. I'd love that.

3 A: Do you want to go to Melissa's party with me on Friday night?

B: ...., thanks. I can't. I'm afraid I'll be away.

4 A: Would you like to sit with us?

B: .... That's very kind of you.

Promises

7 Tick (✓) the statements which are promises.

1 We'll make sure to be there to pick you up at the airport, don't worry.

2 It's hot in here. I'll open the window.

3 I'll walk the dog every day; you can rely on me.

4 We'll drive to Manchester tomorrow for the meeting with Ian. The train's too expensive.

5 I'll never leave you. I love you.

Requests

8a Match each situation 1–10 with a request a–j.

1 _b_ 2 ...... 3 ...... 4 ...... 5 ...... 6 ...... 7 ...... 8 ...... 9 ...... 10 ......

1 You've forgotten your watch.

2 There's been an accident.

3 You've finished your meal in a restaurant.

4 There's only one chair free in a café.

5 You aren't happy with the service on a phone helpline.

6 You are going to have to work late.

7 You want to know how much a new kitchen would cost.

8 You're lost.

9 You need the report by tomorrow.

10 You're hungry.

a Can you call an ambulance?

b Could you tell me the time?

c Would you mind if I sat here?

d I would be grateful if you would send us an estimate as soon as possible.

e May I have the bill please?

f Could you pick up the children? I won't get out of work until seven o'clock.

g Would you mind making me something to eat?

h Do you think you could get it to me by tomorrow morning?

i I want to speak to whoever is in charge, please.

j Could you tell me how to get to Blessington Street, please?

8b Which request a–j is more likely to be written than spoken? ....

9a Pete is a new student at Brooklawn University. It's his first day and he needs help from different people but his requests don't suit the situation. Write a more suitable request in each case.

1 I want more information about this course.
Could you _give me more information about this course, please?_ ....

2 I need you to tell me where the library is.
Would you mind ....?

3 Will you tell me how to spell the lecturer's name?
Could you ....?

4 I need your pen. Mine is broken.
Can I ....?

5 I'd be most grateful if you could tell me the name of the textbook.
Would you mind ....?

9b Ask someone politely to:

1 open a window ....
2 get you a sandwich ....
3 make you a cup of tea ....
4 be quiet ....

Suggestions

10 Fill in each gap in the dialogue with a phrase from the box. Sometimes more than one answer is possible.

~~how about~~   let's   why don't   what about

A: What shall we do tonight?

B: (1) _How about_ going for a walk in the park?

A: I'm too tired.

B: Okay, so (2) .... stay in and watch a film.

A: Good idea, and (3) .... we order a pizza?

B: We had pizza on Friday. (4) .... ordering a curry?

11 Write a suggestion for each situation.

1 Your friend's bike has been stolen.
You say: Why don't _you call the police?_ ....

2 You and your friend are shopping. It's nearly lunchtime and you're hungry.
You say: How about ....

3 Your friend needs to save money for her holiday.
You say: You could ....

4 You'd like to go to a concert with a friend on Saturday but you're not sure whether she likes classical music so you don't want to be too forceful.
You say: I thought ....

5 A friend is annoyed because her sister keeps taking her clothes without asking.
You say: ....

6 Your son is doing his homework at breakfast because he didn't do it yesterday evening after school.
You say: ....

7 It's a beautiful sunny day. Your friend calls at your door.
You say: ....

8 You and your flatmate have been tidying your flat for two hours. You're tired.
You say: ....

9 Your friend has invited her boss and his wife to her house for dinner and she is trying to decide what to cook.
You say: ....

10 You're trying to think of a good present for your friend's birthday.
You say: ....

English Grammar Today Workbook

Warnings

12 Fill in each gap to complete the warning for each situation using a phrase from the box. Use each phrase once only.

> ~~I wouldn't~~   I don't think   I must warn you   Don't
> Mind   Watch out!   Whatever you do

1 It's dangerous to stand so near the fire.

   .... *I wouldn't* .... stand so near the fire if I were you.

2 It's dangerous to cross the road when the pedestrian light is red.

   .... cross at a red light.

3 The grass is wet.

   .... you should sit on the grass.

4 A tram is coming in your direction.

   .... There's a tram coming.

5 There's a very low door into the old house.

   .... your head.

6 It gets very cold as you go higher into the mountain.

   .... to bring warm clothing.

7 It isn't safe to walk home alone at night.

   ...., don't walk home alone at night.

13a Match each warning 1–4 with a public notice a–d.

a   b CAUTION   c CAUTION   d CAUTION

1 Danger: 2 Beware of the   3 Caution: wet   4 Danger: strong
   falling   dog!   floor   currents
   rocks

13b What would you say to someone to warn them about each sign?

1 ....   3 ....

2 ....   4 ....

Spelling

Plural nouns and -s forms of verbs.

1 **Form plurals for these nouns.**

1 dog ..... *dogs* .....   6 life .....   11 potato .....
2 chair .....   7 church .....   12 hero .....
3 duck .....   8 box .....   13 wife .....
4 party .....   9 eye .....   14 half .....
5 story .....   10 judge .....   15 video .....

2 **Make -s forms of these verbs.**

1 carry ..... *carries* .....   6 die .....
2 wash .....   7 buzz .....
3 say .....   8 enjoy .....
4 go .....   9 wave .....
5 wish .....   10 eat .....

Final -e

3 **Find and correct the seven spelling mistakes. One sentence has no mistakes.**

1 I was hopeing we could meat.

2 The children are both making a cake.

3 She's now a very fameous film star.

4 We like it to be shadey on the beach.

5 He will definitely be at the party this evning.

6 I normally like arguements but I completly agree with you both.

Doubling of consonants

4 **Which of these words double the final consonant when we add endings? Think of one example for each word.**

1 stop ..... *stopped* .....   6 begin .....   11 prefer .....
2 slim .....   7 show .....   12 fax .....
3 travel .....   8 open .....   13 forgot .....
4 big .....   9 visit .....   14 occur .....
5 upset .....   10 look .....   15 offer .....

Typical errors

5 Correct the six spelling mistakes in this email.

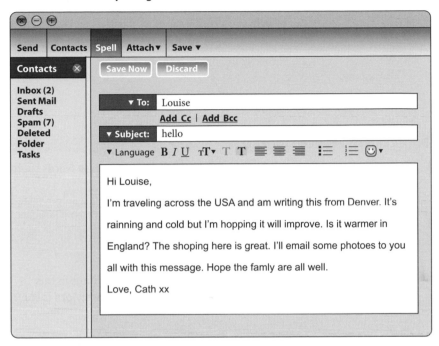

Send | Contacts | Spell | Attach ▾ | Save ▾

Contacts ⊗

Inbox (2)
Sent Mail
Drafts
Spam (7)
Deleted
Folder
Tasks

Save Now | Discard

▾ **To:** Louise

Add Cc | Add Bcc

▾ **Subject:** hello

▾ Language **B** *I* U ₁T▾ T T ≡ ≡ ≡ ☱ ☱ ☺▾

Hi Louise,

I'm traveling across the USA and am writing this from Denver. It's rainning and cold but I'm hopping it will improve. Is it warmer in England? The shoping here is great. I'll email some photoes to you all with this message. Hope the famly are all well.

Love, Cath xx

i before *e* except after *c*.

6a Fill in the gap in each word with *ie* or *ei*.

1 ch ...... f
2 p ...... ce
3 c ...... ling
4 rec ...... ve
5 f ...... ld

6 rec ...... pt
7 n ...... ghbour
8 n ...... ce
9 l ...... sure
10 w ...... gh

6b Which of these words follow the rule *i* before *e* except after *c*? Which words are exceptions?

Two, to or *too; its* or *it's; there, their* or *they're*

7 Fill in each gap with the correct word from the brackets.
1 It was .... dark .... see the road. He'd been walking .... slowly and was still .... hours away from the village. (two, to, too)
2 .... a shame that this shirt has lost .... colour since we washed it. (it's, its)

3 .... was a long queue outside the cinema so Jean and Ken invited us to watch a DVD at .... house. .... not very far from the cinema. (there, they're, their)

4 .... trying to help people get back to .... homes after the floods. .... is a lot of work to be done. (there, they're, their)

5 A: .... car are we going in?
B: Matt and Khedija's.
A: Okay, so .... driving?
A: Matt, I think. (who's, whose)

British English and American English

8 These words are all written in American English. How are these words spelt in British English?

theater	center	color	defense	neighbor	program

....

9 Underline the seven words that have American English spellings in this postcard from an American tourist in London. Write how each word is spelt in British English.

Hi everyone,
Arrived safely in London. Hotel is great but the behavior of some drivers in the city center is terrible (!) but we love the color of all the spring flowers in the parks here. Just off to cash our travelers' checks at the bank and then we are going to buy mom some jewelry in a place called Covent Garden. Tomorrow we're visiting Maud and her husband at the Harbour hotel on the River Thames. It's just across from the Tower of London. Love,
Louise

Brad & Family
1020 Lincoln Drive
NYC
USA

Spoken and written English: register

1 In each sentence, underline the words and phrases which you are more likely to hear in spoken English than read in formal written English.

1 Well, er, he is not sure what to do.

2 Mmm, I agree it is best not to say anything.

3 Right, what time shall we go to the cinema?

4 Yeah, it's a bit too cold for me today.

5 It's not, you know, the best thing to do.

6 She was wearing a sort of pinkish coat and a white blouse.

7 Phoned yesterday but guess you were out at the match or something.

8 So, have we decided when we need to leave for the station?

9 Oh, it's not that we don't want to help, I mean, everybody wants to help, don't they?

10 And all the time my mum's like "why don't you ring your gran?"

2 Carol finds spelling difficult. She asks Jill to read a report she has written to help her check for spelling errors. At first, she's a little nervous about asking Jill. Underline the most likely words and phrases in the dialogue.

Carol: (1) *mmm / er*, can I ask you a favour?

Jill: (2) *anyway / mmm*

Carol: You know how awful my spelling is.

Jill: (3) *yeah / thought so*, you have told me before.

Carol: (4) *well / mmm*, I've written this report for my boss and I'm, (5) *er / anyway*, not sure really about my spelling.

Jill: (6) *anyway / okay*, I'll have a look at it for you.

Carol: (7) *thought so / well*. Thanks. I owe you one.

Jill: (8) *anyway / well*, your spelling is much better than you think. I'm sure it'll be fine.

3 **Write a short dialogue using the outline below. The dialogue has been started. Use at least three of the following features of spoken language.**

Yeah	great yeah	really?	Absolutely	how interesting
oh	that's lovely, thanks	sounds good	so	er

Jim and Jill are at a conference. They don't know each other very well. Jim comments that it's an interesting conference. Jill agrees. Jim offers to get Jill something to drink. When he returns with the drinks, he asks Jill about her course at university.

Jim: Great conference, isn't it?

Jill: Great, yeah.

Jim: ....

Jill: ....

Jim: ....

Jill: ....

Jim: ....

Jill: ....

4a **Which dialogue, A or B, is more informal?**

A

Fergus: What did you do last weekend?
Elliot: I went shopping actually.
Fergus: Oh, who did you go shopping with?
Elliot: I went shopping with my wife.

B

Fergus: What did you do last weekend?
Elliot: Went shopping actually
Fergus: Oh, who with?
Elliot: With my wife.

4b **Continue the dialogues in the appropriate register.**

Fergus: Did you buy anything nice?
Elliot: (2) ....
Fergus: (3) .... ?
Elliot: [laughs] Yes, surprisingly, I
    have got some money left.
Fergus: Lucky you! That sounds good.

Fergus: (1) .... ?
Elliot: Yeah, three new suits.
Fergus: Gosh, any money left
    for your holiday next week?
Elliot: [laughs] (4) ....
Fergus: (5) ....

5 **Rewrite these spoken comments as written English.**

1 There were two hundred or so people at the meeting.
   There were approximately two hundred people at the meeting.

2 It was too difficult to read, wasn't it, that chemistry book?

   ....

3 There's too many cars in the car park.

   ....

English Grammar Today Workbook

4 I've got loads of essay marking and stuff to do.

....

5 You know who I'm talking about probably.

....

6 That kind of tower of flats in the centre of town, by the library, is that where they both live?

....

6 **Rewrite this text message as a more formal email or written note.**

Text message 123 (1) Abc **Hi. Just back in Liverpool. Train v slow** **and stopped everywhere. Got some** **reading done and saw the thing u said** **on cooking!!! Glad 2 c see yr gran too** **and 2 know she's getting better. Better** **stop. Got report 2 write 4 work** **tomorrow. Thnx for gr8 time. Hope 2 C U** **both again v soon. Luv Sally** Options Close	....

7 **Read this extract from an informal description of the poet W. H. Auden. Then write three sentences about him as a formal biographical statement.**

Well, he was born in York, I think it was, in 1907 and went to school in Holt in Norfolk, I think, yes, in Norfolk where he actually started writing his first poems when he was sixteen or thereabouts. He went to university, that's Oxford University by the way, where he got even more involved in poetry publications. I'm actually interested in his poetry in the 1930s when he wrote about the Spanish Civil war and, I think, went out to Spain to fight in the war himself.

....

....

....

8 The following statements are all spoken remarks. Rewrite them into more formal English by turning the verbs or adjectives into nouns.

1 What time are they flying?
What time is their ....*flight?*........

2 Their technical knowledge has improved.
There has been an .... in their technical knowledge.

3 They'll install it free.
The .... will be free.

4 Whenever I'd visited previously, I had always been welcomed warmly.
On my previous ...., I had always received a warm
....

5 Especially at political meetings, people get violent.
There can be ...., especially at political meetings.

6 The party had finished and at last it was peaceful.
The party had finished and at last there was ....

9a Put the sentences a–c in the correct order in this weather forecast. Then fill in each gap with a word from the box.

strong	showers	breezy

1 .... 2 .... 3 ....

An Atlantic depression is approaching the country so the weather will be distinctly unsettled over the coming few days.

a All parts of the country should have sunny periods from time to time today but there will be some .... from early morning.
b It will be cool and .... everywhere by evening, with winds moderate to .... in the south west and across Wales.
c By the end of the morning, showers will become more widespread across the country.

9b Use the information from the forecast to write an email to a friend who is arriving in England tomorrow. Tell them what the weather will be like when they arrive.

....

....

....

10 Match the sentences 1–6 with a–f. Then say in what context you would expect to see the sentences.

1 *c instructions for medicines*   2 ....   3 ....

4 ....   5 ....   6 ....

1 Take two tablets every four hours.

a All shoes and socks must be removed before entering.

2 Add the butter and onions to the saucepan.

b The author of over 25 plays and several books of poetry, he won the Nobel Prize for Literature in 2005.

3 You are entering a holy site.

c Do not exceed the stated dose without consulting your doctor.

4 Man critically ill after overnight mountain rescue.

d Allow them to cook gently on a medium heat for about 15 minutes, or until they are soft and lightly browned.

5 The playwright Harold Pinter was born in 1930.

e A man is seriously ill in hospital today after exposure to extreme cold during a mountaineering expedition with friends in the Swiss Alps.

6 Sow between April and May in a prepared seed bed.

f Cover lightly with soil and keep moist.

11a List the ingredients you need to follow this recipe.

Apple and onion soup

1. Add the butter and onions to a saucepan and allow the onions to cook gently on a medium heat for about 15 minutes, or until they are soft and lightly browned.
2. Add the apple, apple juice and cider vinegar. Boil until the apple juice has reduced by about half.
3. Add the thyme, bay leaf, chicken stock, potato and a little salt. Bring to a simmer, and then cook for about 15 minutes over a low heat.
4. Remove the bay leaf, and purée the soup in a blender or food processor until smooth.
5. To serve, put the hot soup into warm bowls and add the fried onion.

Ingredients:

....

11b Now write your own favourite recipe either as a formal recipe or an informal description to a friend.

....

....

....

Subjects

1 Underline 11 more subjects in this text.

Jobs of the future

In 2010, <u>a UK government report</u> looked at jobs of the future. It predicted that the occupation of space pilot could be normal in the year 2030. Space tourism will be so common that large numbers of space pilots will be needed. Other pilots will fly spaceships for the exploration of new planets. Besides space pilots, 'vertical farmers' will be a common job. These farmers will grow food in tall buildings instead of on the ground. We will also need highly specialised doctors; for example, operations will be carried out in order to give people extra memory, just as we can increase the memory of a computer. The jobs of the future will be very different from those of today.

2 Fill in each gap with the correct form of the verb in brackets.

1 Some friends of my brother's.....................(be) at our house yesterday.

2 Every student.....................(have) to get a part-time job these days in order to pay their fees.

3 Both these sweaters.....................(look) nice on you. Why not buy them both?

4 The number 27 bus.....................(not go) to the station. You need the 29.

5 ....(do) your best friend live near you or is she in another part of town?

6 When it arrived, the edges of the box.....................(be) damaged, but luckily the contents.....................(be) okay.

7 All parents.....................(worry) about their children.

8 I stayed in that hotel three times, and each time.....................(be) better than the time before.

9 My experience of being in hospital was good. The doctor and the nurses.....................(be) wonderful.

10 Could you come here and advise me? Which of these jackets ....(look) best on me, the blue one or the green one?

3 Correct the six mistakes in the sentences. Tick (✓) the two correct sentences.

1 A: Is this your brother in this photo?
  B: No, that's not he. That's a friend of mine.

2 There is several reasons why I don't want to study maths.

3 Mr Jones's office is upstairs.

4 Jim and Eric are here! I guessed it was they when I heard the taxi arrive.

5 The plumber and the electrician is coming tomorrow to do some work in the kitchen.

6 There are a cinema and a theatre in Dixon Square.

7 Are there any restaurants near here?

8 The banks and the post office is closed today – it's a public holiday.

4 Complete each sentence so that it is true for you.

1 If I could choose any career, I would like to be ....

2 My favourite academic subjects ....

3 Personally, I think mathematics ....

4 In my room, there are ....

Tags

1   Underline the tags in the conversation.

Lucy and Amy are at a party and have just met for the first time. They are talking to Amy's husband Chris about Anna, who is a mutual friend.

Amy: It's a lovely day for a barbecue, isn't it?

Lucy: It is. Do you know Anna well?

Amy: [looks at Chris] Yes, we've worked together for about five years, haven't we? [Chris nods in agreement]

Lucy: Really?

Amy: You didn't work with her in Rome too, did you?

Lucy: Yes, but only for a couple of months.

Amy: Oh, right. A couple of months. And you work with her in London now, right?

Lucy: Yes.

2   Fill in each gap with a tag from the box.

isn't it	didn't he	haven't they	does he	can't you
could you	shall we	were they	will you	won't she

1   Tom doesn't look very fit, ...?

2   It's getting very cold now, ...?

3   You couldn't lend me £20, ...?

4   Let's go out for dinner, ...?

5   She'll be okay travelling on her own, ...?

6   They've been really helpful, ...?

7   They weren't married when we first met them, ...?

8   You can see the island in the distance, ...?

9   Don't be late, ...?

10 Robert used to be a hairdresser, ...?

3   Fill in each gap with an appropriate tag.

1   It must be ten years since we saw them last, ...?

2   Wait for me on the corner, ...?

3   Let's call the doctor, ...?

4   She always wanted to go to Moscow, ...?

5   Nobody likes her dress, ...?

6   Everybody's enjoying themselves, ...?

4 Draw an arrow over the tag to indicate whether it is likely that the speaker is fairly sure of the answer and uses falling intonation (↘) or is less sure of the answer and uses rising intonation (↗)

1 A: I've stayed at that hotel before. It's in Walker Street, **isn't it?**
   B: Yes, it is.

2 A: She has such a lovely voice. She sang beautifully, **didn't she?**
   B: Yes, she did.

3 A: There's half an hour till the next train so I've got time to buy a magazine, **haven't I?**
   B: Yes, of course.

4 A: Oh dear, I've forgotten. The play doesn't start at 8:30, **does it?**
   B: No, it's 9 pm, I think.

5 A: Nice day today, **isn't it?** B: It is, but it's too hot for me.

6 A: I sent the invitation by email last week. She got the invitation, **did she?**
   B: Yes, she did.

5 Make each tag more formal.

1 The film starts at 6.30, yeah?

2 You've got the keys for both suitcases, right?

3 So you came by train, right, and then changed your mind.

4 We ought to write to thank them for the presents, shouldn't we?

6 Write what you would say in each situation using the verbs in brackets and a tag.

1 You warn someone not to forget to collect your aunt from the station.
   (don't forget)

   ....

2 You suggest to a colleague that you work on a project together.
   (let's work)

   ....

3 You need to borrow a laptop. The hotel reception might have one and you ask one of the reception staff.
   (haven't got)

   ....

4 You ask a friend if they could look after your dog while you are away.
   (couldn't look after)

   ....

There is **and** *there are*

1a **Fill in the gaps with words from the box to describe pictures a–e.**

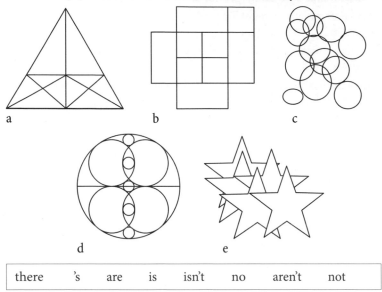

a   b   c

d   e

there	's	are	is	isn't	no	aren't	not

1 How many triangles .... there in a?

2 .... are both squares and rectangles in b.

3 In c, ... one circle that is bigger than the other circles?

4 I think .... ten circles in d.

5 .... a line through the middle of the biggest circle in d, making two semi-circles.

6 There .... five star shapes in e, ...?

7 .... a hexagon (⬢) in any of the pictures, is there?

8 There .... any diamond shapes, ...?

9 There's .... an equal number of squares and rectangles in B, is there?

10 There's .... square in e.

1b **Write down how many of each of these shapes there is in each picture.**

square	rectangle	triangle	circle	star

There are 11 squares in b. ....

....

....

2 Study the pictures for one minute. Then cover them and write down what you can remember. Use *There is* or *There are* and describe as much detail as you can.

....

....

....

....

....

....

Used to and *would*

1 Fill in each gap with a word from the box. You can use each word more than once. You don't need to use all of the words.

didn't	use	did	use	to	used

1 I .... to play the flute when I was younger.

2 Paula used .... sing in a choir.

3 He didn't .... to get so tired. Now he always has a sleep in the day.

4 They didn't use to open on a Sunday, ... they?

5 When she was little, she used to love singing, ... she?

6 Did you .... to go to the cinema much when you were younger?

7 I always .... to phone people. Now I tend to email them.

8 .... Cara use to live near you?

9 He .... to eat oranges with the peel still on, didn't he?

10 You're right. Rory .... use to be blond when he was little.

2a Fill in each gap with the correct form of *used to* or *would* and the verb in brackets.

I can remember some things from my childhood. I (1) .... (play) in the garden with my brothers a lot. We (2) .... (climb) the trees – we (3) .... (have) a tree house. My dad <u>taught</u> me how to ride a bike. I (4) .... read in my room a lot too. My mother (5) .... (pick) me up from school and we (6) .... (talk) while we were waiting for my brothers to finish school. When I got a bit older, I (7) .... (walk) home from school with my friends. We often (8) .... (go) on holiday by the sea. I can remember one holiday when I was very young, when my grandmother <u>showed</u> me how to make a motorboat out of sand. Every holiday after that, I (9) .... (spend) hours playing in the sand. And I also remember another holiday where we <u>stayed</u> in a house with a circular staircase, surrounded by apple trees.

2b Look at the past simple verbs underlined. Can you use *would* or *used to* instead? Why or why not?

....

....

3a We asked some people about the differences between shopping and eating habits in Britain in the 1950s and now. Write sentences about what life used to be like. Use *used to* and *didn't use to* where appropriate.

Every high street had a fishmonger, a butcher, a baker and a greengrocer.

We went to the local shops to buy all our food.

We ate our food together around the table. We never ate in the sitting room. Now, we sometimes eat in front of the TV.

We ate lots of bread and potatoes. We didn't eat pasta.

We cooked everything ourselves. We didn't buy ready-made food.

The shops were small independent shops, owned by families. There weren't any big supermarkets owned by a large company.

The shopkeeper served you what you wanted. You didn't pick it.

....

....

....

....

3b Think of any things in your life that have changed and write sentences about them.

....

....

....

4 Write five sentences about how the world was different before we had computers. Think about the internet, entertainment, shopping, ways of communicating and any of your own ideas.

1 We used to write more letters. Now we use email a lot.

2 ....

3 ....

4 ....

5 ....

Used to and *be used to*

5 Match the beginnings with the most likely endings.

1 .....e..... 2 .... 3 .... 4 .... 5 .... 6 ....

1 Anna is used to getting up early.

a driving this car yet. It's a bit big for me.

2 Anna used to get up early to milk the cows.

b helping people in mountain accidents.

3 Helicopters are used to

c rescue people from mountain accidents.

4 Helicopter rescue pilots are used to

d drive this car but I gave it to my sister.

5 I'm not used to

e She's a farmer.

6 I used to

f Phil does it now.

6 Seven of these sentences have mistakes with *used to* and *would*. Correct the mistakes and tick (✓) the correct sentence.

1 We're used to work at night. It's part of the job.

2 It's a new phone. We're not use to it yet.

3 She would work in Paris a couple of years ago.

4 How are you settling in to the new school? Are you getting use to it?

5 Didn't there use to be a cinema there?

6 Tim didn't used to like olives, used he?

7 Tanya use to be a really good tennis player.

8 She was used to be an actor.

Verbs

1 **Put the verbs in the box into one of the three groups.**

~~become~~ do seem might have appear would look may

Linking verbs	Auxiliary verbs	Modal verbs
become		

2 **Fill in each gap with the correct form of *do, be* or *have*.**

1 A: ......*Do*...... you like jazz?
   B: No, I .... like jazz. I .... never liked it.

2 A: .... you working on Saturday?
   B: No, I .... work on Saturdays, normally.
   A: Good. .... you seen the new *Spider-Man* film?
   B: No, I ....
   A: .... you want to go and see it on Saturday, then?

3 A: Jeff has .... looking for you. Where .... you been?
   B: I .... been anywhere. I .... been here all the time!
      What .... he want?

4 A: What great shoes! I .... like them! Where .... you buy them?
   B: In Shoemart. I .... like them at first, but I .... now.

3a **Complete the missing parts of the verbs in the table.**

base form	*-ing* form	past form	*-ed* form
reach	reaching	reached	reached
think		thought	
write		wrote	
fall	falling		fallen
show	showing	showed	
rise	rising		risen
begin		began	
move		moved	

3b **Which verbs in 3a are irregular?**

....

3c Fill in each gap with the correct form of a verb from the table.

1 She _____moved_____ into her new house last week. She loves it.

2 She _____ she would never be able to afford her own house because of the high prices.

3 Property prices _____ last year and houses are now much more expensive than five years ago.

4 Prices had _____ to rise in January and continued to rise throughout the year.

5 House prices _____ their highest point in December of last year.

6 In the two years up to last year, house prices had _____ from £200,000 to £180,000 on average.

7 A survey in 2010 _____ that people were extremely worried about house prices rising.

8 An economist _____ an article for the *Clarion* newspaper predicting that house prices would remain high for another two years.

4 Fill in each gap with the words in brackets. Use the present simple for state verbs or present continuous for action verbs.

1 We _'re having_ (have) a party on New Year's Eve. Would you like to come?

2 A: Where are you from originally, Herbert?
B: I _____ (come) from Manchester.

3 A: What _____ (you think) about?
B: Oh, nothing special. I'm just daydreaming.

4 A: That bag looks heavy!
B: Yes, it _____ (weigh) more than 15 kilos.

5 A: What _____ (your parents think) about you getting married?
B: Oh, they say I'm too young!

6 A: What nationality do you think Maria is?
B: I'm not sure. She _____ (look) Spanish to me.

7 A: Hi Brian, is this a good time to call? B: Well, actually, we _____ (have) lunch right now. Can you ring back in about an hour?

8 A: Hurry up! The bus _____ (come)! B: Okay, okay! Don't panic!

5a Form compound verbs by adding a word from the right-hand column to a word in the left-hand column.

day_dream_	grade
over _____	list
high _____	~~dream~~
up _____	come
short _____	wash
hand _____	light

5b **Use the correct form of a compound verb from 5a to fill in each gap.**

1 I'm sorry, I didn't hear what you said. I was _daydreaming_ .

2 I always _____ this sweater. I don't like putting it in the washing machine.

3 I want to _____ my mobile phone and get the latest model.

4 Have you been _____ for that job you applied for?

5 We had to _____ a lot of problems before we succeeded.

6 I always _____ new words in my English course book.

6 **Find and correct the mistake in each of the sentences.**

something strange happened

1 ~~Someone happened something strange~~ near our house yesterday. A woman stood in the middle of the road and started singing and dancing.

2 She offered me some cakes, but I didn't want.

3 He bought me a pair of headphones for my birthday but I've never used.

4 A police officer caught me parking in a no-parking zone and fined 100 euros.

5 I sent Paul an email to wish good luck in his job interview.

6 She asked if I wanted to have lunch with them. I said I'd like, but I was very busy.

7a **Choose an appropriate phrase from the box to respond to each statement or question.**

I don't want any   I hope not   I don't want to
I'd love to   I don't want one

1 A: Is it going to rain?   B: _I hope not_ .

2 A: Why didn't you order soup?   B: Because _____ .

3 A: Do you fancy going to the cinema tonight?   B: Yes, _____ .

4 A: Shall I buy you a baseball cap for your birthday?   B: No thanks, _____ .

5 Do you think the price of petrol will go up?   B: _____ .

7b **Now use phrases from the box in 7a to give your own responses to these questions.**

1 Why aren't you coming to the party? _____ .

2 Do you want to join us for dinner tomorrow evening? _____ .

3 Go on! Have a go on the bungee jump! _____ .

4 There's ice cream in the fridge. Why don't you have some? _____ .

5 Here, have a biscuit. _____ .

8 Rewrite each sentence using a phrasal verb from the box instead of the verbs in bold. Sometimes there is more than one possible word order.

look up	sort out	make out	~~hand out~~	set off
hang on	take on	carry on		

1 Would you **distribute** these forms, please?
   would you hand out these forms, please? ***or*** ... *hand these forms out* ...

2 We need to **resolve** some minor problems before we finish.

3 Shall we stop now and **continue** tomorrow?

4 **Wait** a moment. I need to put paper in the printer before you can print your document.

5 I **contacted** an old school friend when I was in Edinburgh last week.

6 The traffic was very noisy and I couldn't **understand** what she was saying.

7 I don't want to **accept** the responsibility of leading a large team of people.

8 We should **leave** early tomorrow, before the rush hour.

9 For each phrasal verb, list two possible objects. Use a dictionary if necessary.

1 look up *a word / someone's phone number*

2 take off .... 4 turn down ....

3 bring up .... 5 lift up ....

10a Read sentences a–f and then answer the questions.

   a I'm going to feed my neighbour's dog and take it for walks when she's away.
   b I'm going to try to not watch TV for a month.
   c I have to face the problem and try to solve it.
   d I really need my car to go to work. The bus service is bad.
   e I had a bad cold but now I'm better.
   f I can't find my credit card. I've searched all my pockets.

1 Which sentence refers to someone **dealing with** something? ....c....

2 Which sentence refers to someone **looking for** something? ....

3 Which sentence refers to someone **looking after** something? ....

4 Which sentence refers to someone **getting over** something? ....

5 Which sentence refers to someone **doing without** something? ....

6 Which sentence refers to someone **depending on** something? ....

10b Choose three of the phrasal verbs in 10a and write sentences about yourself.

1 ....

2 ....

3 ....

11a Add a preposition to complete each sentence.

1 That man reminds me ⟨ *of* my uncle Jeremy.

2 I'd like to thank you your kindness to me when I stayed at your house.

3 The thieves robbed the poor woman all her money.

4 The company provided me a laptop when I started work.

5 Some people look down people who are poor or uneducated.

6 I am very tolerant but I will not put with racism!

7 I knew Joanna was getting divorced. Rita let me on the secret.

11b Write whole sentences that are true for you, using the verbs in brackets.

1 (reminds me of) ....

2 (look up to) ....

3 (look forward to) .... ,

4 (do without) ....

12 Put the words in brackets in the correct order.

This year (1) *has definitely not been* (not/been/definitely/has) a good year for me. I (2) .... (have/should/finished) my degree course but I (3) .... (had/waiting/been) to get the results of some extra courses I (4) .... (had/taken). When I (5) .... (finally/told/was) the results, I realised I (6) .... (have/actually/would) to take two of the subjects again, and that (7) .... (mean/then/would) that I (8) .... (not/would/be) able to graduate. If I had passed all the exams, I (9) .... (would/graduating/have/been) at the end of this month, and I (10) .... (have/been/even/offered/might) a place on the Master's course for next year. It's just bad luck, I suppose. Maybe next year will be better!

Verbs: everyday verbs (*get, go, wish, want*)

1 **Use the following words and phrases to describe the meaning of *get*.**

a become   **b** receive   **c** travel to *or* arrive at   **d** bring   **e** persuade

1 Can you **get** me some more milk, please?

2 We're trying to **get** David to ring Joan before he leaves.

3 She's quite old now and **gets** tired easily.

4 Did you **get** an invitation to Anne's party?

5 We've only half-an-hour to **get** to the airport.

2 **Match the beginnings 1–8 with endings a–h.**

1 ...d... 2 .... 3 .... 4 .... 5 .... 6 ....

1 If you're late
a getting your new MP3 player?

2 When are you
b to get Jack to tidy his room.

3 What time
c We're getting the car ready for you now.

4 I'm just going
d just get a taxi.

5 We need
e we get the TV working? What's wrong with it?

6 Sorry to keep you waiting.
f get a bus to the office so she took a taxi instead.

7 Why can't
g did they get home?

8 She didn't want to
h to get Adam some breakfast.

get and *go*

3 **Fill in each gap with the correct form of *get* or *go*.**

1 It's started to .... very cold in the evenings.

2 We'd better hurry. It's .... late.

3 He's only 25 but he's started to .... bald.

4 The weather suddenly started to .... worse.

5 Hurry up! The traffic lights have already .... green.

6 We'd better go home now before the children .... too tired.

Have and *have got*

4 **Match each sentence with the topic (a–f) that describes the use of *have*.**

a Things we own: I *have* three black cats.

b Hygiene routines: She's *having* a shower.

c Actions or events: They *have* a party in May every year.

d Conversations: I *had* a long chat with him.

e Food: I *had* the fish and Jim just *had* a salad.

f Problems: Their car *had* a puncture …

1 I hope they both had a good night's sleep. Topic c

2 I need to have a shave.

3 We're just going to have something to eat. Want to come?

4 We should have lunch together next week.

5 We had a really good game of squash.

6 Have a nice holiday.

7 They had a long discussion about it and are now speaking to each other again.

8 She's having real difficulty in understanding the lecture.

9 They have a meeting at 2 pm.

10 They must be very wealthy because they have two houses, one in Singapore and one in Bangkok.

5 **Tick the more informal sentence, a or b.**

1 **a** They haven't got a car. **b** They don't have a car.

2 **a** How many cousins does he have? **b** How many cousins has he got?

3 **a** I've got no idea. **b** I have no idea.

4 **a** The dog needs to have more exercise. **b** The dog needs to get more exercise.

5 **a** He had his car repaired. **b** He got his car repaired

6 **a** We wish to make a complaint. **b** We want to make a complaint.

7 **a** The BBC wants to apologise for the interruption to your programme.
b The BBC wishes to apologise for the interruption to your programme.

8 **a** They don't want their competitors to have that information.
b They don't wish their competitors to have that information.

Wish and *hope*

6 **Five of the sentences have mistakes. Correct the mistakes and tick (✓) the correct sentences.**

1 They wish that they visit us in April next year.

2 I don't wish Jean to know that I'm looking for a new job.

3 I wish they'd told us they'd moved house.

4 I wish we have a bigger apartment.

5 I wish it doesn't rain for the wedding next week.

6 I just wish they wouldn't talk so much in private.

7 I know both singers are ill but I hope they don't postpone the concert.

8 I hope Jill to phone this evening.

Want

7 **Four of the sentences have mistakes with *want*. Correct the mistakes and tick (✓) the correct sentences.**

1 What do you want that we do?

2 Do you want some more fruit juice?

3 A: Is Adam going on holiday with you?   B: No, he doesn't want this year.

4 Don't they want to try the new Vietnamese restaurant in town?

5 She took her driving test in France even though her father didn't want her to.

6 We simply want them give us our money back.

7 They are not wanted to attend the meeting

Look, watch and *see*

8 **In each sentence, put the words in the right order.**

1 the view / window / from / at / Come and look / this
   Come and look at this view from the window.

2 he / very well / yesterday / look / didn't / We / saw / him / but

3 to / It / looks like / going / snow / it's

4 you / Can / back / come / tomorrow? / to watch her match

5 What / brother / does / look like / her?

6 had / She / has / a / shock / she / looks / as though / a bit of

9 **Fill in each gap with the correct form of *look, look at, see* or *watch*.**

1 What would you like to .... on TV this evening?

2 I can't .... the pictures properly without my glasses.

3 Can you .... my letter of application and tell me what you think?

4 A: We're just going to the cinema.
   B: Are you? What are you going to .... ?

5 She .... me in a very strange way and asked me why I was here.

6 .... , David. You've been late every morning this week so I shall
   have to speak to the boss.

7 Can you .... if there have been any phone messages for me?

Do and *make*

10 **Complete the sentences with the verb *do* or *make* and a word or phrase from the box.**

a cake	your homework	Japanese	the cooking
aerobics	~~long journeys~~	an appointment	the crossword

1 His new car can *do / ~~make~~* ..*long journeys*.. very economically.

2 She's decided to *do / make* .... as her second language at school.

3 Why do I always have to *do / make* .... ? You don't even do the
   washing-up.

4 He's in the kitchen *doing / making* .... at the moment; I'll ask
   him to call you back.

5 I know you don't like maths but it's nine o'clock and you haven't
   done / made ....

6 Jill and Cara *do / make* .... in the gym; and Alicia does ballet.

7 She *did / made* .... to see the doctor next week.

8 Every morning before breakfast he *does / makes* .... in the
   newspaper.

Verb patterns

1 **Underline the correct form of the verb to complete each sentence.**

1 I can't help *thinking* / *to think* she's making a big mistake.

2 We can't afford *to buy* / *buying* a new car.

3 I promised *calling* / *to call* her as soon as my plane landed.

4 We should leave early to avoid *to get* / *getting* stuck in the morning traffic.

5 I think I would enjoy *playing* / *to play* in a rock band.

6 He refused *to listen* / *listening* to his parents' advice.

7 I've arranged *going* / *to go* out with my team-mates on Saturday.

8 Do you feel like *to eat* / *eating* out tonight?

2 **Write what you would you say in each situation. Use verbs in the *to*-infinitive form or the *-ing* form, as appropriate.**

1 Your workmate has lost his mobile phone. You saw it earlier on his desk.
I remember *seeing it earlier on your desk.*

2 You said something that offended somebody. You want to apologise.
I'm sorry. I didn't mean ....

3 You are travelling with a friend in your car. You think it might be good to get something to eat on the way.
If you get hungry, we can stop ....

4 Your friend thinks you and she should get the 6 am train to London. Explain that it will be necessary to get up at 5 am if you do that.
If we get the 6 am train, it means ....

5 Someone is interrupting you all the time. Ask them to stop.
Could you please stop ....

6 You asked a friend to book tickets for a concert. Check whether they did it.
Did you remember .... ?

3 **Read the dialogues and complete each statement with the correct verb pattern, either object + *to*-infinitive or object + base form.**

1 Bill: Oh come on, come to the party with us. It'll be fun.
Hannah: Oh well ... okay.
Bill persuaded *Hannah to go to the party.*

2 Rana: You really upset me. Now say you're sorry!
Frank: Okay, okay. I'm very sorry.
Rana made ....

3 Doorman: You can't go in without a tie.
James: Oh, really? Oh well, never mind – I'll go somewhere else.
The doorman wouldn't let ....

English Grammar Today Workbook

4 Sally: Don't let me forget to phone Carol.
Julian: Okay.

Sally asked Julian to remind ....

5 Wilma: It would be lovely if you came with me to the hospital.
Sam: Really? Okay.

Wilma wanted ....

4 Underline the correct verb pattern to complete each sentence.

1 When you didn't answer the phone, we assumed *you being out* / *that you were out*.

2 Next time you're in Cambridge, we insist *you to stay* / *that you stay* with us.

3 I want *that you stay* / *you to stay* till Kevin arrives, if that's okay.

4 I suggest *you to arrange* / *that you arrange* an appointment with Dr Silver as soon as possible.

5 I imagine *you to be tired* / *you'll be tired* when you get here after such a long journey.

6 We heard him *sing* / *to sing* at the concert the other day. It was lovely; we enjoyed it so much.

7 We all hope *you to be* / *that you'll be* happy in your new job.

8 I saw him *arriving* / *to arrive* with someone but I couldn't see who it was.

5 Complete the sentences with the correct verb pattern, using the outlines.

1 She complained / boss / too much work.
She complained to her boss that she had too much work.

2 I told / my lazy brother / ought to get a job. ....

3 The teacher explained / the students / have to take an extra exam.

....

4 He asked / the police officer / go with him. ....

5 The Colonel ordered / troops / advance. ....

6 The secretary pointed out / Andrew / he had not signed his application form. ....

7 Trevor said / his mother / he intended / move out of the family home.

....

8 The chairperson informed / the committee / the next meeting would be on 30th March. ....

Verbs which are easily confused

Come and go

1 **Fill in each gap with the correct form of *come* or *go*.**

1 Are you ..... *coming* ..... to my house for lunch tomorrow?

2 I'll .... to your office at ten o'clock and show you the report, okay?

3 We're .... to the cinema tonight. Would you like to .... with us?

4 A: I'm .... to Paris next week. B: Oh, that's nice. I've never been there. Who are you .... with? A: A friend from work.

5 Julian .... to see me yesterday. I hadn't seen him for months.

6 A: Did you .... anywhere interesting at the weekend?
B: Yes, we .... to the London Transport Museum. It was great.

Bring, take, fetch, lend and borrow

2 **Read the remarks by different speakers and then answer the questions.**

Printha: "Are you going to the kitchen? Can you get me a glass, please?"

Nigel: "You can have my guitar till the weekend."

Arlene: "Thanks for the dictionary. I'll give it back to you this afternoon."

Krishnan: "I'll buy you some flowers on my way to your house."

Paco: "I'll buy some flowers for Mona when I go to see her in the hospital."

1 Who is borrowing something from someone?   *Arlene*

2 Who is bringing something to someone?   ....

3 Who is lending something to someone?   ....

4 Who wants someone to fetch something?   ....

5 Who is taking something to someone?   ....

3 **Write what you would say in each situation. Use *bring, take, fetch, lend* and *borrow*. Sometimes more than one answer is possible.**

1 You would like to use a friend's bike.
Can I ..... *borrow your bike?* .....

2 You spill some juice. You need a cloth to clean it up. Ask a friend to get one.
Can you .... , please?

3 Your friend is going to play tennis. She hasn't got a racket. You have one.
I can ....

4 You have a parcel for Harry. Your friend is going to Harry's office.
Can you .... for me, please?

5 Your friend is coming to your house. You'd like to see his new laptop.
When you come to my house, can you .... with you?

Expect, wait for and hope

4 Five of the sentences have mistakes. Correct the mistakes and tick (✓) the correct sentences.

1 I waited the bus but it didn't come.

2 Tanya is expecting a baby.

3 We expect the parcel to arrive tomorrow.

4 I expect I pass all my exams.

5 Kieran is hoping that he'll get an interview for the job in Oslo.

6 I can't come out. I'm waiting that my mother arrives.

7 I don't hope I fail my driving test.

8 A: Will he accept the job?   B: I expect so. It's a good one.

9 We're waiting for Archie to tell us if he's coming tonight.

10 People wait for supermarkets to be cheaper than small shops but it's not always true.

Fall, fall down and feel

5 Underline the correct verb in each sentence.

1 I slipped on the ice and *feel / fell / felt*. I injured my hand and knee.

2 House prices have *fallen down / fallen / felt* this year.

3 She left work early because she said she *felt / fell / feel* unwell.

4 My poster has *felt / fell / fallen down* from the wall. I need some tape.

5 I always love autumn, when the leaves *fell / fall down / fall* from the trees.

Look, see, watch, hear and listen

6 Match the beginnings 1–8 with endings a–h.

1 ....d.... 2 .... 3 .... 4 .... 5 .... 6 .... 7 .... 8 ....

1 We watched	**a** a poem I've written?
2 I listened	**b** the news? Jenny's getting married!
3 Have you seen	**c** at photos of countries I've never been to.
4 I always enjoy looking	**d** a really good documentary on TV last night.
5 Did you hear	**e** at that report I left on your desk?
6 Did you watch	**f** to an interview with the minister on the radio.
7 Would you like to hear	**g** *The Wicker Man*? It's a very scary film.
8 Did you look	**h** TV last night?

7 Use the correct form of the verbs in the box to replace the words in bold.

watch	come	~~expect~~	go	look at
feel	listen to	see	fall	hear

Hi Patrick, Greetings from our holiday cottage.
Everyone (1) ~~believes~~ *expects* the weather to be fine all the time in the summer in the
Mediterranean, but right now the weather's awful! As I look out of my window, I can
(2) **observe** big, black clouds and it's raining heavily. I can't go out. All I can do is
(3) **turn on** the TV. Sometimes I (4) **switch on** the radio instead. Five centimetres of
rain (5) **came down** yesterday. It was such an awful day and I (6) **was** so depressed.
All I did was (7) **read** some magazines I found in the living room. The day started well
and the weather was dry, but then I (8) **caught the sound** of some thunder in the
distance, and soon the rain started. You said you would like to (9) **visit** here for a few
days. Don't! (10) **Travel to** somewhere sunny instead!
Ivor

8 Describe what the people in each picture are doing.

1 They.. .

2 They.. .

3 He.. .

4 She... .

Used to, be used to and *usually*

9a Tick (✓) the correct explanation, a or b, for each sentence.

1 Emily used to get up at seven o'clock.
   a Emily normally got up at seven o'clock and she still does.
   b Emily got up at seven o'clock in the past, but not now.

2 Liam was used to getting up early.
   a Liam was accustomed to getting up early. **b** Liam normally got up early.

3 Freda usually got up late on Saturdays.
   a Freda got up late on Saturdays, but now she gets up early.
   b Freda normally got up late on Saturdays.

4 They usually eat hot spicy food.
   a They don't eat hot spicy food anymore. **b** They normally eat hot spicy food.

5 I used to play football.
   a I normally play football. **b** I don't play football anymore.

6 She's used to working long hours.
   a She worked long hours, but not anymore.
   b She is familiar with working long hours.

9b Complete each sentence so that it is true for you.

1 I used to ....
2 I usually ....
3 I'm used to ....

10 Find and correct the six mistakes with *used to, be used to* (and *usually*).
Sometimes more than one answer is possible.

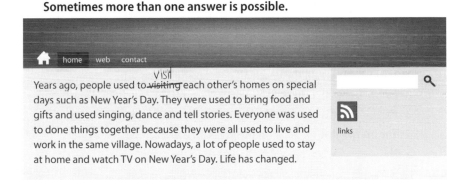

home   web   contact

visit
Years ago, people used to ~~visiting~~ each other's homes on special
days such as New Year's Day. They were used to bring food and
gifts and used singing, dance and tell stories. Everyone was used
to done things together because they were all used to live and
work in the same village. Nowadays, a lot of people used to stay
at home and watch TV on New Year's Day. Life has changed.

links

Say and *tell*

11 Tick (✓) the correct option, a or b, for each situation.

1 You want directions to the museum. What do you ask someone?
   a Can you say to me the way to the museum?
   b Can you tell me the way to the museum?

2 You want to thank some friends for a gift. What do you say?
   a I want to tell you all thank you for the lovely gift.
   b I want to say thank you to all of you for the lovely gift.

3 You want to report a conversation you had with Kevin. What do you say?
a Kevin said me he was ill last week. **b** Kevin told me he was ill last week.

4 You want to find out what happened in a conversation between your friend and Lela. What do you say?
a Did Lela say that she was still going out with Jeremy?
b Did Lela tell that she was still going out with Jeremy?

Verbs that sound similar

12a *Raise* or *rise*? Write the correct form of *raise* or *rise* in these pairs of sentences.

1 The temperature __rose__ to 35 degrees yesterday.
The scientists .... the temperature to test the material.

2 That restaurant has .... its prices again. They do it every month!
House prices have .... by 5% this year.

3 If you have a question, ... your hand.
When the speaker finished, he invited questions and several hands ....

4 The boss has promised to .... my salary next year.
My salary should .... by about 4% next year.

12b *Lay* or *lie*? Complete the grammar chart.

meaning	base form	past form	-ed participle
be horizontal	lie	lay	
place something horizontally	lay		
not tell the truth			lied

Fill in each gap with the correct form of *lay* or *lie*.

1 We just __lay__ on the beach all day, taking in the sun.
2 I don't feel well. I think I should .... on the couch for a few minutes.
3 He .... his hand on the boy's shoulder and said, "Don't worry."
4 The cat has just .... on the grass all day sleeping.
5 He .... when he said he had been in the army.

12c *Wake, wake up, waken, awake* or *awaken*? Underline the most appropriate verb each sentence. More than one answer may be possible, but one answer may be more likely than another.

1 *Wake / Awake* me at half past six, will you? My taxi's coming at seven.
2 I *awakened / woke up* at seven. Normally I don't *wake up / awaken* till 8.30!
3 They walked silently, in order not to *wake up / waken* the child as she lay asleep in her cot.
4 *Awaken / Wake up*! It's 8.30. You've got a class at nine. Come on!
5 The music *woke up / awoke* memories of my childhood in Scotland.

English Grammar Today Workbook

Do and make

13a Put these nouns into two groups, 'do nouns' and 'make nouns'.

~~coffee~~	effort	phone call	favour	mistake
homework	job	damage	shopping	noise

do nouns	*make* nouns
	coffee

13b Fill in each gap with the correct form of *make* or *do* and a noun from the box.

1 Would you like some .... coffee .... ? I'm just going to .... make .... some.

2 Who's going to .... the .... today? We need milk, potatoes and bread.

3 Please stop .... so much .... ! I'm trying to study!

4 I often .... grammatical .... in English. This book will help me.

5 I failed the exam last time. This time I'm going to .... a real .... to pass.

6 There was a very strong wind last night and it .... a lot of .... to the trees in our garden.

7 I can't come out tonight. I have to .... my .... for tomorrow.

8 Are there any .... I can .... for you? I want to help out.

9 I need to .... a .... Can I borrow your phone?

10 Could you .... me a .... ? Could you lend me 50 euros till next week?

Rob and steal, remind and remember, fit and suit

14 Match the beginnings 1–6 with endings a–f.

1 ..c.. 2 .... 3 .... 4 .... 5 .... 6 ....

1 This jacket doesn't fit me;	**a** to text his workmate.
2 Four men in a blue car robbed	**b** of my brother.
3 Tom reminded me	**c** it's too small.
4 Two men with guns stole	**d** red just isn't my colour.
5 This jacket doesn't suit me;	**e** a High-street bank this morning.
6 Tom remembered	**f** 20,000 euros from a shop yesterday.

Word formation

As these exercises test many different words, you may need to use a dictionary.

Prefixes

1 Add a prefix from the box to each adjective in the list below to create a negative meaning.

| in- | il- | im- | ir- | un- | dis- |

1 experienced _inexperienced_   6 complete................   11 relevant................
2 fair.................................   7 regular................   12 literate................
3 possible.........................   8 certain................   13 satisfied................
4 expected.......................   9 legible................   14 legal................
5 polite............................   10 contented................

Adjectives and suffixes

2 Fill in each gap with a suffix from the box.

| -able | -ful | -ly | -y | ous | -less |

1 She's very care _ful_   with money.
2 They live in a large apartment in Tokyo and are very wealth.......... .
3 On many parts of the island the water is not drink.......... .
4 Everyone at the club was very friend.......... towards us.
5 He always worked hard at school and is now fam.......... as a musician.
6 They've just got a new puppy and it's very play.......... .
7 The roads can be very danger.......... at nights.
8 The paintings they bought at the auction are worth.......... .
9 The company became unprofit.......... and had to close down.
10 Her friends were all on holiday and she suddenly felt very lone.......... .
11 That's very thought.......... of you. Thank you.
12 I've just lost five games of badminton. I'm completely hope.......... .

Nouns into adjectives

3 Use a suffix from the box to change the nouns into adjectives. Make a sentence with the adjective you have formed.

| -ive | -ent | -ic | -ous |

1 aggression _aggressive – Some breeds of dog can be very aggressive._

2 confidence ....

English Grammar Today Workbook

3 fame ....

4 ambition ....

5 electricity ....

Nouns and prefixes

4 **Use a word or phrase to explain the meaning of each prefix in bold. You may need to use a dictionary.**

1 They were all taking part in an **anti**-war protest. anti = against

2 The workmen did the job very well but we felt we were **over**charged. over = ...

3 The team didn't arrive on time and was **dis**qualified. dis = ...

4 We're meeting again in **mid**-August, aren't we? mid = ...

5 At the World Cup, all his friends were **pro**-Italy. pro = ...

6 He made the first solo **trans**atlantic crossing by sailing boat. trans = ...

5 **Add a suffix to each word to create a noun. If the word is already a noun, make a new noun using a suffix.**

1 artist	6 friend...............	11 Morocco............
2 performance	7 refuse...............	12 republic............
3 child............	8 lonely............	13 piano............
4 London............	9 communicate............	14 Marx............
5 China............	10 govern............	

Verbs and prefixes

6 **Make a word to fill each gap by taking a prefix from the first box and adding it to a word in the second box to make a verb.**

dis		understand
re		large
over		eat
en		appear
mis		number
out		heat

1 She was speaking very quickly and I must have   misunderstood   her.

2 I'm sorry the soup is cold but you can .... it.

3 They haven't been seen for two years. They've ....

4 With so much food in front of us, it was very easy to ....

5 I'd like to have these photographs ....

6 We all went to the match but their supporters 119

Verbs and suffixes

7 Complete this table.

	adjective	verb	noun
1	strong	strengthen	strength
2	sweet		sweetness
3	tight		tightness
4	high		height
5	sympathetic		sympathy
6	simple		simplicity
7	ripe		ripeness
8	soft		softness
9	modern		modernisation
10	short		shortness

Nouns and verbs

8 Complete this table with the correct nouns and verbs. Sometimes more than one answer is possible.

	verb	noun: activity	noun: occupation or role
1	translate	translation	translator
2	sail	sailing	
3			actor
4	explore		
5		employment	
6			entertainer
7	teach		
8		driving	
9			organiser
10		management	

English Grammar Today Workbook

Adverbs and suffixes

9 **Form adverbs from the following words:**

quick, calm, impossible, north, natural, unhappy, back

....

Conversions, compounds and abbreviations

10 **Write a sentence using the words in bold in the word class indicated. Your sentence may be about any topic.**

1 Did you get my **email**? *verb*: I'll email her at once. ....

2 I'll have to **text** her. *noun*: ....

3 Okay, we'll meet on Tuesday. That's a **definite**. *adverb*: ....

4 I can't afford that new video **phone**. *verb*: ....

5 We're in a hurry. I'll **microwave** the dinner for us. *noun*: ....

11 **Fill in each gap with an adjective compound.**

1 The flight lasted twenty hours.

It was .... a twenty-hour .... flight.

2 He was wearing a shirt with short sleeves.

He was wearing a .... shirt.

3 The girl has brown eyes.

She's a .... girl.

4 These sweets are free of sugar.

They are .... sweets.

5 Janine writes with her left hand.

Janine is ....

12 **Write abbreviated or shortened forms of the words in bold.**

Please buy me.

Today **advertisements** are everywhere. They are on **television**, on **mobile telephones**, on **compact disks** and you even see them on your seats in **aeroplanes**. Many **magazines** have lovely colour **photographs** but in the corner you see an advertisement for a camera! The **European Union** and the **United Kingdom** government are trying to reduce the number of advertisements we see all around us but it is a very big job.

Words and expressions which are easily confused

As or *like*

1   Underline the correct word in each sentence, *as* or *like*.

1   She looks *as / like* a friend of mine that I was at university with.

2   He works *as / like* a waiter in a restaurant, so he doesn't earn very much.

3   *As / Like* captain of the team, he has a lot of responsibility.

4   She is acting *as / like* the chairperson of the committee until they elect a new one.

5   She was acting *as / like* a child. She should grow up and stop behaving so stupidly!

6   Father to child: "*As / Like* your father, it's my responsibility to see you do things properly."

7   Mother to child: "*As / Like* your father, I have a responsibility towards you."

8   It seems *as / like* a good idea to me.

All, every and *the whole*

2   Match the beginnings 1–7 with the most appropriate endings a–g.

1 All	**a** day's work was lost because of the bad weather.
2 Every	**b** students in my class are female.
3 A whole	**c** the apple was bad so I threw it away.
4 The whole	**d** children love fairy stories.
5 All the	**e** child loves to play and to invent games.
6 All of	**f** class had to take the exam again.
7 The whole of	**g** my relatives live far away.

3   Complete each sentence so that it is true for you.

1   I love all ....

2   I usually .... every ....

3   I couldn't eat/drink a whole .... ; it would be too much!

4   I like all of ....

5   I wouldn't like to spend the whole of .... studying English.

First, firstly, last, the end

4   Use the expressions from the box to complete the conversations. Use each expression once only.

firstly	in the end	at last	at first	first	at the end	lastly

1   A: Where did you go on your tour of Spain?

B: Well, ... we went to Madrid, then Barcelona, then Valencia.

English Grammar Today Workbook

2 A: Sorry I'm late! The traffic was awful.

B: James! You're here .... ! We've all been waiting for you!

3 A: Did you ever find that memory stick you lost?

B: Yes. I looked everywhere and .... I found it under the sofa.

4 A: How's Louisa's new job going?

B: Well, ... she didn't like it, but she loves it now.

5 A: Do you need a pen? Here, borrow mine.

B: Thanks. I'll give it back to you .... of the lesson.

6 Lecturer: There are three things to remember when upgrading the operating system on a computer: ...., all data must be backed up before beginning, secondly, the upgrade must be compatible with the computer's operating system, and ...., personal settings will need to be transferred.

Each and every

5 Underline the correct word. If both are possible, underline them both.

NOTICE BOARD

(1) *Each / Every* year, the school awards a prize for the student who performs best in the exams. The prize is £300. Last year, three students had the same high marks, so (2) *each / every* student received £100. There is also a prize for the 'top class' in the school. All the different classes compete with (3) *each other / one another* for the highest total grades, and the winning class receives a gold medal.

This year, there will be a new prize, the 'best pair-work' prize. The idea is that two students get together and help (4) *each other / one another* in some way, for example to research a project or make a poster. The best pair will win a silver medal. The exam and pair-work competitions are open to (5) *each / every* student in the school, so apply now! See the school's homepage for details.

Already, still and yet

6 Tick (✓) the correct explanation a or b of each sentence.

1 It's four o'clock already!
a I expected it to be four o'clock.   **b** I didn't expect it to be four o'clock.

2 Is your brother still in college?
a I know your brother has been in college.
b I don't know if your brother has been in college.

3 She hasn't bought her ticket yet.
a I expect her to buy a ticket.   **b** I don't expect her to buy a ticket.

7 Put *already* in the correct position in each sentence.

  1 He had seen the film.

  2 The Liverpool train has left the station.

  3 I'm beginning to regret buying my new bike.

  4 We know the answer.

  5 The troops were marching towards the border.

8 Put *still* in each sentence. Give two possible answers in each case, one which is neutral, and one which is more likely in informal spoken language.

  1 He's a bit young.   4 Are you at university?
  2 Is this important?   5 I'm waiting for her reply.
  3 I haven't posted that letter.

9 Put *yet* in the correct position in each sentence. Sometimes more than one answer is possible.

  1 Have you phoned your sister?   4 Hasn't she arrived?
  2 He's not back.   5 Is it five o'clock?
  3 The government has not responded to the report. (give two answers)

10 Three of the sentences have mistakes with *still*, *yet* and *already*. Correct the mistakes and tick (✓) the correct sentences.

  1 She won't still eat anything and it's very worrying.

  2 Yet they haven't decided where to go but I hope they decide soon.

  3 They've already been and done the shopping.

  4 We waited for an hour but they didn't still come.

  5 Already the stadium was beginning to fill as the supporters came crowding in.

11 Fill in each gap with *already, still* or *yet*.

Okay, what else is there to do? We've got the food. The music is done. I've (1) .... phoned to check that Dale is bringing his guitar. I'll tell you what I haven't done (2) .... though. I haven't done the decorations (3) .... , oh, and Maura (4) .... hasn't said what time she's coming. That's a bit of a problem. She needs to be here early. She's (5) .... forgotten the present once.

12 Complete each sentence so that it is true for you.

  1 I haven't .... yet.

  2 I still don't know ....

  3 This year I have already ....

  4 I still want to ....

  5 .... hasn't finished yet.

ANSWER KEY

Adjectives

1 1. long 2. No adjectives 3. <u>late</u> for the school bus 4. daily
5. hard 6. nice
Note: in 1, *hard* is an adverb but it is an adjective in 5. In 3, the second *late* is an adverb.

🦋 **EGT** Adjectives 8

2 3. **Dutch** painting 4. ... are they **Dutch**? 5. very **religious** ... 6. **religious** buildings 7. ... people are less **polite** 8. **polite** young men 9. ... are very **friendly** 10. **friendly** pets 11. ... very **scientific** 12. **scientific** experiments

🦋 **EGT** Adjectives 8; Adjectives: order 10; Adjective phrases: position 13

3 1. a 2. a 3. b 4. a 5. b

🦋 **EGT** Adjectives: with *-ing* and *-ed* (*interesting, interested*) 9d

4 2. tiring 3. terrified 4. depressing 5. amazing 6. surprising 7. relaxed
8. interesting 9. confusing 10. exciting 11. embarrassing 12. fascinated
Note: in 9, *confused* is also possible but *confusing* is more likely.

🦋 **EGT** Adjectives: with *-ing* and *-ed* (*interesting, interested*) 9d

5 1. b 2. b 3. b 4. b 5. a

🦋 **EGT** Adjective phrases: position 13

6 1. ~~very~~ 2. ✓ 3. ~~absolutely~~ 4. ✓ 5. ✓ 6. ~~very~~ 7. ~~quite~~ 8. ~~reasonably~~

🦋 **EGT** Gradable adjectives and words and phrases that go before them 13c

7 2. He owns an enormous, white vintage car.
3. ... a large, Chinese, woollen rug and a lovely, old, Italian u-shaped mirror.
4. ... a lovely, rectangular, antique wooden coffee table.
5. ... beautiful, slim girl; a blue and pink silk dress. (*or* ... pink and blue ...)
6. ... long, white sandy beaches.

🦋 **EGT** Adjectives: order 10

8 2. It's a fast, smooth, punctual train. 3. This is an attractive, light, fashionable phone. 4. It's a warm, comfortable, black jacket. 5. It's a quiet, reliable, economical washing-machine. 6. It's a comfortable, classic leather armchair.

9 *Suggested answers*
a It has a large, well-kept vegetable garden. The house has five large, newly-decorated bedrooms. It has a spacious and homely kitchen with dark, English oak cupboards

b This is a beautiful, modern, elegant city-centre flat with two large, centrally-heated bedrooms and a stylish, spacious kitchen. There are new, flat-screen TVs in both living rooms.

10 1. economical   2. economic   3. historical   4. historic   5. classic   6. classical

11 *Possible answer*
The young family are about to take a long train journey to a warm country. The little girl with dark hair is wearing a big, warm coat and her brother is wearing a thin jacket. Both children have interesting books and toys to play with on the train. The mother looks happy.

Adjuncts (Adverbials)

1   1. for six years   2. in the end   3. under the bed   4. At first   5. slowly   6. very carefully

 Adjuncts 15; Prepositional phrases 276

2   1. A   2. P   3. C (the verb *put* must have an expression of place to complete its meaning)   4. A   5. C (prepositional phrases after main verb *be* are complements)   6. P

 Adjuncts and complements 15; Postmodifiers 235d

3   1. She left the house early in the morning. *or* In the morning, she left the house early.   2. He plays the violin and the viola very well.   3. ✓   4. I always take the bus to work.   5. During the lesson the teacher told the students to be quiet. *or* The teacher told the students to be quiet during the lesson.   6. ✓   7. I'll post the letter tomorrow.   8. ✓

 Adverbs and adverb phrases: position 23

4   *Possible answers*

1. my bag.   2. eight o'clock during the holidays.   3. on my day off / at the weekend.   4. my friend Julia in town / in the evenings / on Fridays / at the coffee shop / at the weekend.   5. try to pronounce/spell the words correctly/accurately.   6. to the library after class.   7. before breakfast / after school / in the morning / in the evening.   8. at the end of the lesson / after class / after work / in the evening / on Fridays.

 Adjuncts 15

Adverbs and adverb phrases

1   2. well   3. suddenly   4. fast   5. … I've always worked <u>hard</u>.   6. warmly   7. beautifully   8. well   9. here   10. upstairs

1b   1. Carefully, the little girl walked to the edge of the river. *or* The little girl carefully walked to the edge of the river.
   3. Suddenly, a face appeared at the window. (may be written with or without a comma) *or* A face appeared suddenly at the window.

6. She was a friendly woman who welcomed us warmly.

9. Could you come and help me here?

10. I'll just run and get that book upstairs for you.

 Adverbs 16

2 1. well   2. happily   3. sad   4. beautifully   5. badly   6. slow; late

3 2. Does she usually work on Saturdays?

3. My brother speaks Russian very well.

4. Suddenly, we saw a police car. (with or without a comma) *or* We suddenly saw …

5. We'll probably get the six o'clock flight. *or* (in informal situations, especially in spoken language) We'll get the six o'clock flight, probably. *or* Probably we'll get the six o'clock flight.

6. They had always wanted a house near the beach.

7. I have been feeling unwell recently. *or* Recently, I've been feeling unwell. *or* (more formal) I have recently been feeling unwell.

8. She loves her parents dearly. *or* (less common) She dearly loves her parents.

 Adverbs and adverb phrases: position 23

4 2. extremely slowly   3. so badly   4. quite happily   5. rather unkindly   6. absolutely smoothly   7. just outside   8. fairly slowly   9. quickly enough   10. Luckily for me

 Adverb phrases 22

5 downstairs (place); excitedly (manner); already (time); always (frequency); soon (time); hurriedly (manner); eagerly (manner); occasionally (frequency); there (place)

 Adverbs: types 19

6 *Possible answers*

2. When I finish work, I usually go to the gym.

3. I like to drive slowly when I am passing through nice countryside.

4. Just before an exam, I usually feel extremely nervous.

5. I sometimes react angrily when people are impolite.

6. I'm quite optimistic about the future.

 Adverbs and adverb phrases: position 23

7 ~~busyly~~ busily; ~~careful~~ carefully; ~~extremley~~ extremely; ~~correct~~ correctly; ~~hardly~~ hard; ~~real~~ really

 Adverbs and adverb phrases: typical errors 24

8 2. easily   3. fast   4. wrong   5. badly; fortunately   6. well

9 2. excitedly   3. angrily   4. calmly   5. tearfully   6. sarcastically

10 2. some time   3. especially   4. perhaps   5. finally   6. At first

Clauses

1a 1 and 4 are not clauses

1b *Possible answers*

    1. The monster ran over the hills and far away.

    4. We thought we had all the time in the world.

> **EGT** What is a clause? 70a

2   2. two   3. two   4. one   5. two   6. one

> **EGT** What is a sentence? 70b

3   *Suggested answer*

    …If I don't do that anymore, I will save a lot of water. Also, I use a new plastic bag every day when I bring lunch to work. So using the same one more often would be a good idea. Finally, I buy a lot of fruit because I love it. I could try to buy fruit that is grown locally and also fruit that is organic.

4

Declarative	Interrogative	Imperative	Exclamative
2, 6, 8, 10	1, 12	3, 4, 5	7, 9, 11

> **EGT** Clause types 71

5   2. Won't they be coming with us?   3. Some people don't like walking for hours.
4. Can I help you?   5. Don't go now.   6. Let's not watch a film tonight *or* Don't let's watch a film tonight.   7. Did they leave early?   8. Why are they selling the house?   9. Be there before 6.   10. Don't leave me alone.

6   *Suggested answers*

    2. Have a seat. *or* (Do) sit down.   3. Let's have lunch.   4. Let's take a break.
5. Come round for dinner. *or* Let's have dinner.

> **EGT** Imperative clauses 71c

7   1. What   2. How   3. Aren't   4. Can

> **EGT** Exclamative clauses 71d

8a   2. **M:** Buy some vegetables **S:** if you go to the market.

    3. **S:** Because they have a house in the country, **M:** they don't spend … .

    4. **S:** Before reading *Harry Potter*, **M:** I went to see the film.

    5. **S:** Having spent forty years in the army, **M:** he was very happy to retire.

    6. **S:** Although he was tired, **M:** he was so happy to have arrived safely in Rome.

> **EGT** Main (independent) clauses and subordinate (dependent) clauses 68b

8b   1. finite   2. finite   3. finite   4. non-finite   5. non-finite   6. finite

> **EGT** Clauses: finite and non-finite 69

9a 2. non-finite; finite   3. non-finite; finite   4. non-finite; finite   5. non-finite; finite
6. non-finite; finite.

9b 1. Being a terrible cook, I usually don't have dinner parties.
2. Watched by an audience of millions, she sang at the Oscars ceremony.
3. Not being very fit, I decided to go for a cycle after work in the evenings.
4. In order to join the club, you just fill out a form online.

Comparison

1 2. bigger   3. darker   4. as big as   5. longest   6. larger

> **EGT** Comparison: adjectives (*bigger, biggest, more interesting*) 77; Comparison: comparisons of equality (*as tall as his father*) 81

2 2. the cheapest   3. shorter   4. higher / highest   5. more expensive   6. further / farther   7. better

3a 1. older   2. happier; than; younger *or* as happy; as; younger   3. busier; than *or* as busy; as   4. the most expensive   5. the most interesting   6. the most dangerous   7. the tastiest   8. the nicest

3b *Answers for the author who wrote the exercise*

1. I've got two older sisters.
2. I'm as happy now as when I was younger.
3. I'm not as busy today as I was yesterday.
4. The most expensive thing I've ever bought is a house.
5. The most interesting book I've ever read is *Midnight in the garden of good and evil.*
6. The most dangerous thing I've ever done is ski down a black run.
7. The tastiest meal I've ever made is a curry.
8. The nicest thing I've done today so far is a walk up a hill with my dog and friends.

> **EGT** Comparison: adverbs (*worse, more easily*) 78

4 2. **f** harder   3. **d** more slowly   4. **a** worse (preferred to *He couldn't have done more badly.*)   5. **c** better   6. **e** further/farther

5 1. better ~~that~~ than me ... ~~more fast~~ faster.   2. ~~the most early~~ the earliest
3. ~~the worse~~ the worst   4. ~~more lately~~ later   5. ~~more fluent as Italian~~ as fluently as Italian *or* more fluently than Italian

> **EGT** Comparison: adverbs (*worse, more easily*) 78

6a 1. more   2. than   3. as much   4. fewer   5. than   6. more (than ten years ago)
7. as much   8. as   9. more   10. than we did (ten years ago)

6b *Answers for the author who wrote the exercise*

I read more books than I used to.
I do more exercise than I did.
I don't go to the cinema as often as I did.
I work more at home and less in school.
I go out with my friends more than when my children were young.

7 1. than   2. as   3. than   4. than   5. Rudi 6, Erin 4, Davide 14, Maria 7, Sinjan 15
6. the least   7. the most

8 *Possible answers*

2. I don't think the inner circle on the right is bigger than the outer circle on the left. I think they're the same.

3. I think the small grey square on the left is as dark as the small grey square on the right.

4. I think the shapes are the same size.

5. The lines are all the same.

6. The square on the right is not bigger than the square on the left.

Conditionals: *If, if only, provided, I'd rather, I wish*

1 2. i   3. a   4. j   5. b (*c* and *d* are possible but b is most likely)   6. g
7. h (*i* is possible but *h* is most likely)   8. c   9. d   10. e

EGT Conditionals 84; Types of conditional: summary 85g

2 1. ~~will~~ would   2. *would swim* is correct but *swam* is possible. Both forms refer to a repeated action in the past.   3. I ~~would know~~ knew, ~~tell~~ would tell   4. ~~will have~~ had *or* have   5. ~~has~~ had   6. ~~will~~ see   7. ~~I go~~/I am going/I will go. *I'll go / I will go* are more common in this structure.   8. ~~would~~ bring. *Brought* is also possible and more common in more polite requests.

3 2. will leave   3. 'll give   4. practised   5. wouldn't be   6. 'd get   7. would behave
8. had been   9. wouldn't have caused   10. hadn't visited

4 2. unless   3. in case   4. in case   5. suppose   6. provided /providing *or* as / so
long as   7. unless   8. in case   9. unless   10. provided / providing *or* so/as long as.
Notes: *Providing* (*that*) and *suppose* are more common in informal English. *Supposing that*, *providing that* and *provided that* can also be used but they are all more formal structures. *As long as* is more common in informal English; *so long as* is more formal and more common in writing.

EGT Conditionals: *if* 85; Other conditional expressions (*unless, as long as*, etc.) 86; *If* 168; *Supposing* 86g; *As long as, so long as, providing*, etc. 86e; *Unless* 86a

5 1. if   2. whether   3. whether   4. whether / if   5. whether   6. whether
Note: in 5 and 6, *whether* (not *if*) follows a preposition.

EGT *If* or *whether*? 169

6 1. if only   2. or else / otherwise.   3. or else / otherwise   4. I'd rather; or else / otherwise (*or else* is the most likely)   5. We'd rather / If only (*would rather* is correct but more formal).   6. If only; would you rather.

EGT *If only* 170; *Else*: *or else* 117c; *Or* and *otherwise* 86f; *Would rather* 395a

7 2. F   3. F   4. F   5. F   6. F   7. I   8. I   9. F
Note: In 7, *here's the vegetables* is more informal than *Here are the vegetables*.

EGT *If* 168

English Grammar Today Workbook

8 *Possible answers*

Some very effective ads use only one conditional clause e.g. *If only all cars were as reliable as my ...*

9 *Answers for the author who wrote the exercise*

1. more free time each day.   2. coming on holiday with me.   3. play tennis better.
4. been so lazy at school.   5. bought a motorbike.   6. knew how to speak Japanese.
7. wouldn't be so strict.   8. visited Hong Kong again.

EGT *Wish 385; If only 170; It's time* ●

Conjunctions

1   2. d Although   3. i because   4. a As   5. h while   6. c before   7. l While
8. b After   9. g though   10. k Since   11. j or   12. e Although

EGT Conjunctions 88

2   1. ~~So~~ I've been running most days this month so I feel really fit.
2. I'm going to Beijing ~~whereas~~ because I'd like to study Chinese medicine.
3. They didn't like their hotel room ~~while~~ so they complained to the manager.
4. ✓ (*although* would be more formal)
5. He wanted to give up learning Russian because it's too hard ~~so he can't do it~~.
6. ✓
7. A: Why didn't you like her? B: ~~Since~~ Because she is always too busy to talk to us.
8. ✓

Note: in 5, two conjunctions are not possible.

3   *Answers for the author who wrote the exercise*

1. I want to take a course in order to improve my Japanese.
2. Since I've been doing yoga exercises, I feel much fitter and stronger.
3. When I'm bored, I watch too much TV.
4. I'd like to visit Sydney, because I'd like to see the Opera House.
5. All my friends speak more than one foreign language whereas I can only speak a little Spanish.

4   1. Even though   2. Either; or   3. Even if   4. not only; but also   5. Even if

EGT Conjunctions: contrasting 91; *Even though* and *even if* 91d; *Either... or...* 115; *not only ... but also*

5   1. While   2. when   3. Although   4. As / Because   5. Even though   6. because
(*cos* is more informal and used mostly in speaking)   7. while   8. Although (*though* is correct but is more informal)

EGT Conjunctions: contrasting 91; *As, when* or *while*? 39; *Even though* and *even If* 91d

6   1 ~~and~~ or   2. ✓   3. ~~or~~ but   4. ~~as~~ but   5. ~~since~~ but   6. ~~and~~ or

EGT *And, but, either ... or*, etc. (coordinating conjunctions) 88a

7 1. but   2. because / as   3. although   4. because / as   5. Even though / As / Because / Although   6. Not only   7. but also   8. both   9. and

> **EGT** Conjunctions: contrasting 91; *As, because* or *since*? 45

8 *Suggested answers*
2. miss the flight.   3. just fell asleep.   4. the hero died at the end.   5. I can use the Internet more.   6. are older.
Note that *in order to* and *so as not to* are more formal.

> **EGT** *In order to* 175; *So* as a conjunction 323e

9 2. so that   3. Whereas   4. So   5. until   6. in order to   7. and

Determiners

1a two billion; each; two million; every; Most; this; many; the; all; the
1b 1. many   2. all   3. a lot of / many; many   4. a   5. the   6. other

> **EGT** Determiners (*the, my, some, this*) 98

2 1. an   2. a   3. an   4. a   5. a   6. a   7. an   8. an   9. an   10. a

> **EGT** *A/an* and *the* 1

3 1. The sun; the garden   2. X; the world   3. X   4. the newspaper; the radio
5. X; the Mojave Desert   6. X; the UK   7. the poor   8. The M1 motorway
9. the Nile; the Amazon   10. the moon

4 The Life is very expensive ... The economy ... The Minister of Education ... the economic situation ... the things will not get better. ... The Unemployment ... getting the jobs ...

5 1. any   2. any; any   3. some (*any* is also possible, but people most commonly use *some* in offers of food and drink); some   4. some; some   5. any; some; any

> **EGT** *Any* as a determiner 34a; *Some* as a determiner 325a

6 1. its   2. this   3. little   4. their   5. our   6. other

> **EGT** Determiners (*the, my, some, this*) 98

7 2. Anoma   3. Ulla   4. Richard   5. Joanna

> **EGT** More than one determiner 100b; *Both* 60

8 2. Every   3. None   4. One   5. Both   6. All

> **EGT** More than one determiner 100b; *No, none* and *none of* 222

9 2. **such** a wonderful present   3. **few** people   4. **enough** money   5. **any** value
6. **another** coffee; **some** biscuits   7. **Several** people   8. My **two** best friends
9. Both **her** parents   10. **Every** one of the customers

10a 2. I don't want these **books**; I want those ~~books~~.
   5. I don't need any more **pens**. I already have several ~~pens~~.
   6. I can't decide which of the two **sweaters** I like. Shall I buy both ~~sweaters~~?

10b *Changes to the sentences which were not crossed out:*
   3. That's mine over there.   4. … he burnt **every one**.
   7. … Lilian would not show us **hers**.   8. Is this one **yours**?

   EGT Determiners used as pronouns 101

11 *Answers for the author who wrote the exercise*
   1. clothes   2. my wife   3. the guitar   4. books about computer programming
   5. raincoat   6. clothes

12 2. Half of the apple is on the table; the other (half) is on the floor.
   3. None of them / None of the girls was wearing shoes. (It is also very common to hear people say: ***None** of the girls **were** wearing shoes.*)
   4. Both of them / Both men / Both of the men were asleep.
   5. Neither of them / Neither woman was wearing glasses.
   6. All of them / All of the boys / All the boys were carrying books.

13 1. little   2. a few   3. few   4. a few   5. a few   6. little   7. a little

   EGT Determiners and types of noun 99

Discourse markers

1 1. So   2. okay   3. Right   4. Anyway   5. well

   EGT Discourses markers 104; Adverbs as discourse markers (*anyway, finally*) 20

2 1. All are possible.   2. right / okay / fine   3. right / now / so / okay
   4. right / now / so / okay   5. actually

   EGT Discourses markers 104; *Actually* as a discourse marker 7b

3 1. Right / Okay   2. Fine / Right   3. Anyway   4. Actually   5. Firstly / Okay

   EGT Discourses markers 104; *Anyway* as a discourse marker 35b

4 2. **Firstly**, it will be bad for the environment. **Secondly**, it will mean heavy traffic. **What's more**, it will look ugly.
   3. I can't work late tonight. **For a start**, I have to babysit for my sister. **On top of that**, I've worked late two evenings this week already, **so** why don't you …
   4. **In general**, at least two teachers are ill every week, **so** we have a list …
   5. It was a long night; **to begin with**, we lost our keys … **And then** we had to phone Jason … **In the end**, it was 3 am when we got to bed!

   EGT Discourses markers 104 (Ordering what we say)

5 *Possible answers*
2. my rent is very expensive and I have to pay bills as well.
3. no one failed.
4. they don't need you like dogs do.
5. I haven't studied any science subjects at school.

EGT Discourse markers that monitor what we say 104b (Saying something in another way)

6 1. Absolutely   2. Definitely   3. Exactly   4. Probably   5. Certainly

EGT Discourse markers as responses 104c; Adverbs as short responses (*definitely, certainly*) 21

7 1. b   2. a   3. b   4. a   5. a

EGT Discourse markers showing attitude 104d

8 1. We should **perhaps** ask … (*or* We should ask for permission, **perhaps**. *or* **Perhaps** we should ask …)
2. There are **roughly** 20 candles … (*or* There are 20 candles left in the box, **roughly**.)
3. Can you **just** close the door?
4. It's **sort of** hot in here.
5. She was **arguably** the best flute player … (*or* She was the best flute player of her generation, **arguably**. *or* **Arguably**, she was …)

EGT Discourse markers: sounding less direct 104e

9 1. b   2. d   3. e   4. c   5. a

EGT Discourse markers: interjections (*Oh! Gosh!*) 104g; Interjections 179

10 1. Firstly   2. Secondly   3. thirdly   4. On the one hand   5. on the other hand
6. Moreover   7. In addition   8. In conclusion

11 1. That's terrible!   2. Oh really?   3. That's a shame!   4. That's amazing!   5. Exactly!

EGT Discourse markers as responses 104c

12 1. Oh really?   2. Definitely   3. That's amazing.   4. Oh no!   5. Absolutely

13 3, 4, 5 are not suitable. These answers are what the author who wrote this exercise would say in these situations:

3. That's really interesting.   4. That's awful.   5. Absolutely.

EGT Discourse markers as responses 104c; Adverbs as short responses 21

14 *Possible answers*
1. We're going to have a new boss.
2. I heard that the only cinema in town is going to close down.
3. I've been offered a new job!
4. The reason why they left so early was because Kevin had to catch an early flight.

English Grammar Today Workbook

Ellipsis and substitution

1   2 …and ~~we~~ danced …   3. … sorry ~~that~~ you …   4. …and ~~they~~ had…   5. …but ~~I~~
can't remember…   6. …or ~~he~~ emailed…   7 …and ~~it~~ ran out of…   8. afraid ~~that~~ he …

    EGT Ellipsis 116; Textual ellipsis 116a

2   2. … but I don't ~~criticise her too much~~.
3. When it is ~~working~~ …
4. … but fortunately everyone else on the boat can ~~swim~~.
5. … and her sister is ~~a fan of the Giants~~ too.

3a *Possible answers*
1. An advertisement for a language school or course   2. A newspaper headline
3. A holiday brochure   4. A recipe   5. An 'accommodation wanted' column in a
newspaper

3b *Possible answer; a small 'personal' advertisement in a newspaper*
Student looking for holiday job. Willing to work very hard. Has own car. Contact
Sean. Tel: 84076231.

    EGT Situational ellipsis 116b; Newspaper headlines ○

4   2. They don't want to ~~buy another car~~.   3. No. Sorry, I didn't ~~ring Tom~~.
4. Yes, she could ~~stay with you~~.   5. Yes, we have ~~got time~~.
6. Yeah, they are ~~getting married~~.

5   2. **Do you** know what …   3. **Are** you ready …   4. **It's** too late … (*you're /
we're too late* are also possible here)   5. **Be** careful …   6. **Do you** need …
7. **There are** lots of things … (*I have* or *I've got* are also possible)
8. A: **Have you** tried phoning …
   B: Yeah but **there's** nobody … (B: *Yeah but there was* … is also possible).

6   2. ~~I~~ wonder…   3. ~~I~~ saw… ; ~~she~~ said she was going to work…   4. ~~It~~ sounds good.
5. ~~I~~ don't agree.   6. ~~We~~ hope you arrived…   7. B: ~~It~~ should be…   8. ~~I~~ expect …

7   2. A: **He** wasn't happy, was he? B: … **he** got really cross.
3. A: **You** wrote to the bank to complain, did you? B: Yes, and **I** got a reply …
4. B: Yeah, **they** went last week.
5. B: **They** got confused … A: Yes, but **it was a** good thing **that** they had a map…

8a 2. neither does   3. neither is Mark   4. so do   5. so is

8b *Answer for the author who wrote the exercise*
I like tennis but don't like swimming. I like golf and cricket but not rugby. I watch a lot
of football on television but don't like playing it. I don't like horse-racing or baseball
but my uncle does.

8c 2. I'm afraid not.   3. I expect not. (*I don't expect so* is also possible here.)   4. I think so.

    EGT Substitution 336; *So as a substitute form* 323c; *Neither do I, Nor can she* 220d

9a *Possible answer*
Good to hear you got there safely. Hope you have a great holiday. Very cold here so
really envy you!

9b *Possible answer*
Navy lifts ban on women in submarines

 Newspaper headlines **○**

10b *Possible answer*
A: How about a beach holiday?
B: Er, don't know. Did that last year. What do you think about a walking holiday in the mountains?
A: Mmm. Not hot enough.
A: OK, shall we try Tunisia?
B: Too far, isn't it?
A: Well, I'd like that. Haven't been there.
B: Ok, good idea. Let's try Tunisia.

Future

1   1. Will; shall   2. will   3. won't   4. 'll; shall   5. will; won't *or* won't; will
6. will   7. won't; will (*shan't*; *shall* is also possible but more formal)
8. shall (*will* is also possible if the speaker is asking for information rather than inviting a suggestion.)
Note: In 2, 4 and 5 *'ll* and *will* are both possible. *'ll* is more informal.

 Future: *will* and *shall* 138; *Will* 384; *Shall* 320

2   2. is going to get
3. is going to decorate
4. I'm going to close *or* I'll close
5. 'll *or* will spend.
6. 's going to rain
7. Are you going to be
8. 'm going to watch
Note: In 4 *I'll* shows an instant decision, made at the moment of speaking. In 6 *It's going to rain* is a prediction based on current evidence and knowledge. In 7 *Will you be at home or in the office…* is more direct. *Are you going to be…* is more polite.

 Future 134; *Will* 384; *Be going to* 135; Future: present continuous to talk about the future (*I'm working tomorrow*) 136

3   1. Do you think ~~she wears it~~ she'll wear it? (*or* she will)
2. ~~go~~ are going to go *or* are going
3. ~~go~~ is going … (*is going to go* is also possible but *is going* is more likely.)
4. I ~~learn~~. I'm learning *or* I'm going to learn. *I'm learning* refers to arrangements that have already been made; *I'm going to learn* announces a future intention.
5. ~~It really hurts him~~. It's really going to hurt … (*going to* is a prediction based on current evidence and knowledge. *It'll really hurt* is possible but less likely)
6. Their theatre group ~~performs~~ is performing … (*Their theatre group is going to perform* is also possible but *is performing* is more likely as it refers to plans that have already been made.)
Note: In 6, *are going to* and *are performing* may also be used since it refers to a group and both singular and plural may be used with groups.

4   1. b   2. a   3. b   4. a   5. a   6. a   7. a
Notes: In 3, *be about to* refers to the very near future. In 3, 5 and 6 *is to* is very formal and official. *About to* is not used with a specific time reference. In 5, the present continuous *The ferry's leaving* could also be used here. In 6, *visits* is possible

English Grammar Today Workbook

but it's more likely to occur in newspaper and media reports: *Vietnamese president visits Singapore.*

5 1. be studying   2. be thinking   3. be buying   4. have bought   5. have read; have finished   6. be seeing   7. be performing   8. be skiing

> **EGT** Future continuous (*I will be working*) 139; Future perfect simple (*I will have worked eight hours*) 142

6 2. 'll have been living   3. will have run   4. will have sold   5. will have washed   6. will have been writing

> **EGT** Future perfect simple (*I will have worked eight hours*) 142; Future perfect continuous (*I will have been working here ten years*) 141

7a something <u>would go</u> wrong … We <u>were planning</u> to stay … I <u>was to speak</u> at the Trade Convention … Sarah <u>was beginning to feel</u> unwell … We <u>were going to take</u> the night flight …

7b 1. were planning   2. was going to drive   3. was   4. would / should never see

> **EGT** Future in the past 140

8 *Suggested answer*
I'm flying from Heathrow to St. Petersburg. **A guide will meet us** and take us to our hotel. On the third day **there is going to be** a visit to the Hermitage Museum and **I'll also be exploring** the city on my own. **We will then be taken** by train to Moscow and **will transfer** to a hotel there. In Moscow **I'm going to be visiting** the Novodevichy Convent and the Kremlin. When we are in St Petersburg, **there'll be a special gala ballet** performance when **caviar will be served**.

Hedges and downtoners

1 2. possibly   3. Maybe   4. sort of   5. I feel   6. We reckon   7. just

> **EGT** Hedges 162

2 1. Maybe (*or* We feel *or* It's possible)   2. We feel (*or* Maybe *or* It's possible)
3. Would you mind   4. It's possible   5. We are likely

3 2. slightly   3. only just   4. a tiny bit   5. barely   6. kind of

> **EGT** Downtoners 108

4 1. a bit (*or* slightly *or* somewhat)   2. somewhat (*or* a bit *or* slightly)
3. only just (*or* hardly)   4. slightly (*or* a bit *or* somewhat)   5. hardly

5 1. b   2. a   3. a   4. a   5. b

> **EGT** Hedges 162; Modal expressions 271b

6 1. barely   2. slightly   3. somewhat   4. only just   5. a tiny bit

7 *Suggested answers*
2. Did you want some more soup?
3. Okay ladies and gentlemen, if you would follow me, please.

4. What was your name, please sir? (using the past tense in this situation is less direct than the present *What is …*) *or* Could I ask for your name, please sir?

5. Did you need more time? *or* Would you like some more time?

6. I was wondering if you could open the window. I'm feeling really warm. *or* Would you mind opening the window …

 Hedges 162; Changing tenses and verb forms 271b

8 *Suggested answers*

Can I ask you about your next album? Will you bring out another album before the end of the year?

Do you like all of your albums? Which one is your favourite?

Do you mind if I ask you about your relationship with the other members of the band? Do you get on well with them?

How about the future? Will you be doing another tour soon?

Would you mind if I asked about your name? What do your friends call you?

 Hedges 162; Two-step questions 271b

Imperatives

1 1, 3, 4, 5, 6, 8, 9, 10

 Imperative clauses (*Be quiet!*) 172

2 *Possible answers*
1. Don't move! *or* Stay where you are! *or* Someone call an ambulance!
2. Sit down everyone.   3. Have a great trip!   4. Turn it the other way.
5. Come with us to the theatre.

3a 1, 2, 4, 5

3b *Possible answers*

1. Be quiet, please.   2. Stand up, please.   4. Turn off the radio if you don't mind.   5. Try not to forget your toothbrush.

4 1. let's not   2. let's not   3. don't   4. don't let's   5. Do not   6. let's

5 1. Go (*or* Come); Have   2. come; stay   3. Try (*or* Have)   4. be; call

 Imperatives as offers and invitations 172h

6a 1, 2, 5

6b 1. Have a seat.   2. Let's not say anything …   5. Let's not forget …

7 1. b   2. b   3. a   4. a   5. b

 Question tags commonly used after imperatives 172g

8 *Suggested answers*
2. Come to the nightclub with us.   3. Try these muffins that Jamie made.
4. Leave your car at home and travel with us.   5. Call to see me in my new office.
6. Let's go to a restaurant this evening.

 Imperative clauses (*Be quiet!*) 172

9 *Possible answers*

    1. B: ~~Ask someone else~~. I'm afraid I don't have a watch.

    2. B: ~~Don't ask me~~. I'm afraid I'm not from here.

    3. B: ~~You~~ Use mine and I'll use this pencil.

Infinitives

1   1. ✓   2. I can't ~~to~~ reach the top shelf.   3. We don't use that knife ~~for to cut~~ for cutting the bread. *or* We don't use that knife to cut the bread.   4. ✓   5. ✓

  6. He wanted to find a good job in New York.

    EGT Infinitives with and without *to* 174

2   1. want   2. to talk   3. to sell   4. to find   5. To be   6. use   7. tidy   8. to take

3   1. to   2. to   3. to   4. to   5. to   6. X   7. X   8. X   9. to   10. X   11. X   12. X   13. X

Modality

1   2. I can speak   3. I could play chess   4. Can you ride   5. Can't you swim?; I can now but I couldn't until I was fourteen.   6. She can't write text messages.

    EGT *Can, could* 66

2   2. can   3. was able to (we don't use *could* to talk about single events in the past)   4. could   5. be able to *or* not be able to (we don't use *can/could* with another modal verb)   6. can't, am not able to *or* won't be able to

    EGT *Can, could* 66; *Be able to* 54b

3   2. C   3. A   4. C   5. A   6. B

    EGT Modality: meanings and uses 209

4   1. might   2. will   3. should   4. must   5. could (or, less likely, *might*)   6. shall (*will* is possible but *shall* is more likely in this formal context)

    EGT Modality: meanings and uses 209; *Could* 95; *May* 202; *Might* 206; *Shall* 320; *Should* 321; *Will* 384

5   2. We ought to help (*should* is also possible)   3. You needn't tell (*don't have to* is also possible but less likely)   4. I simply must call (or *have to*)   5. Does she need to study   6. Should we offer   7. I have to live

    EGT Modal verbs: uses 209b

6   2. think   3. seems   4. tends *or* seems   5. sounds (*seems* is possible but less likely)

    EGT Modality: other verbs 211

7   1. appears   2. feel   3. reckons   4. gather   5. suppose   6. looks

    EGT Modality: verbs expressing possibility 211a

8   2. A (this is formal)   3. B   4. A   5. B   6. B

    EGT Modal verbs: uses 209b; *Can:* uses 65b; *May:* uses 202b

9 *Answers for the author who wrote the exercise*
1. I can   2. I can't   3. I can't   4. I'm able to   5. I'm not able to

10 *Answers for the author who wrote the exercise*
1. I was able to   2. I wasn't able to   3. I could   4. I could   5. I could

11a *Possible answers*
2. there **may** soon be   3. **might** solve   4. **may not** have to
5. **seems to** work   6. **should** be   7. **could** benefit

11b *Possible answer for space travel*
Space travel **may** become common in the next 50 years, with the result that people
will be able to take holidays in space. However, long flights could cause problems so
scientists will have to find solutions before astronauts can reach distant planets. Apart
from space holidays and exploration, space travel **may** lead to important scientific
discoveries about the earth. We **could**, for example, learn a lot about the global climate,
or we **might** learn more about the oceans by observing them from space.

 Modality: meanings and uses 209

12   2. N   3. S   4. S   5. N   6. W   7. N   8. W

 Modal verbs: uses 209b

13 *Answers for the author who wrote the exercise*
1. I ought to back up all my files every week.   2. I should be in bed by 11 o'clock.
3. I could get up earlier.   4. I ought to email my friends more often.
5. I don't need to go to the dentist for a check up.   6. I should take a holiday.
7. I don't have to drive to work.   8. I don't need to work harder on my English.

Modal verbs: *can, could, may, might, be able to*

1   1. Can; can't   2. could   3. Can/Could   4. Could; can   5. Can; Could
6. could   7. can   8. can/could

 Can 65; *Could* 95

2   1. May I help you, sir?
2. Could you ride a bike when you were five?
3. Might it help if I came a little earlier tomorrow?
4. Can you read these bus times for me? I don't have my glasses.
Note: *Can/could I help you sir?* and *Could you read these bus times for me?* are also
possible.

 Can, could or *may*? 66

3   1. a   2. b   3. b   4. a   5. b   6. a   7. b   8. b

 Can, could or *may*? 66; *Could, may* and *might* 96

4   1. Can your brother ~~to~~ play the piano?
2. … but the police ~~could~~ were able to capture them within a few hours.

3. A: ~~May~~ Can/Could you help me to put these chairs out for the meeting?
4. It's snowing in New York, so her flight this evening ~~can~~ could be delayed. (*may* and *might* are also possible)
5. Were you able to get in touch with Harry yesterday?
6. There are a number of things you cannot (written as one word) …

 Can 65; Could 95; Be able to 54b

5 *Possible answers*
1. When I was a child, I could sing a song in German but I've forgotten it now.
2. By the end of this year, I'll be able to apply for a place at university.
3. One day I might take a year off and travel round the world.
4. Tomorrow I may go and see a film with a friend.
5. If I practised every day, my English could get better.
6. I can't speak Chinese but I can cook some Chinese meals.

6 2. She fell off the boat into the river but she **was able to** swim to the bank.
3. **You may well be** right, but I still think we should be careful.
4. **Human beings could** travel to distant planets one day.
5. **Will you be able to** pick Georgie up from school tomorrow?

 May as well and *might as well* 203

7 1. Could / May / Might I make suggestion. (*Might* is more formal than *may* and *may* is more formal than *could*.)
2. You could talk to Professor White. He is very helpful.
3. May I help you to sort these papers out? (or *Could* or, very formal, *Might*)
4. Could you meet / Are you able to you meet us for lunch tomorrow? (*Are you able* is more formal than *could*.)
5. May / Could / Can I take your coat, madam? (*Could* is less formal than *may*, and *can* is less formal than *could*.)
6. I'm sorry, I can't help you.

 Could, may and *might* 96; Requests 316

8 2. Can / Could you come to a meeting to plan a presentation? (*Could* is more formal)
3. Can you speak any other languages? *or* Are you able to speak any other languages?
4. May I leave work early today? (*Can, could* or, very formal, *might* are also possible)
5. We might as well stay at home this evening since the weather is so bad. *or* We may as well stay … (*We could stay at home* is also possible)
6. Take sun cream with you because people can get sunburnt at this time of year.

 Could, may and might 96; Requests 316

Modal verbs: *must, have to, have got to, need*

1a 1. must / have to   2. have to   3. do you have to   4. must / have to
5. Do you have to (Preferred to *must*)   6. has to / must   7. have to
1b 1. mustn't   2. don't have to   3. don't have to   4 Don't you have to   5 mustn't

 *Must 216; Have to 156*

2 1. d But I said it had to be cheap.   2. a You don't have to shout.
3. b I 'll have to / must check my diary.   4. c You must / 'll have to / 've got to
go to bed.
Note: In 2 *don't have to* means it isn't necessary to shout. *Mustn't* is also possible
but sounds more formal.

3 1. had to go   2. had to hire   3. 'll have to get up (*must* is also possible)
4. ('ll) have to let / must let   5. did you have to apologise

4 1. need   2. needn't have   3. needn't   4. doesn't need   5. needs   6. don't need

 Need 218

5 *Possible answers*
You have to wear a swimming hat all the time. You *mustn't take your belongings
with you. In fact you have to leave them in a locker. You *mustn't dive in the shallow
end. You *mustn't take any food, drink or animals into the pool area. You need to take
all the swimming equipment back to the reception when you leave. You *mustn't go on
the slide if someone else is already on there. Children under 14 have to be accompanied
by an adult.
Note: *We also use *can't* instead of *mustn't* to show that something is not allowed.

 Can 65

6 *Possible answers*
2. They must still be in the front door. *or* I must have left them in the front door.
3. He must be very disappointed.
4. There has to be a leak somewhere. *or* I must have left a tap on.
5. There must be some problem / an accident. *or* There must have been an accident.
6. Everyone / They must be out somewhere. *or* Everyone / They must have gone out.

 Must: uses 216b

7 1. b   2. a   3. b   4. b

8 1. They'll have ~~got~~ to   2. I ~~must~~ had to work   3. ~~Does she must~~ Must she
talk ... *or* Does she have to talk   4. There ~~don't must~~ mustn't be any noise
5. You~~'ve to must~~ You have to get / You must get / You need to get
6. She ~~don't~~ doesn't need to / needn't come for very long.   7. We didn't need to
bring   8. You must ~~to~~ come and   9. You ~~needn't~~ don't need a coat

9 1. e conclusion   2. c obligation   3. f conclusion   4. a obligation
5. d conclusion   6. b obligation (or lack of it)

 Modality: meanings and uses 209

Modal verbs: *should* and *ought to*

1a 2. should eat   3. should include   4. should make up   5. shouldn't keep
6. should try   7. should be able to   8. shouldn't choose   9. shouldn't wait

English Grammar Today Workbook

1b 1. ought to be   2. ought to eat   3. ought to include   4. ought to make up   5. ought not to keep (not as common as *shouldn't*)   6. ought to try   7. ought to be able to   8. ought not to choose   9. ought not to wait

EGT *Should* 321; *Ought to* 253

2 *Possible answers*

You should eat fresh fruit and veg as soon as you can. You shouldn't store it for a long time.

You shouldn't overcook fruit and veg. It's best to use a steamer or a microwave.

You should try to use as little water as possible to cook fruit and veg. You should use the cooking water in a soup because you'll keep some of the lost vitamins and minerals.

You ought not to leave any vegetables open to the air, light or heat after you have cut them up. You should cover and chill them but you shouldn't leave them in water.

You should try to avoid adding fat or rich sauces to vegetables or sugar to fruit. You should try to keep it natural.

Note: In all cases *ought to* and *ought not to* are possible but less common.

3 *Possible answers*

2. He should be wearing a coat. *or* He ought to have worn a coat.

3. We ought to put more lights in this room. *or* You ought to turn the light on.

4. They should open more checkouts. *or* There ought to be more people working.

5. There should be a lid on the kettle.

6. The hairdryer shouldn't be near water.

4 1. Shouldn't you ~~to~~ go now?   2. ~~Do we ought~~ Ought we to tell   3. ✓ (*should* is often used as the tag for *ought to*)   4. They ~~don't ought to have~~ ought not to have stayed so late. *or* shouldn't have   5. we ~~would~~ should get   6. what ~~would~~ should be done   7. They should ~~bought~~ buy / have bought   8. I ~~sould~~ should finish   9. should ~~be~~ have been fixed   10. He should have had better advice

5 *Possible answers*

2. It shouldn't be longer than half an hour. *or* It should only take half an hour.

3. You should find a parking space nearby.

4. It shouldn't have taken so long. *or* It should only have taken an hour.

5. It should have been sunny. *or* It shouldn't have been raining.

6. You shouldn't have!

7. Should I phone Flora to let her know?

8. I shouldn't have stayed up so late last night. *or* I should have gone to bed earlier.

9. He ought to have locked the garage door. *or* He should have locked the garage door.

10. I ought to have left a note. *or* I ought to have told someone where I was going.

6 *Possible answers*

2. If you want to cancel the agreement … (*or* If you'd like to cancel …)

3. Should you need the emergency services … (*or* If you should need …)

4. I would really like to come with you. Thank you.

5. I should think that an hour would be plenty of time. *or* I think that an hour should be plenty of time.

6. Should we tell someone that we're leaving?

Modal verbs: *will, shall* and *would*

1   1. will   2. 'll   3. won't   4. Will   5. will   6. will   7. won't   8. will not

 Will 384; *Shall* 320; *Would* 393

2   *Suggested answers*
2. I'll have a black coffee, please.   3. Will you close the door, please?   4. That'll be Cath.   5. Will you stop making that noise?   6. I'll phone you tomorrow. *or* I'll phone mum tomorrow.

3   2. e   3. e   4. h   5. c   6. b   7. f   8. a   9. g (*or* e)

4   *Suggested answers*
Hamish: I'll organise food. Shall we have cheese, biscuits and grapes?
Carlo: I'll design the tickets. I'll be able to print them at work.
Katie: I'll write the quiz questions.
Jo: I'll help Katie with the quiz.
Frank: Shall I ask *The Bridge* if they're free? *or* I'll ask *The Bridge* if they're free.
Lara: We'll have to get a licence. I'll do that.
Helen: Will everyone help with the setting up and clearing up? *or* Would anyone be
      able to help with …

5   1. I'll ~~must~~ have to finish *or* I must finish   2. I'll explain to you how to get there.
3. I'll do my best to get the job.   4. I hope he ~~shall~~'ll reply to my e-mail.
5. ✓ (quite formal)   6. When you ~~will~~ arrive   7. ~~will be~~ is arranged.   8. It ~~will~~'d be a great idea *or* It ~~will be~~'s   9. B: Yes. ~~I'll~~ I will.   10. we ~~shall~~'d be delighted.

6a 2. The food was terrible. I think **I'll** write and complain.
3. We **shall** see each other on Friday, **shan't** we?
4. **Will** you bring us the bill when you're ready?

6b 1. **I'd** suggest   2. **I'd** advise   3. **I'd** recommend

Modal verbs: *would, would like, would rather, would prefer*

1   *Answers for the author who wrote the exercise*
2. I'd have a coffee with some friends.
3. I'd have some felafels and hummus in a restaurant near where I live.
4. I'd meet Nelson Mandela, because he has amazing strength of character.
5. I'd be walking in the hills near my house with my dog.
6. I'd go somewhere hot and sunny with my family because it's cold and wet here.

 Would 393

2   1. to make   2. Would   3. I'd like   4. likes   5. Would   6. like to

 Would like 394

3a 2. I'd liked to have learnt the piano when I was young but I didn't get the chance.
3. I'd like to have asked more questions at the meeting but we didn't have time.
4. My sister would like to have been a doctor but she didn't get the grades.
5. We'd like to have gone skiing last year but it was too expensive.

4a 2. Would you rather have fruit than a cooked breakfast?
3. Would you rather start work early and finish early than start late and finish in the
      evening?

4. Would you rather read a book than watch tv?

5. Would you rather jump in a pool of freezing water than do a parachute jump?

Note: *Would you prefer to* is also possible in each sentence.

 Would rather 395a

4b *Possible answers*

2. Millie would much rather have fruit and yoghurt than a cooked breakfast.

3. Millie and Aran would rather start work early and finish early than start work late and work in the evening but Roland would much rather start work late.

4. Shara would rather read a book than watch TV.

5. Only Millie would prefer to do a parachute jump than jump into freezing water.

5   1. a   2. a   3. a and b   4. a

Modality: expressions with *be*

1   1. It is likely to rain in the next few hours.

2. The Norbeth museum is due to open on 23rd May.

3. The plane is about to land.

4. I can't talk now. We're about to have dinner.

5. There are likely to be long delays because of the fog.

6. The Dublin flight is due to arrive at 13:30.

 About 2; Modal expressions with *be* 53d

2   2. Jim is bound to be late. He always is!

3. You're supposed to send your CV with your application.

4. *Zendo* is set to become the biggest maker of sports goods in Europe.

5. She was going to apply for the job but she changed her mind.

6. She wasn't able to finish her report in time for the annual meeting.

7. It is a bad plan and it is certain to fail.

8. The meeting was to start at 3 pm, but it didn't start till 3.30. (*or* The meeting was to have started …)

 Modal expressions with *be* 53d

3   2. Which room are we supposed to go to for the next class?

3. Is everyone allowed to use the photocopier, or just the staff?

4. Are we meant to sign these forms?

5. Were people forced to vote for the President or did they have a free choice?

6. Is it likely that we'll make contact with people from other planets this century?

4   *Suggested answers*

2. Are you likely to be in the library tomorrow?

3. Are you due to take any exams this term?

4. Am I / Are we allowed to use the computer lab during the lunch break?

5. Is the dictionary meant to be used in class or just for homework? *or* Are we meant to / allowed to use the dictionary in class or just for homework?

5   *Answers for the author who wrote the exercise*

2. I was supposed to make an appointment at the dentist's but I forgot.

3. I'm likely to go away on holiday during the next few months.
4. I'm sure to check my emails today or tomorrow.
5. It's bound to rain a lot this summer!

Modality: tense

1a

can		would	✓	should	✓	might	✓
must		may		will		could	✓

Note: We can refer to past time by using *can't, must, mustn't, may* and *may not +*
have + -ed participle.
It **must have been** *difficult for you when your school closed.*
He **may have left** *a message on the answerphone; I'll check.*
She **can't have been** *at the meeting yesterday – she's away in Hong Kong.*

1b 2. P   3. P (by adding *have + -ed* participle)   4. Pr   5. F
6. Pr (*will* here is used for habits in the present)

 Modality: tense 210

2 1. would; might   2. could   3. would; couldn't   4. had to; could   5. can; will

3 2. I **should have been** in London, but because of the snow …
3. I'**d** normally go online and read the news, then I'**d** answer a few emails.
4. We **had to** wait a long time before getting our money back. (*or*, less likely,
We **had had to …**)
5. **Were you able to** help out in some way to organise the school show?
6. We **ought to have got** in touch with her immediately.

 Must 216; Should 321; Will 384; Would 393; Have to 156; Be able to 54b; Ought to 253

4 2. She said she used to go to work by bus but now she drives.
3. They said that they would need more money. (or, if it is still true, *They said that*
they will need more money.)
4. She said she might/may have sent it to the wrong address. (*May* is more formal.)
5. She said I could use the office computer. (*Might* is also possible, but formal)
6. He said the package had to be delivered by five o'clock. (*Must* is also possible if *five*
o'clock is still in the future)

 Reported speech: indirect speech 314, Backshift 314f

5 *Answers for the author who wrote the exercise*
1. have studied law instead   2. stayed longer in Thailand   3. phoned my brother
yesterday   4. sing lots of songs by heart   5. play tennis   6. afford a new car

Negation

1a 2. don't   3. aren't; can't   4. not   5. no   6. didn't; not   7. never
1b 1. can't; nothing / no   2. not   3. aren't; either   4. un-; none   5. never
6. didn't; wasn't; couldn't   7. unlikely; doesn't / won't; won't / doesn't

 Negation 219

English Grammar Today Workbook

2   2. Don't take an umbrella.

3. Haven't we met before? *or* Have we not met before? (more formal)

4. Mightn't he be late? (quite formal)

5. There are no useful books in the library on the subject. (*or* There aren't any …)

6. None of my friends like cooking. *or* Some of my friends don't like cooking. *or* None of my friends don't like cooking. (**Note** the double negative. It means the same as 'All of my friends like cooking.')

7. Jules and Petra won't be coming.

8. Nothing happened when I rang the bell. (*or,* less likely, Something happened when I didn't ring the bell. *or* Nothing happened when I didn't ring the bell.)

9. I hope you're not going to ask for more money.

10. Not to have asked Julio for his help would have been difficult. (*or* To have asked Julio for his help wouldn't have been difficult.)

3   2. If you're not **in the least bit** interested, let me know.

3. She didn't say anything **at all** to me. *or* She didn't say anything to me **at all**.

4. **Not for a moment** did I think I'd get the job. *or* I didn't think **for a moment** I'd get the job.

5. She **rarely** asked for advice. *or* **Rarely** did she ask for advice. (even more formal)

6. A: Do you mind if we sit here? B: No. **Not in the least.**

EGT Negative adverbs: *hardly, seldom*, etc. 219f; Negation: emphasising 219g

Nouns

1a   egg; hole; shell; pin; pan; water; water; egg; minutes; salt

1b   1. water, salt   2. minutes

EGT Nouns 226

2   2. teeth   3. children   4. sheep   5. women   6. mice   7. feet   8. fish

EGT Nouns: Forming the plural of nouns 229b

3   gender gap; lifestyle; fast food; junk food; blood pressure; heart attacks; health scare; wake-up call

EGT Nouns: Compound nouns 227

4a   shopkeeper; runway; website (sometimes written as two words); windscreen; bottle opener (*bottle-opener* is also possible); bathroom; greenhouse

4b   1. website   2. shopkeeper   3. runway   4. greenhouse   5. windscreen   6. bottle opener   7. bathroom

5a   2. binoculars   3. sunglasses   4. shorts   5. scissors   6. pyjamas   7. glasses   8. trousers

EGT Nouns only used in the plural 231b

5b   2. pyjamas   3. scissors   4. binoculars   5. sunglasses   6. trousers   7. shorts   8. glasses

6   2. flies / bees / mosquitoes /insects (any flying insect)   3. sheep / birds / geese / doves (any bird that flies in large groups)   4. flowers   5. rules / regulations / guidelines   6. cows / cattle / goats / sheep / deer / elephants

EGT Collective nouns (group words) 231c

7   2. Congratulations   3. surroundings   4. earnings   5. belongings   6. dislikes

🍁 Nouns only used in the plural 231b

8   2. is   3. is / are   4. is   5. seems / seem   6. was / were
9   firefighter; flight attendant; actor; waiter; head teacher; Chair/Chairperson

🍁 Nouns and gender 232

10   2. for   3. in   4. into *or* on   5. of   6. of   7. for   8. to   9. into   10. to

🍁 Nouns and prepositions 233

11   2. X   3. a rise in temperature   4. a sense of frustration   5. X   6. feeling of loneliness

🍁 Noun phrases: Complements 235c

12   *Answers for the author who wrote the exercise*
a keyboard (compound); headphones (plural only); sticky tape (uncountable) my glasses (plural only); a cup (countable); sheets of paper (piece word plus uncountable); a phone (countable); a mouse (countable); books (countable); hand-cream (uncountable, compound)

Nouns: countable and uncountable nouns

1a   2. accommodation   3. money; currency (*cash* also possible)   4. luggage; baggage

🍁 Countable and uncountable nouns 228

1b   *Possible answers*
2. hotel, guest house, youth hostel, bed and breakfast, inn
3. Dollar, Euro, Yen, Peso, Krona, etc. *or* coins, notes, bills, travellers cheques.
4. suitcase, bag, rucksack, briefcase

2   1. travel; journeys   2. currency; notes   3. luggage; suitcase
4. accommodation; hotel   5. information; timetable

3a   **countable:** tool question orange wallet piano
uncountable: equipment news furniture advice rice bread progress soap
3b   1.   Have you made any ~~progresses~~ progress …
2.   ✓
3.   I cooked ~~much~~ a lot of rice. Would you like some?
4.   Some of ~~these furnitures are~~ this furniture is very old.
5.   There is ~~a~~ some soap in the cabinet.
6.   This website sells sports ~~equipments~~ equipment. I bought a tennis racket from there.
7.   I have ~~an~~ (some) interesting news for you. *or* … an interesting piece of news
8.   ✓
9.   ✓
10. My parents always give me good **advice**.

4   1. b   2. b   3. a   4. b   5. a   6. b

English Grammar Today Workbook

5   2. flash of   3. X   4. bar of   5. loaf of   6. X   7. piece of / bit of / item of   8. piece of

 Piece words 270

6   *Possible answers*
2. **beautiful weather** when we were in Ireland.   3. **knowledge** of Russian. I did a
course.   4. **experience** of working with children.   5. **poem** about my home town.
6. **homework** where we have to correct the grammar in sentences.   7. **trips** to Japan.
8. **research** into the causes of heart disease.

 Countable and uncountable nouns 228

Objects: direct and indirect objects

1   2. a French-English dictionary   3. an ice-cream seller; a big strawberry cone
4. None (linking verbs such as *be, seem, become* take complements, not an objects)
5. more coffee   6. None (*feel* as a linking verb takes a complement, not an object)
7. me; me   8. me

 Objects 241

2   She gave (me) the link to the site … (everyone) your opinion on world events … The website
offers (users) a list of possible words … You register your email address … the website
sends (you) a message … Then you text your reaction-word to the website on your phone
or enter your word … they send (you) the 'Word of the day' … I send you the link?

 Indirect objects 241b

3   2. Martin bought **his daughter** a computer when she passed her exams.
3. We owe **the bank** a lot of money.
4. Come over tomorrow and I'll cook **you all** a Chinese meal.
5. I'm going to visit Peter in hospital. I'll take **him** some chocolates.
6. My friend Carolina taught **me** the words of a Spanish song.

4   2. Hugh cooked his classmates a wonderful Japanese meal.
3. Luke didn't want to lie to me so he told me the truth.
4. It was our wedding anniversary and our son bought us some chocolates.
5. Kevin needed somewhere to stay so I offered him the spare room in my flat.
6. I couldn't get Arlo on the phone so I sent him an email.
7. Alan liked Jane very much so he sent her a Valentine's Day card.
8. Rita was thirsty so I fetched her a glass of water.

5   1. The children made their dad a cake.   2. Jane sang us a folk song.   3. Sylvia read /
is reading her daughter a bedtime story.   4. Tim bought his wife a bicycle for her
birthday.   5. Richard brought Megan a bunch of flowers.   6. The little boy showed
everyone his drawing.

6   *Answers for the author who wrote the exercise*
1. I sent my grandmother a birthday card last week. 2. I once owed a friend some
money, but I paid it back. 3. I showed my teacher my essay. 4. I always give my best
friend a birthday present. 5. I would never lend my camera to my brother.

Passive

1   2. are manufactured   3. was written   4. was being watched   5. is being
televised   6. be invited   7. should be heated but not boiled   8. were given
9. must be decorated 10. been seen

 Passives 257

2a 1. had been told   2. would be shown   3. could be seen   4. had been given
5. wasn't being helped   6. would be given   7. had been treated   8. was sent

2b 1. past perfect   2. modal simple   3. modal simple   4. past perfect
5. past continuous   6. modal simple   7. past perfect   8. past simple

3   1. ✓ *He got injured* is more common.
2. all the workers got sacked.
3. ✓
4. ~~My hair got cut~~. I had my hair cut.
5. ✓ *I had my mobile stolen* is also correct. *Got stolen* is more informal.
6. ✓ *They always had their holidays paid for by his parents* is correct but more formal.
7. The window got broken. (*I had the window broken* means that the window was
broken on purpose because I asked for it to be broken.)
8. I had the car cleaned.
Note: 1–6 and 8 could be used with *get* in place of *have*. *Get* is more informal. The
standard passive can also be used in all these examples.

4   B: No, but it er explains why **the papers are always criticising them**.
A: They've all got big expensive cars and houses and stuff too.
B: I suppose **they don't want people to ignore them**, do they?
A: Oh well, I'm just jealous. I know **my boss will never pay me** that much.

5   2. Climate change deal has been agreed by European leaders.
3. 500 homes have been damaged by floods.
4. 200 job losses have been announced by a major bank.

6   1. has been created (*or* was created)   2. is being unveiled *or* will be unveiled
3. have also been made *or* were also made   4. painted by   5. being asked

7   The desk was cleared and covered with newspaper. A volcano was made out of clay.
Red clay was used around the top of the volcano to make it look like lava. A hole was
made at the top of the volcano and one teaspoon of baking soda was added. A few
drops of red food colouring and washing-up liquid were put in. Some vinegar was
added and we stood back!

8   1. e with   2. f with   3. d by *or* with   4. a by   5. b in   6. c by

 Passive: other forms 257f

9   1. i   2. f   3. i   4. f

10 *Possible answers*
2. is estimated   3. is believed   4. has been made   5. was told

11 2. Bookings can be made up to seven days before the event.   3. It's hospital policy,
I suppose, so we might not be allowed to see her.   4. We tried again in case we
couldn't be heard.   5. She must have been hurt by what I said to her.

English Grammar Today Workbook

12 *Possible answers*

1. a company answerphone message   2. a hotel   3. a TV serial   4. a bill
5. a train / aeroplane door or window   6. a letter from a club or society

 Passive: uses 257e

Past: past simple, past continuous and present perfect simple

1a 1. e had; was; took   2. d didn't go; had   3. b went; had   4. a looked; needed
5. c travelled; didn't like

1b Sentences 3 and 5 talk about something that happened more than once. *on Saturdays* means 'every Saturday'. In 5, *usually* expresses habit.

 Past simple (*I worked*) 260

2a 1. opened; 1153   2. used; 45 billion   3. 1800; was   4. invented; 200
5. became; 1900   6. signed; million   7. split; had; 120   8. received; 1982; did

2b **Regular forms:** opened used invented signed received
Irregular forms and the three parts of the verbs:
be was/were been   split split split (all forms the same)
become became become   do did done

 Past simple: irregular verbs 260c

3 1. I ~~work~~ worked   2. ~~He did go~~ Did he go (Questions can sometimes have statement form – see 00 – but the correct question form is as here)   3. didn't ~~ate~~ eat out   4. ~~ringed~~ rang   5. You ~~wasn't~~ weren't   6. ~~fail~~ failed

4 2. he was telling   3. We were chatting   4. I was trying   5. were you running?
6. He wasn't listening   7. was driving   8. I wasn't lying

 Past continuous (*I was working*) 259

5 *Possible answers*

2. was crying   3. she was going upstairs   4. I was cooking an egg
5. The sky was getting cloudy   6. No-one was watching

6 2. weren't laughing; saw   3. rang; was falling   4. was watching; took
5. was telling; started   6. were doing; found

 Past continuous or past simple? 261

7 … probably ~~know~~ knew about 5,000 characters. An educated adult ~~was~~ needed to recognise at least 15,000. I ~~was realising~~ realised that I had no idea how many English words I ~~was knowing~~ knew. Unfortunately I ~~learnt not~~ didn't learn many Chinese characters when I ~~was~~ lived / was living there.

8 1. broke   2. walked   3. didn't feel   4. waited   5. didn't taste   6. Did you see him?

9 1. a   2. a   3. b   4. a / b   5. b   6. a

Past: past perfect simple and past perfect continuous

1 2. had (already) started   3. had learnt   4. had written   5. had (already) won

 Past perfect simple (*I had worked*) 263

2 He'd taken the bread out of the oven. He'd folded the clothes. He hadn't taken the clothes upstairs. He had done the washing up. He'd fed the dog. He'd thrown out the flowers but he hadn't emptied the rubbish. He'd cleaned the windows. He hadn't washed the floor. He hadn't turned off the light.

3 2. I went to the party even though Dad had told me not to go.
  3. They hadn't done any preparation but they both passed the exam.
  4. I ate a big breakfast after I had been to the gym. *or* After I'd eaten a big breakfast, I went to the gym.
  5. I went to bed early because I'd had a tiring day.
  6. June went to the hospital as she had promised she'd visit Linda.

4 2. Helen said that they had wanted to see that film but it had been too late.
  3. Paul realised that he had left his credit card in the shop.
  4. They complained that the service hadn't been great and the food had been cold.

  EGT Past perfect simple 263; Reported speech 312

5 He'd been travelling; He'd been feeling; he'd been snacking; She'd been working; He had been really looking forward to

  EGT Past perfect continuous (*I had been working*) 262

6 2. She had been painting the wall. 3. He had been clearing up broken glass.
  4. She'd been making bread. 5. She'd been crying. 6. He hadn't been feeling well.

7 1. heard 2. tasted *or* been tasting 3. known 4. read *or* been reading 5. hated

  EGT Past perfect simple or past perfect continuous 264

8 1. I ~~ever saw~~ 'd ever seen (*ever saw* is correct in American English) 2. If we ~~saw~~ had seen you … 3. … had been ~~stolen~~ stealing 4. They ~~hadn't been hearing~~ hadn't heard … 5. She ~~had watched~~ had been watching …

9a 2. was playing *or* had been playing 3. decided 4. had crossed 5. lived / were living / had been living 6. had been talking 7. hadn't known / didn't know
  8. jumped 9. took 10. was spreading / had spread 11. were trying
  12. didn't believe / hadn't believed 13. realised 14. was happening / had happened 15. had been travelling / had travelled 16. gathered / had gathered / were gathering 17. had raised 18. were walking 19. cheered / was cheering 20. started 21. went

  EGT Past simple 260; Past continuous 259; Past perfect simple 263
  Past perfect continuous 262

Possession

1 1. … the children's clothing department? 2. The boys' bikes… 3. ✓
  4. The men's changing room … 5. ✓ 6. …Britain's highest mountain 7. ✓
  8. ✓ (*Rhys' sister* is also correct). 9. Brendan's mother's friend …
  10. … the government's decision.

Note: in 2 *boy's bikes* would be correct if one boy had more than one bike.

🔖 **EGT** Possession 272

2 2. She borrowed her sister's jacket.   3. Richard is my mother's brother.
4. Ellen's laptop for a week.   5. Fluffy is the name of Linda and Owen's dog.
6. Westminster Abbey is one of London's oldest buildings.

3 1. a   2. b   3. a   4. a   5. a

4 *Possible answers*
Lisa's favourite food is steak.   John's favourite holiday destination is Morocco.
Lisa's favourite film is *Pulp Fiction*.   Ivan's favourite hobby is playing football.
Jacob's favourite type of music is pop. Lisa's favourite holiday destination is Barcelona.
John's favourite hobby is hiking.   The parents' favourite film is *Pulp Fiction*.
The parents' favourite hobby is hiking. The boys' favourite food is fish and chips.

5 2. Kevin is a close friend of mine. (*I am a close friend of his* is also possible)
3. Paul is an uncle of hers.
4. Mrs Lovett is a neighbour of ours.
5. Jason is a brother of Maria's (*or* Jason is a brother of hers)
6. John Whyte is a cousin of theirs.

6 1. a   2. b (*a* is possible but less common)   3. b   4. a   5. a

Prepositions

1 1. across   2. to   3. on   4. above   5. over   6. by   7. after   8. along   9. over
10. between   11. over   12. through   13. next to   14. in front of   15. for   16. about

🔖 **EGT** Prepositions 275; Prepositional phrases 276

2a 1. in   2. for   3. in / at   4. in   5. in   6. in   7. into   8. by   9. during   10. in
11. at   12. at (*in* is also possible)   13. by   14. during / on   15. on   16. in
17. until / for   18. In   19. until

2b *Answer for the author who wrote the exercise*
I plan to travel **to** Sweden next year as I want to learn Swedish **in** six months and then
travel **around** the country before going **to** Denmark **for** a few weeks.

3 1. at; before / after   2. at   3. for; in   4. to; on / near   5. in; on   6. at; in / near
7. By / In   8. on; for   9. by / before / on   10. until / till

Note: In 9, *by* means 'not later than'; *before* means 'at any time before'.

4 1. during   2. in   3. in; for   4. for   5. for; since.   6. till (*till* is a more informal use
of *until*)   7. among   8. between   9. below   10. under

5a **Means of travel**: by train, on foot
Circumstances or the way things happen: by accident, by mistake,
on purpose, in a hurry, in pain, in secret, in love, out of danger
A particular day/part of day: in the evening, at breakfast, on Sunday
Being somewhere else: out of the office, on business
Note: *out of danger* could also be interpreted as 'being somewhere else'

6 *Suggested answers*
On the left, lots of cars are parked **outside** the shops. Lots of people are walking **along** both sides of the street and going **in** and **out** of the shops. Most are walking **on** the pavement, although two people are walking **across** the road. Not many people have walked **onto** the road. The first lampost you see in the picture is **in front of** the Canton bazaar. The Far East café is **opposite** the Canton Bazaar. The sign just **below** the Canton Bazaar says that you can buy furniture **in** the bazaar. Lanterns are hung **across** the street and **outside** each shop. There is a Canadian flag flying **over** one of the buildings.

7 1. in   2. X (*discuss about* is a typical error).   3. with   4. for   5. of
6. about   7. for; from   8. after   9. on   10. with   11. X *He married Julie* is correct;
…is married **to** Julie's brother.   12. for   13. of   14. of   15. on (this preposition can also be omitted in informal English)

8 2. about changing *or* of changing   3. of stealing   4. in working   5. on being able
6. about losing   7. at winning   8. for making

9a 2. them from getting   3. reminds me of walking
9b 1. her for   2. you on   3. us with

10 2. Where was she coming from?   3. Who with / What for?   4. Who for?
5. Who's it by? / What's it about?   6. What for? / Who to?   7. Who with?

Note: 6, *to whom* is very formal and is more common in writing.

11 towards; with; over; of; in.

Possible answer
During the next few days you'll be very relaxed and you'll spend time with friends who are interested in your ideas about future holidays in exciting places.

Present perfect simple and present perfect continuous

1 2. They've broken a window   3. I've just run 10km.   4. He's eaten too much.
5. They've won the game.   6. He's just come back.

EGT Present perfect simple (*I have worked*) 284

2 2. has been; since   3. 've/have lived; since.   4. 've/have known; for.
5. have worked; for   6. has seemed *or* has been; since   7. 've/have wanted; since

3 2. Martha has had three different jobs since school.   3. We've already booked the flights and hotels. *or* We've booked the flights and hotels already.   4. He still hasn't found a job.   5. I haven't had breakfast yet.   6. Have they finished already? *or* … already finished?   7. Haven't you done your homework yet?   8. How long has she lived there?

4a 2. has (never) bought   3. have sent   4. have (often) read
5. have (never) booked   6. has read

4b *Possible answers*
Five people have never read the news online. Nine people have often done their food shopping on the internet. Twelve people have bought a train ticket online only once. Four people have never done their shopping online. Seven people have sent a gift to someone once using the internet.

4c *Answers for the author who wrote the exercise*
I've only ever booked a holiday online once.
I've never done my food shopping on the internet.
I've sold a bed on the internet.
I've often read the news online.
I've often bought train tickets and sent gifts to friends using the internet.

5 *Answers for the author who wrote the exercise*
The most exciting city I've visited is New York.
The best job I've done was cooking in a restaurant.
The tastiest food I've eaten is in a Lebanese restaurant.
I can't remember the worst film I've ever seen.
The best book I've read this year is *When will there be good news* by Kate Atkinson.
The most surprising thing that has happened to me is winning a competition to stay in a lovely hotel.

6 2. have/ 've been worrying   3. have/'ve been thinking   4. haven't been waiting
5. have/'ve been answering   6. has / 's been applying   7. haven't been making
8. hasn't been playing   9. have they been living   10. has he been telling

7 2. It's been raining for three days. (*or* since Saturday)   3. They've been travelling
around South America for six weeks.   4. Have you been working?   5. I haven't/have
been playing games all morning.   6. Have you been practising?

 Present perfect continuous (*We've been waiting*) 283

8 1. b   2. a   3. a   4. b   5. a   6. b   7. b   8. a   9. a/b   10. a/b
Note: 9 and 10 mean the same thing.

 Present perfect simple or present perfect continuous 285

Present simple and present continuous

1 1. lives   2. beats   3. speak   4. does (a human head) contain   5. doesn't have; has
6. don't see; see   7. visit   8. watches   9. makes   10. don't sleep   11. does (a
typical 6-year-old child) need   12. doesn't; isn't

 Present simple (*I work*) 279

2 1. ~~replys~~ replies   2. ~~do~~ does   3. ~~travelling~~ travels; ~~learning~~ learns   4. ~~does'nt~~
doesn't   5. ~~go~~ goes   6. ~~doesn't washes~~ doesn't wash   7. ~~Don't~~ Doesn't
8. ~~it takes~~ does it take

3 2. He sometimes cries in the night. *or* Sometimes he cries in the night. *or* He cries in
    the night sometimes. (baby)
3. She usually has 12 in each class. (teacher)
4. She doesn't get up before 10 o'clock at weekends. (teenager)
5. I don't work much in the summer. (ski instructor)
6. Do you always ride before breakfast? (cyclist)
7. Where does it hurt? (doctor)
8. How do you make bread? (trainee chef)

4 1. returns   2. follows   3. doesn't know   4. live   5. tells   6. explores
7. talk   8. has   9. includes   10. interviews   11. gives   12. reveals
13. brings   14. Do you think

5 *Suggested answer*
First you turn on the oven to 180°C. Then you mix the butter and the sugar together in a bowl. Next you crack the eggs into another bowl and whisk them. Now you add the egg to the butter and sugar and you mix it all together. Then you sift the flour into the mixture and stir it with a metal spoon. When it's ready, you pour the mixture into the cake tin and you put it in the oven.

6 1. 'm working   2. 're waiting   3. 're coming   4. is (Claire) crying   5. is (he) travelling   6. are (you) being   7. 'm not complaining   8. Isn't (she) living *or, more formal*, Is she not living   9. 're not moving   10. 'm not trying

> **EGT** Present continuous (*I am working*) 278

7 *Suggested answer*
We're not printing documents unless we have to. We're switching off lights when we leave a room. We're turning off computers when they're not in use. We're separating rubbish into glass, paper and plastic. We're recycling more. We're not charging mobile phones unless it's necessary. We're looking for new ways to use less water. We're using alternative energy supplies. We're having a 'no cars' day on March 21st. We're lowering the temperature of the heating by 1°C this winter.

8 **present simple forms:** leaves; departs; doesn't stop; stops; meet; which train is further; pass; they are exactly; start; are; doesn't matter

present continuous forms: is travelling; is going; is carrying; 're going

> **EGT** Present simple or present continuous? 280

9 1. Do you think; smells   2. 're speaking   3. attach *or* 'm attaching (less formal)   4. don't frighten   5. seems   6. laughs   7. knows

10a

	regular	now	future
1. I cook and he does the washing up.	✓		
2. You're being extremely difficult.		✓	
3. She's always complaining.	✓		
4. The train doesn't get in until after midnight.	✓		✓
5. I understand what you're saying.		✓	
6. I respect your views but I don't agree with them.	✓	✓	

10b

	regular	now	future
1. I'm cooking and he's doing the washing up.		✓	
2. You're extremely difficult.	✓		
3. She always complains.	✓		
4. The train isn't getting in until after midnight.			✓

5. I'm understanding ...
6. I'm respecting ... I'm not agreeing We don't use some verbs in the present continuous, e.g. state verbs, mental process verbs, verbs of describing senses, verbs expressing feelings and speech act verbs.

EGT Verbs not often used in the present continuous 280b

11 *Answers for the author who wrote the exercise*
I really enjoy cooking and eating. We're trying to use the car less. We often go by bike into town. My family say I'm always working.

Pronouns

1 2. me; them   3. us   4. hers   5. Me (*I am too* is also possible; *me* is more common in speech)   6. it's (*he* is possible but *it* is more common)   7. them
8. They; they (we use *they* to refer to a wider group of people, institutions, authorities etc.)   9. It; you (*you* here is a generic *you*, meaning people)   10. them

EGT Pronouns 287; Pronouns: personal (*I*, me, *you*, him, *it*, they, etc.) 289

2 1. yours   2. theirs   3. mine   4. it; ours   5. it   6. yours   7. us; ours   8. his

EGT Pronouns: possessive (*my, mine, your, yours*, etc.) 291

3 1. hurt me myself   2. ✓   3. ✓   4. her by herself (*by herself* means alone, *on her own*)   5. ourselves (*hurry* is not a reflexive verb)   6. ✓   7. themselves each other
8. ✓   9. each other each other's   10. ✓   11. yourself yourselves
12. ourselves themselves

EGT Pronouns: reflexive (*myself, themselves*, etc.) 292

4 1. one   2. one   3. ones   4. some   5. None   6. some

EGT Determiners used as pronouns 101

5a 2. someone   3. someone *or* everyone   4. something   5. everyone   6. no one
7. somewhere   8. nowhere   9. nothing   10. Everywhere *or* Everything
Note: *Somebody, everybody* and *nobody* are also possible. They are more informal than *someone, everyone* and *no one*.

5b *Possible answer*
Eventually I found somewhere to sleep. Someone lent me some money so I was able to buy something to eat from a machine. Everything suddenly felt better.

EGT Pronouns: indefinite (*-body, -one, -thing, -where*) 288

6 1. This   2. this   3. those   4. these; This / That   5. that   6. This   7. that
8. this   9. this; that   10. this; this / that (in US English *who's this?* is more common here)

EGT Determiners used as pronouns 101

7 1. e (one)   2. d (ones)   3. a (one)   4. c (ones)   5. b (one)   6. f (ones; ones)

8 2. I must get new **ones**.   3. I've got another **one** in my bag.   4. Why don't you take this **one**?   5. Sorry, I can't lend you **any**.   6. **Any; some**

9a **It** has become more popular than ever. **It** can be entertaining; people can get addicted to **it**… People spend hours in front of **them** and can become lazy. How much time do you spend in front of ~~your~~ **yours**?

> 🔖 EGT Substitution 336

10a The pronoun *you* is used because it makes us all think that we might be there.

10b *This is the car for you* brings the car closer to you. *That is the car for you* lets you see the car further away. Both are possible.

11 *Possible questions*
  2. Where is the Taj Mahal?
  3. When did the Second World War end?
  4. Who wrote *All's Well That Ends Well*?
  5. Where in New York is the New York Stock Exchange?
  6. What is the tallest building in Paris?
  7. What was the film called that won the 2009 Oscar?
  8. Who was the first man who walked on the moon?

> 🔖 EGT Relative pronouns 311; *That*: relative pronoun 344b; *When* as a relative pronoun 375c; *Where* as a relative pronoun 376d; Questions: interrogative pronouns (*what, who*) 303

Punctuation

1 1. Monday; Tuesday   2. My; John; Thailand; Hong Kong; Professor Hammond; Peninsular Hotel; Chinese   3. Italian; The New York Times

> 🔖 EGT Punctuation 293; Punctuation: capital letters (B, D) and full stops (.) 293a

2 1. It's a big city. It's a busy, exciting, dangerous place.
  2. She's a kind, helpful and intelligent girl.
  3. We travelled through Chile, Brazil, Argentina and Paraguay. Eduardo, our guide, stayed with us for the whole journey.
  4. ✓
  5. Because the sea was so rough, the ferry for Dublin was not able to leave.
  6. ✓
  7. ✓
  8. A: Okay, so, we'll see you outside the cinema in town, shall we?
    B: Thanks for asking but I can't tonight. Perhaps next week?

> 🔖 EGT Punctuation: commas (,) 293c; Punctuation: question marks (?) and exclamation marks (!) 293b

3 1. reasons for the fall of the Roman Empire: economic, social, …
  2. Her new book is called *Everyday English Cookery: A Guide for Beginners*.
  3. English is widely used in public life in S.E. Asia; in Singapore it is …
  4. ; of course, it's the only way to start …

> 🔖 EGT Punctuation: colons (:) and semi-colons (;) 293d

4 1. ✓

2. He asked, "What are the dates for the concert?" He asked: "What are the dates for the concert?" is also possible. Quotation marks can be single or double. We use a comma or a colon before the spoken words.

3. ✓ *They said:* is also possible.

4. ✓

5. Gosh! That sounds very dangerous. Now, listen to me!! This is important.

6. Oh no! Please don't ask me to talk to the whole class. I get really really nervous!

Note: using exclamation marks is a personal choice and it is fine to omit them.

🐦 **EGT** Punctuation: quotation marks (' ' or " ") 293e; Punctuation: question marks (?) and exclamation marks (!) 293b

5 1. don't 2. Isn't 3. Who'd 4. ~~Orange's~~ Oranges 5. mustn't
6. They've; they're 7. ~~Who's~~ Whose jacket; ~~your's~~ yours 8. ~~it's~~ its decision

6 2. 2,350 3. 8.5 4. 3,000m 5. 10kg 6. 9.30 am; 5 pm
7. www.theswimmingclub-humus.org 8. jane.cooper@cambuni.co.uk

Note: In 1 other answers are possible: 17.8.1977 *or* 17-8-1977. In the USA it would be 8/17/1977 *or* 8.17.1977 *or* 8-17-1977.

🐦 **EGT** Punctuation: dashes (–) and other punctuation marks 293f; Punctuation: numerals and punctuation 293g; Saying email and internet addresses 293h

7 Have you seen that film, you know, 'No Country for Old Men', that won an Oscar for best film in March 2008?
Note: We often use italic font for titles of books, films and songs when we type (i.e. *No Country for Old Men*).

Questions

1 1. c 2. f 3. a 4. e 5. b 6. d

🐦 **EGT** Questions 295

2 1. g 2. e 3. h 4. b 5. f 6. c 7. d

3 *Possible answers*

1. Where are you from? *or* Where do you come from?
2. Do you live in Tokyo? *or* Are you from Tokyo?
3. How long does it take to get from Tokyo to Osaka?
4. You're working in Osaka?
5. Do you like your job?

4 *Possible answers*

2. The car's broken down so we can't go to town.
3. A tree has fallen and the road is closed.
4. We've used all the firewood. This is the last log.
5. She invited five people to the dinner party but no one is going.

🐦 **EGT** Questions: statement questions (*you're over 18?*) 301

5 1. That's your uncle?   4. He's decided to leave college?
2. You've made a cake?   5. You've passed your driving test?
3. You're going to learn how to play the guitar?

6 *Possible answers*
2. Is the light on or off?   3. Are you going out on New Year's Eve or staying in?
4. Is she/he Swedish or Norwegian?   5. Is the shop open or closed?
6. Do you like your tea with or without sugar?

> 🍁 EGT Questions: alternative questions 298

7 2. Do you cycle at the weekend?   3. Is there a new lock on the door?
4. Are we going to have to sell the car?   5. Will they be home by dinner time?
6. Do you think she is jealous? *or* Might she be jealous?

> 🍁 EGT Questions: *yes-no* questions 296

8 *Possible answers*
2. Can it take photos?   3. Can you check your emails on it?
4. Could it sleep five people?   5. Is that your dress? (*or* Is that a new dress?)

9 2. Is there one near here? (*or* Is it near here?)   3. Are you working at the reception?
(*or* Do you work …)   4. Have you seen them?   5. Is it okay to put them on the
floor? (*or* Shall I put them on the floor?)

10a 1. Are you going out tonight?   2. What do you have to go to town for?
3. Have you seen the latest Bond film?   4. Is this the right way to do it?
5. Why aren't you buying her a birthday present?

10b 1. You seen my blue pen?   2. This the way to the bathroom?   3. Where (to)?
4. Who with?   5. (You) driving to Birmingham?

> 🍁 EGT Questions: short forms 304

11 *Possible answers*
2. I paid her four thousand pounds for it.
3. Helen shouted at the manager's wife on the phone.
4. They went to Burkina Faso.
5. He said that he didn't like my painting.
6. They gave all their savings and their house to charity.

> 🍁 EGT Questions: echo questions 299

12 2. Her birthday is next week. What day is it?
3. Carmen's married to… What's her husband's name?
4. There's a little café somewhere around here. Where is it?
5. They have two daughters. One is called Liz and what's the other one called?

13 1. Who   2. whom (*whom* is not used very frequently and is very formal)
3. Which   4. What   5. Whose

> 🍁 EGT Questions: interrogative pronouns 303

14 1. S   2. O   3. O   4. S   5. S

> 🍁 EGT Questions: interrogative pronouns 303; Questions: *wh*-questions 297

English Grammar Today Workbook

Questions: *how* and *what ... like?*

1   1. How   2. How often   3. How much   4. How many   5. How old   6. How far
7. How long   8. How about   9. how   10. How lovely

 How 164

2   2. h   3. e   4. f   5. d   6. c   7. b   8. a
Note: the difference in meaning between *What does he like?* and *What is he like?*

 How is ...? or *What is ... like?* 165

3   2. How about going for a walk tomorrow?   3. What was it like?
4. How was your day? *or* How was work? *or* What was work like today?
5. How awful/terrible! *or* What a shame!   6. What's she like?

Questions: *wh-* questions

1   2. e   3. d   4. f   5. c   6. a   7. b

 Questions: *wh-* questions 297

2   2. Which; Camille   3. How; 3   4. Which; Russian   5. Which; Jaime, Camille,
Fidelma, Sofia   6. Where; Brazil   7. Who; Fabricio   8. Why; Probably because
she's going to Shanghai.   9. When; April   10. What; She's going to an IT conference.

3   *Suggested answers*
2. Why were they laughing? *or* Why are they laughing? *or* Why did they laugh?
3. Who cooked yesterday?   4. Who does the washing up in your house?
5. Who has eaten all the cake? *or* Who ate all the cake?   6. Whose coat is this?
7. How do you open the window?   8. Which colour do you prefer?
9. When will you come to see us next? *or* When are you going to come to see us next?

4   *Suggested answers*
2. What has he just announced? *or* Why is he in the news?
3. What's the name of the rocket? *or* What's the rocket called?
4. How long is the flight? *or* How long does the journey last?
5. How much does the trip cost?
6. Who is going to be on the first flight?
7. Why are there two large windows next to each seat?
8. Where do the first flights leave from?

5   *Possible answers*
What has been the best experience of your life?
What's your favourite food/film/thing to do/colour?
Which do you prefer, ... or ....?   What are your influences?
Why did you ... ?   Why do you ...?   Who do you ...?

Relative clauses

1a   1. which/that   2. who/that   3. whose   4. which/that   5. which
6. who/that; who   7. which   8. whose
1b   1, 4 and 6 (There's a girl I work with who comes ...)

 Relative clauses 307

2 *Suggested answers*

2. A surgeon is a doctor who performs operations.

3. A pentagon is a shape that/which has five sides.

4. An orphan is a child whose parents have died.

5. A tin opener is a tool which you use to open tins or cans.

6. A spa is a place where you go to relax, often in water.

7. Anti-virus software is a program that protects your computer.

8. A bargain is an object that you buy for less money than you expected.

3 *Suggested answers*

2. A carpenter is a skilled person who makes things out of wood.

3. A protractor is an instrument which we use to measure and draw angles.

4. A paper clip is a useful thing that keeps pieces of paper together.

5. A bee is a small insect that collects pollen, which it makes into honey.

4a 1. b   2. b   3. b   4. b   5. b   6. a

4b 2, 3, 4, 5

4c 1 and 6

4d *Suggested answers*

2. a The students only enjoyed the weekend activities, which they did with their friends.

3. a The candidates, who all got over 80%, went to medical school.

4. a He's very like his brother, who lives in London.

5. a I sat down at the table, which was right in front of me.

6. b The house has two large bedrooms which are bright and spacious.

 Relative clauses: defining and non-defining 308

5 2. Each person has to answer some questions which have to be about capital cities around the world.

3. This is Norma, whose husband works with Jen.

4. Not far away from here, there's a great organic supermarket where I often go to buy vegetables.

5. The courses, which cost £300, are three days long. *or* The courses, which are three days long, cost £300.

6. Gina decided not to go out because she was too tired, which is understandable.

6 1. ~~that~~ which

2. ~~whom~~ who

3. reading ~~it~~

4. very well,

5. Miguel's words, which he

6. … which ~~they~~

7. Another thing ~~what~~ that we … *or* ~~what~~

8. ~~who's~~ whose name

9. ~~she~~

10. seen ~~it~~.

11. friend ~~his~~ whose parents

 Relative clauses: typical errors 310

English Grammar Today Workbook

7 B: What's that?

A: You know the girl **(who) you were talking to at lunch**?

B: Yeah, Elena, she's the one **whose sister I went to school with**. Why?

A: She's the woman **(who) I used to work with** – the one **(who) I had the big argument with**.

8 *Possible answers*

What do you call a thing which you use to bang in a nail?

What's the word for a person who looks after the financial aspects of a company?

What's the word for a shop where you can buy lots of different types of things?

9 *Possible answer*

The accommodation, which is set on a tranquil hill around a traditional village, is unique and luxurious. It is a mix of timber lodges, studios and cottages. The studios and cottages, which are in the village, are built in a traditional Welsh style. The sports club, which is near the village, is open every day. There is a sports hall where you can play badminton, volleyball and tennis. There is a viewing area, which overlooks the sports hall, for people who want to watch not play. The staff, who all are friendly and very experienced, are always happy to answer your questions.

Reported speech

1 2. Bryan told Heidi to stop making so much noise while he was studying.

3. He said (that) it was a terrible film.

4. She said, "The train leaves at 7.10 every morning."

5. We told her (that) she needed help.

> **EGT** Reported speech 312; Reported speech: direct speech 313; Reported speech: indirect speech 314

2

present continuous	→	past continuous
present perfect simple	→	past perfect simple
present perfect continuous	→	past perfect continuous
past simple	→	past perfect simple
past continuous	→	past perfect continuous
future (*will*)	→	future in the past (*would*)
past perfect	→	past perfect (no change)

3a 2. "Is there a bookshop near here?" he asked. *or* He asked, "Is there … "

3. "I'll never do that again," she promised. *or* She promised, "I'll never … "

4. "The food is cold," he complained. *or* He complained, "The food is cold".

5. "Well, my name is Terrence but everyone calls me Terry," he explained.

3b 2. He asked if / whether there was a bookshop near there. 3. She promised never to do that again. 4. He complained that the food was cold. 5. He explained that his name is Terrence but that everyone calls him Terry". (**Note**: no change of tenses here because what was said is still true)

4 1. ill," 2. Grace thought: *or*, 3. ready?'

4. "Oh no!" 5, 'Let's … 6. … I wanted.

> **EGT** Reported speech: punctuation 312b

5 1. … she said to us *or* she told us   2. ✓   3. She said to me *or* she told me
4. They ~~told~~ asked me *or* They said to me … (we use *say* not *tell* when reporting
questions)   5. ✓   6. My mother ~~tell~~ told me never to walk home alone.

🍁 **EGT** Reported speech: reporting verbs 312c

6a 2. never to speak to me again if I told anyone *or* that he would never speak …
3. that she had copied her essay from the internet. *or* to having copied …
4. to know the truth   5. that they had to let them in.   6. us to fill in the form using
a black pen.

6b 2. Fernando suggested that it might cost too much. Luis agreed but Frances disagreed.
3. Emily complained that their room was too warm and that the air conditioning
wasn't working. The hotel manager apologised and said that s/he would see what s/
he could do.
4. Kevin thought (that) renting a car would cost too much. Agata argued that there
were four of them so it wouldn't (cost too much). Kim agreed with Agata.
5. Kate asked Bill if / whether he had seen Tania. Bill replied that he hadn't seen her
since that morning.

🍁 **EGT** Reported speech: indirect speech 314; Reported speech: reporting verbs 312c

7 2. 'Is Prof. Vaughan in his office?' the student inquired.   3. Nathan wondered what
time the last train was.   4. 'We might take a break,' I suggested.
5. 'It's a wonderful restaurant,' he commented.   6. He whispered not to wake
the baby.   7. They ordered us to get in line.

🍁 **EGT** Indirect speech: reporting statements 314a; Indirect speech: reporting
questions 314b; Indirect speech: reporting commands 314c

8 1. ~~is~~ was feeling   2. we ~~have~~ had sent …   3. ~~went~~ had been to *Il Bacio's or* …
had gone *or* they went to *Il Bacio's* … they did.   4. ~~have~~ had been walking
5. ~~will~~ would start   6. ~~has~~ had been doing.   7. ~~aren't~~ weren't

🍁 **EGT** Reported speech: indirect speech 314

9 2. that he hates airports and that he loves hiking so his ideal holiday is walking for
miles every day. (no change because what he says is still true. *Dave said that he hated
airports and that he loved hiking so his ideal holiday was walking for miles every day*
is possible but less likely as it sounds like it is no longer true.)
3. that she has decided to save up for a big holiday next January. (no change because
her plan for next January is still true).
4. that he and his wife had been doing house exchanges for the last four years and
that it had worked out really well (*or* … and he said that …).
5. that they are / were going camping this year in France with the kids. (no change
necessary because Ian's plan is still true)
6. that she had been going to Italy for the last three summers but that next year she is
/ was going to do something different. (no change necessary as it's understood she
is talking about her future plans).
7. that they had swapped their house with a couple from San Francisco for two weeks
last year and that it (had) worked out really well.

8. that they had been on skiing holidays in the past but not with the kids. (*or* ... had gone on ...)
9. that he couldn't afford to go on holiday since he had bought his house.
10. that he likes / liked to stay in Britain. (no change necessary as it is still true)

10 2. we had to   3. we should   4. if we could (*or* whether we could)
5. would be a good idea   6. said (that) she might (*or* suggested that she might)

Speech acts

1 2. instruction   3. offer   4. promise   5. request   6. suggestion   7. warning

> **EGT** Commands and instructions 76; *Will*: uses (promises) 384b; Offers 243; Requests 316; Suggestions 341; Warnings 372

2 1. b   2. b   3. b   4. a   5. b

3a 2. beat   3. Heat   4. fry   5. add   6. Grate   7. leave

> **EGT** Commands and instructions 76

3b *Answer for the author who wrote the exercise*
Cheese on toast: Place a slice of bread under the grill and toast it on each side. Then put cheese on top of it and put it back under the grill until the cheese melts.

4 1. offer   2. invitation   3. offer   4. invitation   5. invitation   6. offer

> **EGT** Offers 243; Invitations 182; Imperatives as offers and invitations 172h

5a 1. Let   2. Shall   3. Want   4. Would   5. Can
5b *Possible answers*
2. **offer:** Shall I pick you up at the swimming pool?
   invitation: Do you want to come swimming with me?
3. **offer:** I could bring some ice cream for dessert.
   invitation: Do have some ice cream with us.
4. **offer:** I can walk your dog while you are away.
   invitation: Would you like to come with me while I walk my dog?
5. **offer:** Want me to wash your car?
   invitation: Come and have a free car wash at our garage.

6 1. Thanks (*Yes* is possible but less likely)   2. Yes   3. No   4. Thanks (*Yes* is possible but less likely)

> **EGT** Invitations 182

7 1, 3 and 5

> **EGT** *Will*: uses (promises) 384b

8a 2. a   3. e   4. c   5. i   6. f   7. d   8. j   9. h   10. g

> **EGT** Requests 316

8b *d* is a written sentence
9a 2. telling me where the library is?   3. tell me how to spell the lecturer's name, please?
4. borrow your pen please?   5. telling me the name of the textbook, please?

9b *Possible answers*
1. Would you mind opening a window, please?   2. You wouldn't get me a sandwich, would you?   3. Could you make me a cup of tea?   4. Could I ask you to be quiet, please?

10 2. let's   3. why don't (*or* how about)   4. How/What about

🌱 **EGT** Suggestions 341

11 *Possible answers*
2. How about lunch?   3. You could spend less on going out.   4. I thought we might go to the concert on Saturday night.   5. Couldn't you lock your bedroom door?
6. Can't you do your homework in the evenings?   7. Let's go for a walk.
8. Why don't we stop now and have a coffee?   9. How about moussaka?
10. What about a gift voucher for her favourite shop?

12 2. Don't   3. I don't think   4. Watch out!   5. Mind   6. I must warn you
7. Whatever you do

🌱 **EGT** Warnings 372

13a 1. d   2. a   3. b   4. c

13b *Possible answers*
1. Mind the falling rocks around here.   2. Watch out! There's a dog in there.
3. Be careful, the floor's wet.   4. Don't swim in there. There are dangerous currents.

Spelling

1 2. chairs   3. ducks   4. parties   5. stories   6. lives   7. churches   8. boxes
9. eyes   10. judges   11. potatoes   12. heroes   13. wives   14. halves   15. videos

🌱 **EGT** Spelling 330; Spelling and plurals 330b

2 2. washes 3. says 4. goes 5. wishes 6. dies 7. buzzes 8. enjoys 9. waves 10. eats

🌱 **EGT** Spelling and verb forms 330f

3 1. ~~hopeing~~ hoping; ~~meat~~ meet   2. ✓   3. ~~fameous~~ famous   4. ~~shadey~~ shady
5. ~~evning~~ evening   6. ~~arguements~~ arguments; ~~completly~~ completely

🌱 **EGT** Spelling: dropping and adding letters 330d

4 2. slimming / slimmer   3. travelling / travelled   4. bigger   5. upsetting
6. beginning   7. not doubled   8. not doubled   9. not doubled   10. not doubled
11. preferred   11. not doubled   13. forgotten   14. occurred / occurring
15. not doubled
Note: spelling *travelling* with one *l* (*traveling*) is correct in American English.

🌱 **EGT** Spelling: doubling consonants 330c

5 ~~traveling~~ travelling; ~~rainning~~ raining; ~~hopping~~ hoping ; ~~shoping~~ shopping;
~~photoes~~ photos; ~~famly~~ family
Note: The spelling of *travelling* with one *l* (*traveling*) is correct in American English.

English Grammar Today Workbook

6a 1.chief   2. piece   3. ceiling   4. receive   5. field   6. receipt   7. neighbour
8. niece   9. leisure   10. weigh

EGT Spelling: *ie* or *ei?* 330e

6b *leisure, neighbour, weigh* are exceptions.
Note: the rule applies mainly to words which have an *i:* sound (e.g. *piece*).

7 1. **too** dark **to** see; **too** slowly; **two** hours   2. **It's** a shame; **its** colour   3. **There** was;
their house; **They're** not   4. **They're** trying; their homes; **There's** a lot
5. **whose** car; **who's** driving?

EGT *There, their* or *they're?* 346; *Too* 352; *To* 351; *It's* or *Its* 186

8 theatre; centre; colour; defence; neighbour; programme

EGT British and American English Spelling 330h

9 behavior behaviour (UK); center centre (UK); color colour (UK); travelers travellers
(UK); checks cheques (UK); mom mum (UK) jewelry jewellery (UK)

Spoken and written English: register

1 1. Well, er   2. Mmm   3. Right   4. Yeah; a bit   5. you know   6. sort of, pinkish
7. Phoned, guess, or something   8. So   9. Oh, it's; don't; I mean, don't they?   10. like
Note: In 4, *It's* is common in both spoken and informal written English. In 6, the suffix
–ish is common with colour adjectives in speech and informal writing. In 7, verbs
(with no subject pronouns) are common examples of ellipsis in speech. This structure
is not common in formal writing.

EGT Discourse markers (*so, right, okay*) 104; *Like* in spoken English 194f

2 1. er   2. mmm   3. yeah   4. well   5. er   6. okay   7. thought so   8. anyway

3 *Suggested answer*
Jim: Er, can I get you something to drink?
Jill: Oh, that's lovely, thanks.
Jim: So, I hear you're at university. What are you studying?
Jill: Psychology.
Jim: Really?
Jill: Yeah, I'm training to be a child psychologist.
Jim: How interesting. You obviously like working with children.
Jill: Absolutely.

4a B is more informal.
4b *Suggested answer*
1. Buy anything nice   2. Yes, I bought three new suits.   3. Have you got any money
left for your holiday next week?   4. Yeah, surprisingly, I have.
5. Lucky you. Sounds good.

EGT Discourse markers (*so, right, okay*) 104; Register ○

5   2. That chemistry book was too difficult to read, wasn't it?

3. There are too many cars in the car park.

4. I have lots of essay marking and things to do.

5. You probably know who I'm talking about.

6. Do they both live in that tower of flats in the town centre, by the library?

Note: In 3, *there's* + a plural subject is common in spoken English. In 5, *probably* in end position is common in speech. In very formal written English, *You probably know the person **about whom** I am talking* is possible.

6   *Suggested answer*

I have just got back to Liverpool. The train was very slow and stopped everywhere. I managed to get some reading done and I saw the article that you mentioned on cooking! I was glad to see your grandmother too and to know that she's getting better.

I'd better stop now as I have a report to write for work tomorrow. Thanks for a great time. I hope to see you both again very soon. Love, Sally.

7   *Suggested answer*

W.H. Auden was born in York in 1907 and went to school in Holt in Norfolk. It was in Holt where he started writing his first poems when he was approximately sixteen years old. He went to Oxford University, where he became even more involved in poetry publications. He wrote about the Spanish Civil war in the 1930s and went to Spain to fight in the war himself.

8   2. improvement   3. installation   4. visit; welcome   5. violence   6. peace

9a   1. a   2. c   3. b

… there will be some **showers** from early morning … will be cool and **breezy** everywhere by evening with winds moderate to **strong** in the south west …

9b   *Suggested answer*

Look forward to seeing you tomorrow. You asked what the weather'll be like. Well, it's not going to be great. There'll be a bit of sun in the morning but it's gonna be showery, cool and quite windy. Bring some warm clothes and an umbrella with you! See you at Dave's tomorrow evening.

10   2. d Recipe   3. a Official notice   4. e Newspaper report

5. b Biography or encyclopaedia   6. f Instructions on a packet of seeds

11a butter, apples, onions, apple juice, cider vinegar, thyme, bay leaf, chicken stock, potatoes, salt

11b *Formal recipe*

Ingredients: two ripe bananas; butter; brown sugar; plain unsweetened Greek yoghurt

Take a frying pan and melt the butter. Add the bananas and sprinkle with the brown sugar. Cook them for one minute. Then turn and cook for a further minute. Serve in a bowl and add the yoghurt (preferably straight from the fridge).

Recipe written for a friend

Hi Jill, Why don't you do fried bananas with Greek yogurt for dessert? It's easy. Just get a couple of ripe bananas and fry them with some butter. Be sure to sprinkle them with some brown sugar. Fry them for about a minute on each side. Then serve with cold yogurt. Plain Greek yoghurt is best by the way. You'll love it. Anna.

Note the differences in layout, vocabulary and the use of personal names between the two texts. The recipe written for a friend also uses personal pronouns, contractions and includes individual comments such as *It's easy* and *You'll love it.* It's also more approximate in its instructions (*for about a minute, by the way*).

Subjects

1 It; the occupation of space pilot; Space tourism; large numbers of space pilots; Other pilots; 'vertical farmers'; These farmers; We; operations; we; The jobs of the future

 Subjects 333

2 1. were   2. has   3. look   4. does not / doesn't   5. Does   6. were; were
7. worry   8. was   9. were   10. looks

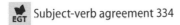 Subject-verb agreement 334

3 1. ~~he~~ him   2. There ~~is~~ are   3 ✓   4. was ~~they~~ them   5. ~~is~~ are coming
6. There ~~are~~ is (although the sentence refers to two buildings, we see each one as single)   7. ✓   8. ~~is~~ are closed

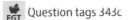 Subject-verb agreement 334; Subject complements 335

4 *Answers for the author who write the exercise*
1. a musician. (don't forget *a*)   2. are history and geography
3. is a difficult subject   4. two chairs and a desk

Tags

1 isn't it?; haven't we?; did you?; right?

 Tags 343

2 1. does he   2. isn't it   3. could you   4. shall we   5. won't she   6. haven't they
7. were they   8. can't you   9. will you   10. didn't he

 Question tags 343c

3 1. mustn't it   2. can you *or* will you   3. shall we   4. didn't she   5. do they
6. aren't they

4 2. ↘   3. ↘   4 ↗   5. ↘   6. ↗

 Intonation 180

5 1. ~~yeah~~ doesn't it 2. ~~right~~ haven't you 3. ~~right~~ didn't you 4. ~~shouldn't we~~ oughtn't we
Note: the tags could also be positive, for example: *The film starts at 6.30, does it?* This usually means the speaker is less sure of the answer.

6 *Suggested answers*
1. Don't forget to collect my aunt from the station, will you?
2. Let's work on the project together, shall we?
3. You haven't got a laptop I could borrow, have you?
4. You couldn't look after the dog while I'm away, could you?

There is **and** there are

1a 1. are   2. There   3. is there   4. there are   5. There's   6. are; aren't there
7. There isn't   8. aren't; are there   9. not   10. no

1b *Possible answers*
There are 28 triangles in a.   There are 12 circles in c.   In d, there's one big circle,
four smaller circles and five small circles. In e, there are five stars.

 There is, there's and *there are* 347

2 *Possible answers*
There's a baby crying in a pram. There's a circle with a cross through it. There are
three cups and a plate of biscuits. There are two fish swimming. There are two squares
with stars in the middle. There are five people waving at a train. There's a house with
three windows and a chimney with smoke coming out. There's bowl of fruits with
three oranges, two apples and some grapes. There's a vase of flowers on a table.

Used to **and** would

1 1. used   2. to   3. use   4. did   5. didn't   6. use   7. used   8. Did / Didn't
9. used   10. did

 Used to 357; *Used to* or *would*? 357b

2a 1. used to play / would play
2. used to climb / would climb
3. used to have
4. used to read / would read
5. used to pick / would pick

6. used to talk / would talk
7. used to walk / would walk
8. used to go *or* We would often go
9. used to spend / would spend

Note: In 3, we don't use *would* to describe a state which is no longer true.

2b You can't use *would* or *used to* because they are single past events not repeated
actions.

3a *Suggested answers*
There used to be small independent shops, owned by families. We used to go to the local
shops to buy all our food. There didn't use to be any big supermarkets. Every high street
used to have a fishmonger, a butcher, a baker and a greengrocer. The shopkeeper used to
serve you what you wanted. We used to cook everything ourselves. We didn't use to buy
ready-made food. We used to eat lots of bread and potatoes. We didn't use to eat pasta.
We used to eat our food together around the table. We never used to eat in the sitting
room. We didn't use to eat in front of the TV.

4 *Possible answers*
Most people didn't use to type. Now most people use a keyboard. People used to use
the phone more. More people used to write letters. We didn't use to expect a reply
straight away. Now we expect an immediate reply.

5 2. f   3. c   4. b   5. a (b possible but less likely)   6. d (c possible but less likely)

 Used to 357

English Grammar Today Workbook

6   1. We're used to working at night.   2. We're not ~~use~~ used to it yet.   3. She ~~would~~ used to work in Paris   4. Are you getting ~~use~~ used to it?   5. ✓
6. Tim didn't ~~used~~ use to like olives, ~~used~~ did he? (Many people consider the first form with a final –d to be incorrect.)   7. Tanya ~~use~~ used to be a really good tennis player.   8. She ~~was~~ used to be an actor.

Verbs

1   **Linking verbs**: seem; appear; look   **Auxiliary verbs**: do; have
Modal verbs: might; would; may

> **EGT**   Verbs: types 364

2   1. B: No, I **don't** like jazz. I**'ve*** never liked it.

2. A: **Are** you working on Saturday?
   B: No, I **don't** work on Saturdays, normally.
   A: Good. **Have** you seen the new *Spider-Man* film?
   B: No, I **haven't**.
   A: **Do** you want to go and see it Saturday, then?

3. A: Jeff has **been** looking for you. Where **have** you been?
   B: I **haven't** been anywhere. I**'ve** been here all the time! What **does** he want? (*or* **did**)

4. A: What great shoes! I **do** like them! Where **did** you buy them?
   B: In Shoemart. I **didn't** like them at first, but I **do** now.

*Note: the full (uncontracted) form *have* is possible but it's very formal.

> **EGT**   Auxiliary verbs 364c

3a   think: thinking, thought, thought
write: writing, wrote, written
fall: falling, fell, fallen
show: showing, showed, shown
rise: rising, rose, risen
begin: beginning, began, begun
move: moving, moved, moved

3b   All are irregular except *reach* and *move*.
3c   2. thought   3. rose   4. begun   5. reached   6. fallen   7. showed   8. wrote

> **EGT**   Verbs: basic forms 361

4   2. come   3. are you thinking   4. weighs   5. do your parents think   6. looks
7. 're / are having   8. is coming

> **EGT**   State and action verbs 364e

5a   daydream; overcome; highlight; upgrade; shortlist; handwash (*or* hand-wash)
5b   2. handwash   3. upgrade   4. shortlisted   5. overcome   6. highlight

> **EGT**   Compound words 83a

6   2. … but I didn't want any. *or* … I didn't want them.   3. … I've never used them.
     4. … fined me 100 euros.   5. … to wish him good luck   6. I said I'd like to …

 Verb patterns: with and without objects 367

7a   2. I don't want any   3. I'd love to   4. I don't want one   5. I hope not
7b   *Possible answers*
     1. I don't want to   2. I'd love to   3. No, I don't want to   4. I don't want any
     5. No thanks, I don't want one

 Verb patterns: with and without objects 367

8   2. **sort out** some minor problems / **sort** some minor problems **out**   3. **carry on**
     4. **Hang on**   5. **looked up** an old school friend / **looked** an old school friend **up**
     6. **make out**   7. **take on** the responsibility / **take** the responsibility **on**   8. **set off**

 Verbs: multi-word verbs 363

9   *Possible answers*
     2. your coat (or any item of clothing); a lid (from a box or jar)
     3. a child / children; a subject (in a conversation)
     4. an invitation / offer / opportunity; a job; radio / music / TV
     5. lift up your arms; a child

 Verbs: multi-word verbs 363

10a   2. f   3. a   4. e   5. b   6. d

11a   2. … thank you for your kindness …   3. … robbed the poor woman of all her
     money   4. … provided me with a laptop …   5. … look down on people …
     6. … put up with …   7. … let me in on the secret

 Verbs: multi-word verbs 363

11b   *Answers for the author who wrote the exercise*
     1. My boss reminds me of an uncle of mine.
     2. I don't really look up to anyone. I think we're all equal.
     3. I always look forward to the holidays.
     4. I couldn't do without my computer. I use it every day.

12   2. should have finished   3. had been waiting   4. had taken   5. was finally told
     6. would actually have (*or* actually would have)   7. would then mean   8. would
     not be   9. would have been graduating   10. might even have been offered
     Note: In the text, the adverbs (definitely, *finally, actually, then, even*) are in their
     most typical positions. However, for greater emphasis, you can put them between the
     subject and the first verb in the verb phrase, for example: *This year **definitely** has* …

Verbs: everyday verbs (*get, go, wish, want*)

1   1. d   2. e   3. a   4. b   5. c

 Get 145

2   2. a   3. g   4. b *or* h   5. b *or* h   6. c   7. e   8. f (d also possible)

3   1. get   2. getting   3. go   4. get   5. gone   6. get

EGT   *Get* or *go* 146

4   2. b   3. c *or* e   4. e (c possible in a very formal event)   5. c   6. c   7. d
8. f   9. c   10. a

EGT   *Have* 154

5   1. a   2. b   3. a   4. b   5. b   6. b   7. a   8. a

EGT   *Have got* and *have* 156

6   1. They wish ~~that they~~ to visit us …   2. ✓   3. ✓   4. I wish we ~~have~~ had a bigger
apartment.   5. I ~~wish~~ hope it doesn't rain …   6. ✓   7. ✓   8. ~~I hope~~
~~Jill to phone this evening.~~ I hope that Jill will phone this evening.

EGT   *Want* meaning 'wish' or 'desire' 371a; *Wish* 385

7   1. What do you want ~~that we do~~ us to do?   2. ✓   3. B: No, he doesn't want to this
year.   4. ✓   5. ✓   6. We simply want them to give us …   7. ~~They are not wanted~~
~~to attend the meeting.~~ We do not want them to attend …

Note: In 7 different subjects are possible, for example: *she / the boss does not* …

EGT   *Want* 371

8   2. We saw him yesterday but he didn't look very well.   3. It looks like it's going to
snow.   4. Can you come back to watch her match tomorrow?   5. What does her
brother look like?   6. She looks as though she has had a bit of a shock.

EGT   *Look* 198; *Be like* or *look like* 194h

9   1. watch   2. see   3. look at   4. see / watch   5. looked at / watched   6. Look   7. see

EGT   *Look at, see* or *watch*? 199

10   2. do Japanese   3. do the cooking   4. making a cake   5. done your homework
6. do aerobics   7. made an appointment   8. does the crossword

EGT   *Do* or *make*? 106

Verb patterns

1   1. thinking   2. to buy   3. to call   4. getting   5. playing   6. to listen   7. to go   8. eating

EGT   Verb patterns: verb + infinitive or verb + *-ing*? 365

2   2. to offend you   3. to get something to eat (*stop and get something to eat* is also
possible)   4. getting up at 5 am   5. interrupting me (all the time)?   6. to book the
tickets for the concert?

English Grammar Today Workbook

3 2. Rana made Frank say he was sorry. *or* Rana made Frank apologise (to her).
3. The doorman wouldn't let James go in without a tie. (*or* 'wouldn't let James in')
4. Sally asked Julian to remind her to phone Carol.
5. Wilma wanted Sam to go to the hospital with her.

> **EGT** Verbs followed by a *to*-infinitive or *-ing* 365; Verbs followed by an infinitive without *to* 365d

4 1. that you were out   2. that you stay   3. you to stay   4. that you arrange
5. you'll be tired   6. sing   7. that you'll be   8. arriving

> **EGT** Verbs followed by a *to*-infinitive or *-ing* 365; Verbs followed by an infinitive without *to* 365d; Verb patterns: verb + *that*-clause 366

5 2. I told my lazy brother (that) he ought to get a job.
3. The teacher explained to the students that they had to take an extra exam. *or ...* explained that the students had to take an extra exam.
4. He asked the police officer to go with him.
5. The Colonel ordered the troops to advance.
6. The secretary pointed out to Andrew that he had not signed his application form.
7. Trevor said to his mother that he intended to move out of the family home.
8. The chairperson informed the committee (that) the next meeting would be ...

Verbs which are easily confused

1 2. come   3. going; come   4. going; going   5. came   6. go; went

> **EGT** *Come* or *go?* 75

2 2. Krishnan   3. Nigel   4. Printha   5. Paco

3 2. Can you fetch / bring (me) a cloth, please.   3. I can lend you a racket.
4. Can you take this to Harry for me, please.   5. can you bring your new laptop with you?

> **EGT** *Lend* or *borrow?* o; *Bring, take* and *fetch* 61

4 1. I waited for the bus ...   2. ✓   3. ✓   4. I expect to pass *or* I expect (that) I'll pass   5. ✓   6. I'm waiting for my mother to arrive.   7. I hope I don't fail my driving test.   8. ✓   9. ✓   10. People expect supermarkets to be cheaper

> **EGT** *Expect, hope* or *wait?* 124

5 1. fell   2. fallen   3. felt   4. fallen down   5. fall

> **EGT** *Fall* or *fall down?* o; *Fell* or *felt?* o

6 2. f   3. g   4. c   5. b   6. h   7. a   8. e

7 2. see   3. watch   4. listen to   5. fell   6. felt   7. look at   8. heard   9. come   10. Go

> **EGT** *Look at, see* or *watch?* 199; *Hear* or *listen (to)?* 161

8 1. They're waiting for a bus.   2. They're watching a DVD.
3. He's listening to music.   4. She's looking at the paintings.

9a 1. b   2. a   3. a/b   4. b   5. b   6. b

9b *Answers for the author who wrote the exercise*
1. I used to live in Wales; now I live in England.
2. I usually get up at about 8.15.
3. I'm used to hearing Spanish because I have some Spanish friends.

   🔖 *Used to* 357

10 They ~~were~~ used to bring food and gifts and used ~~singing~~ to sing, dance and tell stories. Everyone was used to ~~done~~ doing things together because they ~~were~~ all used to live and work in the same village. Nowadays, a lot of people ~~used to~~ usually stay …

11 1. b   2. b   3. b   4. a

12a 1. rose; raised   2. raised; risen   3. raise; rose   4. raise; rise

   🔖 *Raise* or *rise*? ⊙

12b be horizontal: lie lay lain
place something horizontally: lay, laid, laid
not tell the truth: lie, lied, lied

2. lie   3. laid   4. lain   5. lied

   🔖 *Lay* or *lie*? ⊙

12c 1. wake
2. woke up; wake up (*awake* is too formal and sounds like literary style)
3. waken (both are possible, but *waken* is more suitable because the sentence has a rather formal, literary style. *Wake* without *up* would also be suitable in this formal context.)
4. Wake up
5. awoke

   🔖 *Wake, wake up* or *awaken*? ⊙

13a *do* nouns: favour, homework, job, damage, shopping
make nouns: effort, phone call, mistake, noise

13b 2. do the shopping   3. making so much noise   4. make grammatical mistakes   5. make a real effort   6. did a lot of damage   7. do my homework   8. jobs I can do   9. make a (phone) call   10. do me a favour

   🔖 *Do* or *make*? 106

14 2. e   3. b   4. f   5. d   6. a

   🔖 *Forget* or *leave*? ⊙

Word formation

1 2. unfair   3. impossible   4. unexpected   5. impolite   6. incomplete
7. irregular   8. uncertain   9. illegible   10. discontented   11. irrelevant
12. illiterate   13. dissatisfied / unsatisfied   14. illegal

   🔖 Word formation 389; Prefixes 389a

2   2. wealthy   3. drinkable   4. friendly   5. famous   6. playful   7. dangerous
8. worthless   9. unprofitable   10. lonely   11. thoughtful   12. hopeless

> **EGT** Suffixes 389b

3   *Suggested answers*
2. confident. She is a very confident public speaker.
3. famous. What does it mean to be famous?
4. ambitious. Politicians have to be ambitious throughout their careers.
5. electric. The electric guitar at the guitar concert was really exciting.

> **EGT** Conversion 389c

4   2. over = too much   3. dis = reverse or remove   4. mid= middle of
5. pro = in favour of, supporting   6. trans = across

5   3. childhood.   4. Londoner (a person from London)   5. Chinese (the language of
China or a person from China)   6. friendship   7. refusal   8. loneliness
9. communication   10. government   11. Moroccan (a person from Morocco)
12. republican   13. pianist   14. Marxist

> **EGT** Suffixes 389b; Conversion 389c

6   2. reheat   3. disappeared   4. overeat   5. enlarged   6. outnumbered

> **EGT** Prefixes 389a

7   2. sweeten   3. tighten   4. heighten   5. sympathise   6. simplify   7. ripen
8. soften   9. modernise   10. shorten
Note: in American English *–ise* verbs are spelt with *z* instead of *s* (sympathize).

8   2. sailor   3. act; acting   4. exploration (*or* exploring); explorer   5. employ;
employer (*or* employee)   6. entertain; entertainment   7. teaching; teacher
8. drive; driver   9. organise; organisation   10. manage; manager

9   quickly; calmly; impossibly; northward(s); naturally; unhappily; backwards

> **EGT** Adverbs: forms 17

10   *Possible answers*
2. I'll send her a text.   3. We'll definitely meet on Tuesday.
4. Ok, I'll phone her at once.   5. I'll put the dinner in the microwave.

11   2. short-sleeved   3. brown-eyed   4. sugar-free   5. left-handed.

12   ads / adverts; tv; mobile phones / mobiles; CDs; planes; mags; photos; EU; UK.

> **EGT** Abbreviations, initials and acronyms **o**

Words that are easily confused

1   1. like   2. as   3. As   4. as   5. like   6. As   7. Like   8. like
2   1. d   2. e   3. a   4. f   5. b   6. g   7. c

> **EGT** *All* or *every?* 28

3 *Answers for the author who wrote the exercise*
1. kinds of music   2. I usually get up at 8.00 every morning.   3. pot of coffee
4. my workmates   5. the summer

EGT *All or whole?* 29

4 1. first   2. at last   3. in the end   4. at first   5. at the end   6. firstly; lastly

EGT *First, firstly or at first?* 128

5 1. Each / Every   2. each   3. one another*   4. each other*   5. every

*****Note:** In 3 and 4, these forms are the traditionally correct forms, but you will hear educated native speakers using both forms.

EGT *Each other, one another* 112; *Each or every?* 113

6 1. b   2. a   3. a

EGT *Already, still or yet?* 31

7 1. He had already seen the film.
2. The Liverpool train has already left the station.
3. I'm already beginning to regret buying my new bike.
4. We already know the answer.
5. The troops were already marching towards the border.
Note: it is also possible to put *already* at the end of all of these sentences.

8 1. He's still a bit young.   2. Is this still important?
3. I still haven't posted that letter.   4. Are you still at university?
5. I'm still waiting for her reply.
Note: In every case, in informal spoken language, *still* can come at the end of the sentence.

9 1. Have you phoned your sister yet?   2. He's not back yet.
3. The government has not yet responded to the report (more formal). *or*
The government has not responded to the report yet.
4. Hasn't she arrived yet? 5. Is it five o'clock yet?

10 1. She still won't eat anything. It's very worrying.
2. They haven't decided yet … *or* They haven't yet decided … *or* They haven't decided where to go yet …
3. ✓
4. We waited for an hour but they still didn't come.
5. ✓ This usage is quite formal. *The stadium was already beginning to fill …* would be common in informal English.

11 1. already   2. yet   3. yet   4. still   5. already

12 *Possible answers*
1. I haven't finished my essay yet.
2. I still don't know what I want to do next year.
3. This year I have already taken two exams.
4. I still want to learn the piano, but I don't have time.
5. This English lesson hasn't finished yet.